Zealous: A Darker Side of the Early Quakers

From Darkness comes Light. Erica Canela, in a model combination of scholarship and readability, explains how Quakerism emerged from the traumas of a world turned upside down in the British Isles in the 1640s and 1650s.

    Thomas Hamm, Emeritus Professor of History, Earlham College. Author of *The Quakers in America*

Zealous is a fascinating examination of early Quakers in Herefordshire and Worcestershire. Canela's highly readable and engaging account reveals the critical role of regional politics and circumstances in shaping local expressions and experiences of Quakerism.

    Robynne Rogers Healey, Professor of History, Trinity Western University

Erica Canela has written the best account we have of the emerging Quaker movement and its social context in two midlands counties: a book at once both lively and authoritative.

    Stephen K. Roberts, History of Parliament Trust, London

Ambitious in its intent, and masterful in its execution. In *Zealous*, Canela has unearthed a hidden story in the most engaging and informative of ways!

    Jackson van Uden, History with Jackson

A vivid and groundbreaking account of how the early Quakers defied seventeenth-century norms to forge a lasting spiritual revolution.

    Estelle Paranque, author of *Thorns, Lust and Glory: The Betrayal of Anne Boleyn*

Insightful and engaging, this balanced account brings their convictions and struggles to life, while revealing the bold, disruptive strategies these spiritual revolutionaries employed to achieve their ends.

    Mark Turnbull, author of *Prince Rupert of the Rhine: King Charles I's Cavalier Commander*

This is a good local study to fill out our existing national history of early Quakerism, with some additional and moving perspectives not found in previous scholarship.

    Professor Ronald Hutton CBE, author of *Oliver Cromwell: Commander in Chief*

Zealous: A Darker Side of the Early Quakers

Erica Canela

First published in Great Britain in 2025 by
Pen & Sword History
An imprint of Pen & Sword Books Limited
Yorkshire – Philadelphia

Copyright © Erica Canela 2025

ISBN 978 1 03611 214 1

The right of Erica Canela to be identified as
Author of this Work has been asserted by her in accordance
with the Copyright, Designs and Patents Act 1988.

A CIP catalogue record for this book is
available from the British Library.

All rights reserved. No part of this book may be reproduced, transmitted, downloaded, decompiled or reverse engineered in any form or by any means, electronic or mechanical, including photocopying, recording or by any information storage and retrieval system, without permission from the Publisher in writing. NO AI TRAINING: Without in any way limiting the Author's and Publisher's exclusive rights under copyright, any use of this publication to 'train' generative artificial intelligence (AI) technologies to generate text is expressly prohibited. The Author and Publisher reserve all rights to license uses of this work for generative AI training and development of machine learning language models.

Typeset by Mac Style
Printed in the UK by CPI Group (UK) Ltd, Croydon, CR0 4YY.

The Publisher's authorised representative in the EU for product
safety is Authorised Rep Compliance Ltd., Ground Floor,
71 Lower Baggot Street, Dublin D02 P593, Ireland.
www.arccompliance.com

For a complete list of Pen & Sword titles please contact:

PEN & SWORD BOOKS LIMITED
47 Church Street, Barnsley, South Yorkshire, S70 2AS, England
E-mail: enquiries@pen-and-sword.co.uk
Website: www.pen-and-sword.co.uk
or
PEN AND SWORD BOOKS
1950 Lawrence Road, Havertown, PA 19083, USA
E-mail: uspen-and-sword@casematepublishers.com
Website: www.penandswordbooks.com

For Neil.
For Everything.

Contents

Acknowledgements		ix
Prologue		xiii
Introduction		xv
Chapter 1	Prelude: The Road to War	1
Chapter 2	Misery, Total Ruin, Poor, Almost Wasted Kingdom	10
Chapter 3	The Sparks of Radical Faith	22
Chapter 4	A Plague of Northern Locusts	26
Chapter 5	An Organised Grassroots Effort	39
Chapter 6	Early Quakers and their Fierce Opponents	58
Chapter 7	The Blasphemous Susanna Pierson	69
Chapter 8	Persecution or Prosecution?	78
Chapter 9	The Evil Multitudes	92
Chapter 10	Writing Like the World is Ending	104
Chapter 11	The Good Argument against Quakerism	118
Chapter 12	Zealous: Humphrey Smith	124
Chapter 13	Legacy	152
Epilogue: On Colonial Shores		155
Notes		157
Bibliography		188
Index		212

Acknowledgements

I am indebted to the brilliant team at Pen & Sword for helping me bring this tiny piece of history to a wider audience, with special thanks to Jonathan Wright. My outstanding editor, Linne Matthews is as kind as she is shrewd and the only person who has ever convinced me to remove Oxford commas – that is no small feat.

Researching and writing this book has been quite the journey and I am grateful I did not have to travel this metaphorical road alone. Without Dr Richard C. Allen, you would not be reading this right now. He brought these seventeenth-century Quakers into my life and for that, I am forever in his debt. I would also like to extend my heartfelt appreciation to Dr Robynne Rogers Healey for her encouragement and wisdom. She constantly reminded me to 'give them the "so what?"' – to write history that people will care about, and that is probably the greatest piece of advice any historian could receive.

Within the circle of great archivists and historians, I have to especially thank Mary Crauderueff, Jackson van Uden, Mark Turnbull and Dr Isabella Rosner – you are all incredibly generous and kind friends. Thank you for responding to my panicked messages and helping me when I needed it most. Public history can be a very competitive space but somehow, I found a community of incredible scholars who support and encourage one another. I have also been sustained by my wonderful friends, with very special thanks to Junnie Cross, Andy Rosenfeld, Ben Squibbs and Akvile Zakarauskaite. You have listened to me talk about Quakers for a long time, but you are still required to read the book! Trevor Latham, Kirsty Dewhirst, Diane Middleton, James Middleton and Dawn Tung, thank you for your constant distractions and reminding me to take breaks when needed. You all are truly a dream come true.

There are very few people in my life who inspire me like my dearest friend, Hacer Tanrikulu – your friendship is one of the greatest joys of my life. No matter what weirdness I throw in your direction, well… you just know how to counter that with superhuman logic and love. I must express my most sincere gratitude to Simon Brinkworth. In many ways, I'm not sure I could have finished this book without your brutal motivation and guidance. You always show up and you always know the perfect thing to say when my brain gets the best of me. You're the best.

And then there's my incredible family. Cindy, Alexia, Tanner, and Averie – thank you for always being there. You are loved beyond measure. I often imagined my dad picking up this book, looking at the cover and saying, 'That's good, mija.' That's probably all he would say and that would have been the greatest review ever. In his absence, I have never been alone. I am fortunate to have been loved and supported by these wonderful people. Thank you for believing in me.

Zealous

/ˈzɛləs /

ADJECTIVE

FILLED WITH OR INSPIRED BY INTENSE ENTHUSIASM OR ZEAL; ARDENT; FERVENT

Dear Reader,

The events in this book take place primarily from 1630 until 1688. During this period, the Julian calendar was used in England. Before 1752 and the adoption of the Gregorian calendar, the new year officially began on 25 March instead of 1 January. Throughout this book, I have converted dates to the Gregorian calendar for standardisation and aligning with modern chronology.

This book contains quotes from meeting minutes, letters, court records and a whole host of printed publications from the period. English spelling has changed over the last 400 years. With this in mind, when the word still looks very familiar, I have not included [sic] to signpost these anomalies.

Prologue

May 1663 – Winchester, England

Humphrey Smith wanted to live, but at this very late stage, this was not Smith's choice to make. He had been imprisoned for eighteen long months. He had so much more to do, yet he also acquiesced to the Lord's will. As he grew more and more sick with typhus, he begged for his soul to be delivered from his oppressors.

Smith's reputation was that of a God-fearing, fervent and zealous man. His prolific writing and preaching galvanised many, and even as he lay dying, he inspired those around him. His life and even his death were commendable.

Humphrey Smith died in early May and from eyewitness accounts, it was a very painful, arguably needless death.

He was a martyr for the early Quaker movement.

His story has been largely forgotten.

Introduction

The mid-seventeenth century in England was a time of great social and religious upheaval. It was against this turbulent backdrop that a group of individuals emerged, challenging the religious norms of the time. Known as the Quakers, or the Religious Society of Friends, these early dissenters sought a direct and unmediated connection with the divine, defying the hierarchical structures of the established Church. By 1680, the group had approximately 40,000 members, defying the expectations of their opponents.[1]

The story of the Quakers is one of radical ideas and unwavering convictions, with an enduring legacy that continues to inspire and resonate in our world today.

It is impossible to look at early Quakerism without looking at the political and religious perspectives that came before. The upheaval, uncertainty and psychological trauma of the civil wars created an environment in which new ideas like Quakerism could thrive. This experience was critical to the success of the earliest Quakers. The story has to start here.

The civil wars would not only shape political futures but also fundamentally change the social, cultural and religious landscape of Britain during much of the 1640s and 1650s. The experience was transformative – for the everyday people who witnessed the devastation, plundering and chaos of war.

The wars provided the basis for radical dissenters to pursue purposes quite different from the formal war aims of the military parties. These dissenters advocated living in 'the here and now' and this created an atmosphere of concern, fear and anxiety. They challenged the fragile government in a way that some dissenters were able to use opportunistically to their advantage.

This book tells the story of the earliest Quakers in the English counties of Herefordshire and Worcestershire. These two regions strongly felt the veritable tug of war between Royalist and Parliamentarian forces and as a result, were fertile grounds for the earliest travelling Quaker ministers from the north of England. Within these counties, Quakerism thrived; and we will get to know influential local figures who have until now been largely forgotten in the early Quaker story. At the onset of their zealous mission, St Mary's Church in Kidderminster, Worcestershire, was led by the deeply influential Puritan minister Richard Baxter. The inevitable clashes between Baxter and the Quakers highlighted the dangerous threat Quakers posed to this unsettled country.

The earliest Quakers were provocative, and intentionally so. The decision to become a Quaker in the 1650s was not to be taken lightly. It was a path strewn with hardship – some self-imposed.

They were zealous. They had to be.

The idea that God was available to anyone at any time impassioned them; they believed that they had found the closest possible connection to God on earth. In the aftermath and uncertainty of the civil wars, people were not sure what was to come next. There was no king, no monarch, so it would not have been too radical to believe that Christ's much-promised return was imminent. There was no time to waste. The Quakers needed to use everything in their power to share what they had discovered, fully aware that the vast majority of people were not ready to hear this message. They had to try. They had to convince their neighbours, friends and foes before it was too late.

Chapter 1

Prelude: The Road to War

What frequent alarms we gave them by fire-balls, lights upon our steeple, by Dogs, Cats, and outworne Horses, having light Matches tyed about them; and turned out upon their works, whereby we put the enemy in such distraction, that sometimes they charged one another.[1]

The chaos and brutality of war is timeless. Throughout history, the emotional trauma of armed conflicts has left lasting scars. The quote above, written in 1645 by Sir Barnabas Scudamore, the Governor of Hereford, describes the mayhem of civil war in the English border counties. These words provide us with a searing visual image that we can almost hear, and even more acutely, smell.

The civil wars (otherwise known as the British Civil Wars or the Wars of the Three Kingdoms) would not only shape political futures, but also fundamentally change the social, cultural and religious landscape during much of the 1640s and 1650s. Herefordshire and Worcestershire were fully engulfed in the wars, and as the 1640s progressed, there was increased political and religious dissent within these two counties. For this reason, they serve as an effective starting point and provide excellent context for this story of radical faith during tumultuous times.

On the ground, the religious and political propaganda from both sides of the conflict encouraged debate in the broader public arena.[2] It is therefore not surprising that radical religious groups emerged during this decade. While many of these groups faded away by the mid-1650s, they were offering a different interpretation of the religious experience, and the Quakers adopted a good number of the ideals they presented. For that reason, it is important to examine the environment that allowed Quakerism to flourish from the 1650s onwards. How did the civil wars influence dissent? As a result of the civil wars, were people more accepting of radical religious identities? And to what extent did the religious groups harness the general anxiety and trauma from the wars for their benefit?

2 Zealous: A Darker Side of the Early Quakers

Before we look at the civil wars and their impact, we need to take another step back to the ascension of Charles I in 1625 and the lead-up to the initial conflict in 1642. Charles inherited a tense and divided Parliament from his father, James I. Parliament had disputed with James over religious innovations, his attempts to rule without Parliament and, of course, money. At the onset, Parliament wanted to limit their new king by refusing him Tonnage and Poundage revenues. These were taxes that provided a major source of revenue for the monarch. The political manoeuvring of Charles I and religious innovations introduced by Archbishop William Laud reignited hostility towards state and Church; and the civil wars would show that the impositions of the 1630s culminated in religious, political and economic divisions that tore families and communities apart.

There remained a deep suspicion that Catholics, or those who challenged the Anglican Church, would destabilise the kingdom.[3] They were persecuted despite the fact that Charles had a Catholic wife. There was only a brief spell of toleration at the start of his reign but that barely lasted a full year. Catholics believed that only they fully understood the 'true relationship between temporal and spiritual power' and that they were the most ardent supporters of the Stuart dynasty and their royal authority.[4] They realised that any persecution they suffered under Charles would pale in comparison to what the Purtians could unleash. On the other hand, William Laud, quite dramatically, equated papists with adulterers or those who committed incest.[5] Once he became Archbishop of Canterbury in 1633, Laud used his powers of visitation to send questions to the lower clergy and churchwardens, demanding reports about conformity and standards of practice to promote new ceremonialism.[6] Known as the 'beauty of holiness', this ceremonialism was viewed as a backward step to pre-Reformation popery.[7] Many viewed Laud's reforms as a way of repositioning the people and the state church, while also walking a fine line between Protestantism and Catholicism, and expecting acceptance throughout the country.

Prior to Laud's visits, visitation returns were circulated detailing ceremonial alterations, alongside a list of questions for the clergy, entitled *The Articles to be Inquired of The Metropoliticall Visitation of William Laud*. While anti-Catholic in tone, *The Articles* also contained much that would frustrate those who leaned towards Puritanism. The document provided very specific details about all of the ornaments and other possessions a parish church should have in place to practise the 'beauty of holiness', including a 'bible of the largest volume, and a Book of Common Prayer both fairely and substantially bound', a 'faire Communion cup with a cover of silver and a Flagon of silver, tinne, or pewter', as well as 'a convenient and decent Communion Table with a carpet of silke' and 'a comely pulpet'. The table was to be used for religious ceremonies only and it was specified that it should not be sat upon, nor should hats be thrown on it.[8] In Dore, Herefordshire, Viscount John Scudamore, a friend of Archbishop Laud, interpreted Laud's reforms to mean that the table should quite literally be immovable. Consequently, he installed a marble altar, 12 feet long and 4 feet wide, which has never been moved.[9] To many, the lines between ceremony and idolatry were becoming increasingly blurred.

The Articles contained a series of questions that were meant to examine all aspects of life, not only the behaviour of the clergy and church possessions. It required information to be provided concerning schoolmasters, churchwardens, physicians and midwives, ecclesiastical magistrates, and parishioners, particularly those who had strayed from state worship. The purpose of the visitation was to thoroughly probe the diocese, expose recusants or those who caused disturbances to the well-being of the Church, and to audit parishes and the preference for ornamentation. The Diocese of Worcester sent their responses to *The Articles* with no annotations, which suggests that either the clergy were amenable to Laud's requests or they avoided answering the questions.[10] There was an increasing level of mistrust between Laud and those who felt his reforms were going too far, namely Puritans.

Puritanism was defined as a desire for plain worship combined with an intense emphasis on an individual's godly behaviour.[11] Puritans sought a deeper reform of ecclesiastical practices as well as holding a fear that the king was the victim of a Catholic plot, but it is worth noting that Puritans were a distinct minority in England.[12] They maintained that Laudians were a secret popish faction trying to reverse the Protestant Reformation in England. Conversely, Laudians argued that Puritans were dangerous subversives determined to destroy legitimate authority in Church and state. Each party feared the religious principles of the other. Yet, at the core of the argument, they did agree in regarding Roman Catholics as the most dangerous of the king's subjects.[13]

Despite this common enemy, Charles I was stumbling into a domestic quagmire after dismissing Parliament in 1629 and imposing his 'Personal Rule'. This followed four years of wrangling between the king and Parliament. Charles's draconian measures ensured that Parliament did not sit between 1629 and 1640,[14] and other measures discouraged discussion of kingship and religious observance. This was demonstrated by the controls imposed on the Church by Archbishop Laud, while Charles's dismissal of Parliament had grave consequences. This was brought to a head with his methods of raising funds without the consent of Parliament following their refusal to grant the king the customary lifelong Tonnage and Poundage revenues.

Ship Money – originally a property tax for the purpose of supporting the navy – was introduced in coastal counties.[15] It was not a new form of taxation, having last been used by Elizabeth I when the Spanish Armada posed a threat. The Privy Council revived it in 1634 to protect the English coast and trade from foreign powers and pirates; these were emergency funds required to build a fleet.[16] The introduction of Ship Money tax to inland counties in 1635 brought the issue to the wider population. It was imposed on all counties annually from 1635 until 1640, regardless of their ability to supply ships.[17] As a national tax, Ship Money was unprecedented because it lacked any parliamentary approval and, as time progressed, it appeared to be a permanent tax.[18] However, from 1635 until 1639, 90 per cent of what was demanded was paid.[19] The burden of responsibility was on the local sheriff to collect the taxes and he was responsible for the debts even after his term ended.[20] Herefordshire and Worcestershire both made timely payments of Ship Money with minimal arrears. For example, under the 1635 Writ, both counties were charged £4,000; Worcestershire had paid in full by 1 January 1638 and Herefordshire was in arrears of only £88.[21] The sheriffs of the two counties performed their duties and the residents diligently paid their taxes.

Political and religious tensions were further raised in Scotland during the Bishops' Wars, which took place in 1639 and 1640. In an attempt to introduce a new prayer book in Scotland, Charles I found himself in a series of disputes with the Scottish Covenanters, culminating in the Scots seizing Newcastle upon Tyne in August 1640.[22] Throughout the conflict, the Covenanters used the press to address the English and ask for support for their cause.[23] Their propaganda was widely distributed and, in February 1639, Charles I issued a royal proclamation ordering any subject who received a 'libellous' Scottish pamphlet to deliver it to a Justice of the Peace.[24] The Bishops' Wars and Charles's Personal Rule highlighted his inability to manage the situation and, unfortunately, demonstrated to some of his more radical subjects that they could not fully trust him.[25] The Personal Rule lasted from 1629 to 1640 and was followed by the Short Parliament, which lasted three weeks from April to May 1640. The Short Parliament was called to request money after the Bishops' Wars. The Short Parliament was quickly dissolved when they refused to grant Charles I funds.

As tensions rose between Charles I and his parliament, there were strong indications that the king would use the army to suppress Parliament. Sir Robert Harley, the Herefordshire MP, and others formed a committee to draft a Protestation, which was in response to the First Army Plot, an alleged conspiracy by Royalists to use the army against Parliament. The Protestation, issued on 4 May 1641, was circulated to local authorities throughout the country.[26] First and foremost, the Protestation was a vow to maintain and defend the Church of England against all 'popery', and a pledge to maintain and defend the monarchy and parliamentary rule.[27] The wording of the document was clever. Emphasising anti-popery was a powerful means to mobilise opinion in favour of Parliament's actions.[28] Compliance with the first version of this Protestation was voluntary and it was not meant for wide circulation. Most were happy to sign it, 'with much willingness'.[29]

The pledge itself was undeniably in support of the Church of England but the wording of the document also strongly implied that Parliament's power was equal to that of the king as the final paragraph ends with, 'His Majesties Royall Person, Honour, and Estate; As also the Power and Privileges of Parliament'.[30] The wording of the Protestation was likely intentionally vague. For example, the term 'popery' was not defined, thereby giving pause to a more learned reader who may have felt that Laud's ceremonial reforms could have been interpreted as such.[31] It can certainly be argued that the primary objective of the House of Commons was to determine how many Catholics were still practising in England and Wales. The Protestation declared that the Church of England was against 'all popery and popish innovations within this Realm'.[32]

The state church was central to community life and the Protestation was a document that was meant to demonstrate the support Parliament had on a local level. The vague wording and seemingly inoffensive pledge were arguably constructed for a high response rate and even though it succeeded in that respect, the political fallout must have been entirely unexpected. There is a consensus amongst historians that the impact of the document was unintentionally devastating. It was designed to unite the country, but instead, it exposed divisions in allegiance and opinion.[33] The Protestation was a means of identifying who was really committed to the pursuit of reformation.

For radicals, it gave further legitimacy to iconoclasm – the belief in the importance of destroying religious images.[34] When the recently restored Parliament was on a six-week recess in 1641, Sir Robert Harley returned to his home at Brampton Bryan in Herefordshire and enforced the House of Commons resolutions on religion. He pulled down the church cross at Wigmore, where he was the patron, and broke the church windows at Leintwardine. He complained to churchwardens at Leominster for not removing and destroying crucifixes and paintings of the Trinity.[35] Moreover, three years later, he knocked out the painted windows at Whitehall in London and replaced them with 'protestant glass' and symbolically broke the altar into pieces, 'for it hath broken the Kingdom into too many pieces'.[36]

On 23 November 1641, John Pym, leader of the Long Parliament, which sat on and off for twenty years, from 1640 to 1660, introduced the Grand Remonstrance, which was essentially an indictment of Charles's misrule since his ascension in 1625. The Grand Remonstrance demanded that Parliament have more control over the king's councillors and the army, and proposed a meeting to determine the future of the Church of England.[37] This explosive document was Pym's attempt to rally his supporters in view of the emergence of a moderate party. Following this divisive indictment, Members of Parliament, to solidify their political position, recirculated the Protestation in January 1642, with the caveat that this was now an oath to be signed by everyone aged 18 years and over throughout England and Wales. It was no longer a voluntary exercise for local government officials – it was the largest political mobilisation and first proto census attempted by Parliament.[38]

The administration of the oath itself was again delegated to local officials. Once the minister and officers of each parish had attended their regional meeting and taken the Protestation themselves, it was their duty to summon or 'warn' their respective parishioners to come to the place appointed, each to make his protestation.[39] A House of Commons resolution declared that those who refused to sign would be deemed unfit to hold office in the Church or Commonwealth and would be accounted as convicted recusants.[40] All those eligible to sign the oath were expected to do so in front of the local sheriff, Justice of the Peace, minister, constable, or churchwarden. It was the responsibility of the justices and sheriffs to ensure that the oath was taken by those in their jurisdiction. Known recusants were confronted with the oath by local officers, and some of the local officers 'took great pains to track recusants down and confront them with the Protestation yet also offered excuses to those too ill or too elderly'.[41]

In many ways, tendering the oath may have appeared to have been an exercise whose sole purpose was to confront known recusants. This may explain the occasional leniency by local officials towards those not deemed a serious threat. Overall, it was an effective oath because there was little reason for a Protestant to refuse to swear it.[42] It was essentially an oath to protect the Church, king and Parliament, and unless the householder did not share a religious identity with Protestants, they had nothing to fear. If there was any hesitation or trepidation about the powers and privileges of Parliament when presented with the oath, they could make their own interpretations about what it meant and could swear the oath without danger.[43]

The Protestation certainly revealed divisions in allegiance and opinion, but its purpose was to separate Protestants and Catholics, not Royalists from Parliamentarians.[44] The House of Commons Protestation was carefully worded to show support for both king and Parliament, but it is not surprising that such a mandatory oath supporting the rights and privileges of Parliament would generate ill feeling amongst the king's supporters.[45] Many members of the gentry in Herefordshire were outraged by the demands of the document and there were also some who, much as they opposed Laud's reforms, did not want a Puritan assault upon the structure of the Church of England either. A majority of the gentry in Herefordshire did disagree with the House of Commons Protestation and drafted their response as an act of support for King Charles: the Herefordshire Protestation.[46]

The Herefordshire gentry declared themselves for the Protestant religion, the king's rightful power, the laws of the land, and the liberty of the subject – all of which they believed had been violated by John Pym's men, including Sir Robert Harley.[47] The cover of the published collection of petitions presented to Charles I stated that the documents, including the Herefordshire petition, were signed in opposition to 'popery, presbytery, anarchy, and confusion' and published to 'precaution the ill-meaning Zealots of this Age'.[48] The gentry expected everyone in Herefordshire to sign their petition. The result was that it was 'subscribed' by 68 knights, esquires and 'Gentleman of Quality', 8 doctors, 150 'minister of good repute', and 3,600 freeholders and inhabitants of the county.[49] The Herefordshire gentry's response signified that the landowners held the upper hand, as without their wealth, no army would be raised, and certainly not an army in support of Parliament. The words used in the Herefordshire Protestation were succinct and their message of support to King Charles was very clear:

> I believe no power of pope or parliament can depose the sovereign Lord King Charles, or absolve me from my natural allegiance and obedience unto his royal person and successors.
>
> The two Houses of Parliament without the king's consent, hath no authority to make laws or to bind or oblige the subject by their ordinances.
>
> That myself will never bear arms in their quarrel; but if I shall be thereunto called, will assist my sovereign and his armies in the defence of his royal person, crown, and dignity, against all contrary forces.[50]

Viscount Scudamore of Dore was the first to sign the Herefordshire Protestation in January 1642.[51] The signers also committed themselves to:

> not discover the secrets of his Majesties armies to the rebel, nor hold any correspondence or intelligence with them. And all designs of theirs against our sovereigns armies, or for surprising or delivering up the cities of Worcester or Hereford, or of any other his Majesties forts, I shall truly discover to whom it shall concern, so soon as ever it comes unto my knowledge and that his Majesties taking up of arms for the causes by himself so oft declared in print is just and necessary.[52]

The text of the Herefordshire Protestation read as a preparatory document for war. The message was well defined as the terminology used included 'depose the sovereign', 'bear arms', 'defence of his royal person' and 'majesties armies'. The Herefordshire gentry would take up arms for the king and maintain their allegiance to him no matter what the cost. If the gentry were dictating the political agenda of the county, it is natural to assume that those whose livelihood depended on them would fall into line and add their signatures to the oath. A list of all those who refused to sign the Herefordshire Protestation was to be sent to Sir William Bellenden, the general commissioner, who was a staunch Royalist.[53] Similar to the House of Commons Protestation, it is likely that Bellenden intended to confront those who refused to sign the Herefordshire Protestation.

Across the county border in Worcestershire, recusants were readily identified in April 1642. There were 86 men and, notably, 129 women recorded.[54] This evidence suggests that the women were more susceptible to the intimidatory tactics of the local authorities in the county. Elsewhere in England, women were vital to maintaining Catholicism and were confidently practising their faith, even when their husbands were conformists, or merely appearing to conform.[55] The vast majority were identified as wives and the sole household recusants, so it is probable that they were practising their faith defiantly, in full knowledge of the risks.

The House of Commons Protestation exacerbated religious conflicts and political allegiance, both in Parliament and within the wider context of the country. It is important to stress that the Protestation did not show outright support for a civil war, but an intense desire to avoid it.[56] Both the parliamentary Protestation and the Herefordshire Protestation strove to maintain peace in England, preserve the state church and protect it from any popish plots.

The Protestations failed to prevent wider conflict. War was inevitable, but no one could have predicted the impact on every aspect of everyday life. The changes would be unprecedented. No one could have known that by the end, King Charles I would be executed and England would be ruled by a Puritan farmer from Cambridgeshire.

Chapter 2

Misery, Total Ruin, Poor, Almost Wasted Kingdom

The civil wars reached all edges of Herefordshire and Worcestershire. These two counties were strategically important during the wars, and particularly the city of Worcester, as it was home to two major battles that bookended the conflict – the Battle of Powick Bridge, on 23 September 1642, and the Battle of Worcester, on 3 September 1651. At the onset, Worcester mobilised quickly, three days after Charles raised his standard in Nottingham on 22 August 1642, thus formally commencing the civil war. The Chamber of Worcester stated that:

> tomorrowe beeing the sixe and twentieth daie of August anno domini 1642 att two of the clocke in the afternoone all manner of persons within this cittie ... that are charged with armour shall bring upp ... and show the same to Mr Mayor and Mr Aldermen whereby it may appeare that every man doth shewe his owne Armour ... fourtie shillings unto the use of the corporacion of the cyttie.[1]

In the same meeting, it was agreed that 'powder, shott, and match' were to be ready, as well as to collect contributions from those willing for the defence of the city. Four days later, on 29 August 1642, the chamber agreed that 'one double fifteene shall be assessed and collected after the usuall manner towardes the repair of the walls and the bridge of this cittie'; those who refused to pay were subject to seizure of their personal goods; this was not the time to make a grand gesture – the county needed to be protected.[2] Several Worcestershire residents were noted in the Quarter Sessions in 1642 for paying towards the 'safety of the County of Worcester'.[3]

In the preamble to the war, Commissioners of Array were dispatched throughout the country. These commissioners assessed the money needed to support military operations. This was agreed at meetings with the local

Misery, Total Ruin, Poor, Almost Wasted Kingdom 11

gentry – they determined the actual amount of money required to be raised and organised the collection of the sanctioned taxes.[4] The commissioners were responsible for training and mustering the county's militia, ensuring they were well armed, and that the officers were 'persons of quality'.[5]

The city of Hereford began preparations shortly after the outbreak of war. War preparations were noted by Joyce Jeffreys, an affluent widow who had lived in both Herefordshire and Worcestershire. Her account records kept through most of the first civil war provide excellent insights into the day-to-day life of a Royalist supporter in Hereford.[6] A month after the war commenced, Jeffreys moved to Kilkinton, near Garnons, west of Hereford, where she noted that she went to Kilkinton 'for feare of ye parliaments army. Septem. 23, 1642', and she recorded payments to local men for helping her move:

> Paid Edward Parsons of heryford for helpping to carry my goods out of my howse in heriford to the cart that brought it to Kilkinton for feare of ye coming of ye parliaments army from Worcester to heriford ... 1s.
>
> Paid Edward Stefens, Carier, for cariing a way my trunks & boxes and bedding from heriford to kilkinton ... 25s.[7]

Jeffreys' account shows a community willingness, albeit for payment, to help each other before the conflict reached their doorsteps. The urgency Jeffreys felt was warranted as the counties were quickly overwhelmed by the armies of both sides. On 30 September 1642, Hereford was attacked and occupied by parliamentary forces, led by Henry Grey, Earl of Stamford.[8]

In October 1642, Thomas Kittermaster of Hereford, a parliamentary soldier, authored a pamphlet describing his side's victory in Drayton, Herefordshire. He claimed that the 'troopes of the Cavaliers came against the said Towne, with an inten[t] to have plundered it and put the inhabitants to the Sword – men, women, and children'.[9]

The pamphlet immediately credits God with the victory over the king's army and protecting the residents of Drayton. From the start of the conflict, innocent people were being directly impacted and the psychological warfare would continue, develop and brutalise over the next nine years. Kittermaster went on to describe the overall Royalist support of the county: 'our country howsoever they seeme strongly for the other Party, yet in their hearts, they are for the King and Parliament, however, they have been abused in idle Pamphlets.'[10] Both sides of the conflict used such publications to promote their own propaganda. In this 'Paper War', both sides aimed for the middle ground with their printed propaganda.[11] In his letter, Kittermaster wrote, 'God, who still guards the fighters of his battails, did likewise to their courage adde their victory. … I beseech God to send us peace and a speedy happy union betwixt the King and Parliament.'[12] Political propaganda was reaching rural counties and having an impact, but these words did little to soothe the local population who were watching their communities morph into hellish landscapes.

Letters written by Lady Brilliana Harley, wife of Sir Robert, reflect the psychological distress of siege warfare. The Harleys were in the minority amongst their peers in the gentry and their family home became an attractive target to the Royalists. In a letter to her son in February 1642, Lady Harley observed:

> Now they say they will starve me out of my house; they have taken away all your father's rents, and they say they will drive away the cattle, and then I shall have nothing to live upon; for all their aim is to enforce me to let those men I have go, that then they might seize upon my house and cut our throats by a few rogues and then say they knew not who did it. They have used all means to leave me have no man in my house, and tell me that then I shall be safe; but I have no cause to trust them. I thank God we are all well.[13]

Later that year, on 13 December 1642, she wrote, 'I fear the provision of corn and malt will not hold out if this continue, and they say they will burn my barns; and my fear is that they will place soldiers so near me, that there will be no going out.'[14] A year later, still under the constant threat of siege, she wrote: 'I am threatened every day to be beset with soldiers.' And in another letter to her son:

> Now they say they will starve me out of my house … they say they will drive away the cattle, and then I shall have nothing to live upon; for all their aim is to enforce me to let those men I have go, that then they might seise upon my house, and cut our throats by a few rogues.[15]

Lady Harley's letters reveal a woman who was fearful and strong in equal measure, but she would be dead in a year, succumbing to pneumonia.

Meanwhile, garrison towns were fortified and defended, or seized, at a considerable cost to the local population.[16] It was largely a struggle between two competing armies, fighting occasional battles, and settling scores of garrisoned bases. This involved the plunder by soldiers in search of supplies and the greed of marauders in search of money or valuables.[17] In 1642, William Bowen, a junior officer under the command of Robert Devereux, Earl of Essex, reported the names of commanding officers killed in the 'great and bloudy skirmish' that took place in Worcester on 23 September. Bowen added that the Cavaliers had 'done the Towne great injuries, as likewise most places wheresoever they came'.[18] The 'injuries' endured by communities in Herefordshire and Worcestershire were unrelenting. In late 1642, a correspondent from Worcester railed against the alleged misbehaviour of some 600 Welsh Royalist soldiers who had recently been billeted in the town.[19] Henry Townshend, Worcestershire gentleman, noted in his diary:

> Cavaliers and soldiers in divers parts of this kingdom (where they come) have plundered the towns, bloodily killing the king's peaceable subjects, rifling their houses, and violently taking away of their goods and in some places deflowered women. … it is generally suspected and feared they have some design upon this city, or at leastwise may occasion the bringing an army upon this city to the Ruin thereof, And for that we have been credibly informed that there is an intent to billet soldiers here, which (we conceive) may be very dangerous to this City.[20]

The presence of allegedly unruly troops would have been a constant factor for many, especially when soldiers were accused of serious offences. There was also disruption to various tradesmen, as shops were plundered, and craftsmen were forced to give soldiers their raw materials and tools.[21] William Sheldon of Beoley in Worcestershire testified in 1653 that ten years earlier, in December 1643, his house at Beoley was:

> burned to the ground and all my cattle and goods were plundered by the soldiers. … I and my wife were forced for our safety to go to the city of Worcester and after a short stay there, removed to a farmhouse

in the parish of Clifton on Teme ... until all our goods were also taken away by soldiers and the house threatened to be burned.[22]

The residents of Herefordshire and Worcestershire were enduring unrelenting trauma. It is therefore unsurprising that the townspeople were unwilling to billet these unruly soldiers. As the soldiers were already angry about their deferred payments, they were often insubordinate and disrespectful, or, worse, mutinous.[23] It was not only the residents of occupied towns and cities that were frustrated: Nehemiah Wharton, a Parliamentarian officer, observed in October 1642 that the residents of Hereford found solace in alcohol and judged that they were:

> totally ignorant in the waies of God, and much addicted to drunkkenness and other vices, but principally unto swearinge, so that the children that have scarce learned to speake doe universally sweare stoutlye.[24]

Soldiers were not only accused of violating the communities, but they were also viewed as corrupting influences. The Earl of Stamford echoed Wharton's sentiments in December 1642:

> The county, as well as this vile city, as so base and malignant, that, although the roguish Army of the Welsh Papists, and other Vagabonds, that were beaten in the First Battle in Warwickshire, so plunder, kill, murder, and destroy Men and Women, take away all their Goods and Cattle; yet, as such is their Hatred to our Condition, that they had rather be so used and ill-treated, than to be rescued or relieved by us.[25]

Wharton also wrote that Worcester was 'so base so papisticall and Atheisticall and Abominable that it resembles Sodom and is the very Embleme of Gomorah'.[26] This statement was quite an indictment of the city and its residents. As early as 1642, a mere four months into the conflict, there were already comparisons to the biblical end of times. Many residents took shelter inside the city walls or moved elsewhere, but those who could not leave would face complete devastation. The Harley family home in Brampton Bryan had been a parliamentary refuge in 1643 as well as an efficient intelligence service, but it too was destroyed in 1644 by Royalist forces.[27]

It would have been quite easy to tar the soldiers of both sides with the same despicable brush but the soldiers were also suffering. They were unwelcomed at every turn, viewed as looters and tormenters of townspeople, and fighting a seemingly endless war. All men from the age of 16 to 60 were expected to serve in defence of the country. Trained men were expected to meet once a month for further training and attend an annual regimental muster in the summer.[28] Some did not attend the Hereford muster for religious and political reasons, as well as opposition to the Royalists. However, to some, the Royalists represented the moderates who were interested in maintaining the status quo.[29]

Once the war started, king and Parliament made a dash to control trained bands of soldiers; in August 1643, Parliament issued an ordinance that empowered deputy lieutenants and committees in each county to raise soldiers with the help of parish constables and any refusal to be drafted would result in imprisonment.[30] Charles I was highly reliant on the goodwill of influential people in each county to help with recruitment.[31] In 1643, it was agreed that £3,000 should 'be raised and paid monthly towards the payment of His Majesty's forces sent and raised for the defence of this County of Worcester'.[32] Alternatively, in 1644, Sir Robert Harley was nominated as the Herefordshire delegate to a committee with the power and authority to 'take the subscriptions of all such persons as will voluntarily lend or contribute any summe or summes of money, plate, horse, or armes towards supplies and provisions' for parliamentary forces.[33] The financial strain on residents was a constant burden. By 1645, the stress associated with the having to respond to the needs of field armies was clearly visible throughout the two counties. In July 1645, in a letter to the 'worshipfull' mayor, aldermen and citizens of Hereford, parliamentary representatives pleaded that it was their:

> earnest desire to prevent the effusion of much Christian blood, which must unavoydably be spilt, if the City should be forcibly entered, and the consideration that a number of Religious and Innocent Persons are likely to suffer with the rest, whose blood, if spilt through your obstinancy, will be required at your hands.[34]

The local authorities were warned to make a clear path for the soldiers, while citizens in the cities and towns were expected to cooperate. Likewise, those who were able to fight were expected to do so or face consequences. In Herefordshire, there was a list of charges against Thomas Penoyre of Clifford for 'forcibly enlisting men for the King's service'. Penoyre had been ordered by Barnabas Scudamore, the Royalist Governor of Hereford, to raise men and arms in the parish of Clifford in June 1645. A warrant was also issued the next month for the arrest of deserters.[35]

These records do not show why the soldiers deserted, or why Penoyre resorted to forcibly enlisting men. These men may have wanted to fight for Parliament instead, or they may have not wanted to fight at all. For example, Worcestershire was a Royalist county with a high proportion of Roman Catholic gentry families, and yet many Catholic residents in the county remained neutral.[36] In 1645, Clubmen, or peacekeeping associations, banded together in the form of self-defence against the atrocities of war; these groups were well organised and arranged for a watch to be maintained and church bells rung when marauding soldiers were spotted. The Clubmen were generally neutral but it was not a unified national movement because their motivation centred on local interests.[37] In addition, theirs was a vertical organisation, uniting all segments of local society from minor gentry and clergy to poorer farmers.[38] They were not anti-government or apolitical, but focused on immediate local regulations and the demands in times of conflict.[39] The Clubmen varied in their political loyalties, some neutralist, some Royalist, some Parliamentarian, but they all wanted the war to end.[40] Clubmen mobilised in ways that drew upon the tradition of popular protest and those forms of protest clearly persisted. In that sense, Clubmen leaders were trying to inflect a more traditional form of communal demonstration as a contribution to the politics of the civil war and were an unwelcome addition to the political scene.[41] It is noticeable that Clubmen revolts took place in Herefordshire and Worcestershire in the first three months of 1645.[42] These movements broke out in parts of the country that had 'more deeply ... tasted the misery of this unnatural, intestine war'.[43]

In Herefordshire, Colonel Edward Massey stated that the local Clubmen wanted his help, but they 'will not yet declare themselves for Parliament but they conceive themselves able to keep off both the Parliament's forces and the King's and also from contribution and quarter in their county'. By this point, the New Model Army, formed in February 1645, was Parliament's centralised army that benefitted from central funding and leadership. This strategic shift would have huge consequences. When the opportunity arose, the Royalists crushed the Clubmen, and the New Model Army also dispatched with little ceremony those they considered hostile.[44] In Worcestershire, the Clubmen were described as 'anti-disorder, not anti-tax. The Clubmen opposed the rampant plundering and free quartering of soldiers used by both sides.'[45] Thus, both Royalists and Parliamentarians used the Clubmen to their own advantage, trying to persuade them to their respective sides. In Worcestershire, the Clubmen appealed to the Grand Jury and highlighted the risks to their wives and children by the marauding soldiers who threatened to burn down their homes and 'ravish' their wives and daughters.[46]

Both counties were often at the mercy of the travelling field armies, particularly the proximity of Herefordshire sandwiched between Royalist Wales and Parliamentarian Gloucestershire. The population there were expected to shelter and feed the soldiers, as well as their horses. In communities dependent on agriculture, feeding horses could potentially ruin crops for a season, while the damage caused by soldiers trampling fields and plundering crops, livestock and other produce was widespread.[47] Herefordshire residents were horrified by the appearance of Scottish troops in the summer of 1645. Local resident Jane Merrick was injured 'working to move earth' for the defences of Hereford prior to their arrival.[48] The Scots were viewed as foreign invaders and the locals refused to supply them with food or assistance of any kind. The troops were forced to fend for themselves after Parliament reneged on an earlier promise to support them. This was noted by the Earl of Leven, who remarked that they had 'large promises' for:

> furnishing and providing our Army with Victuall and with all materials necessary for a siege; in both we have been exceedingly disappointed. … they never received a farthing, but for the most part, have beene left to their owne shift, and constrained to eat fruit and the Cornes that were growing upon the ground, and now for these six or seven months past, have received but one month's pay.[49]

In Hereford, there were 9,000 Scottish soldiers and 2,000 horses, and, as Thomas Juxon witnessed, with the local plundering, their number of horses doubled before they left the town.[50] This, in turn, led to them being denounced on all sides as voracious plunderers.[51] Indeed, over a century and a half later, a noted Herefordshire antiquary recalled that the pillaging of the Scottish troops made a lasting impression on the residents.[52]

The most disturbing feature of such incidents, from the gentry's point of view, was the atmosphere of defiance that they witnessed and the growing sense that, with the king and his parliament unable to settle their disputes, the law was quickly becoming ineffectual.[53] This lawlessness would have a grave effect on these local communities and, in turn, their political and later religious identities.

There was an increasing sense of hopelessness, made worse with each passing year. As money became tighter as the war progressed, troops were not paid and sought recompense to the detriment of the local community, especially as they commandeered supplies and demanded free quartering. Slowly, the lines between official requisition and blatant plunder became increasingly prominent.[54] When control of Hereford returned to the Parliamentarians in December 1645, Colonels Thomas Morgan and John Birch stated:

> The Townesmen have suffered by the Souldier, by reason we entred it by force, and that the Enemy shot out at the windowes and in the streets, the Soudlier was so inraged that we could not prevent them from plundering.[55]

Townsfolk and villagers alike were ready to defend themselves after years of exploitation from both sides. Morgan recorded that 'we found the city of Hereford, by our intelligence to be so strong, both in its selfe and the resolution of the Defendants, that much hazard would be in the gaining of it'.[56] In *Mercurius Belgicus*, the Royalists noted that:

> The loyal city of Hereford was by the persidiousnesse of some within, and the bribery of others without, delivered up to the rebels without any siege, or almost any bloodshed, whereby the persons and goods of many Gentlemen of quality and other loyall subjects fell into the hands of the mercilesse Victors.[57]

This bloodless surrender suggests that the people were suffering from conflict fatigue and lacked the will and energy to engage the incoming troops. The frontispiece of this document contains the Latin phrase '*Incerti sunt exitus pugnarum, Marsque esi communis, qui sepe spoliantem, jam & exultantem evertit,*

& perculit ab abjecto' ('the uncertain outcome of warfare') and it ends noting that 'there remains now nothing to compleat this short, sad story'.[58] The Puritans perceived the civil wars as a 'struggle by the godly few against the enemies of true religion'.[59] Puritan minister Richard Baxter of Kidderminster recalled the 'marvellous preservation' of soldiers' pocket bibles stopping bullets and frequently cited this as an example of divine providence.[60] Describing God's divine plan in 1645, Barnabas Scudamore determined that God had sent them:

> singular men of all professions, very usefull, and necessary for us in this distresse, and so accidentally to us, as if they had on purpose been let downe from Heaven, to serve our present and emergent occasions.[61]

As the wars progressed, there was a need to be fighting on God's side, as demonstrated by Parliamentarian Colonel Thomas Morgan's statement to William Lenthall, Speaker of the House of Commons. Following their success in Hereford, he stated that he had been:

> commanded by the Committee of both Kingdoms, to make an Attempt upon Hereford: In which Design it pleased God to bless us, and the Souldiers going on with undaunted resolution, made our entrance with small losse; divers of the Enemy making resistance in the street, were slain, and the rest taken prisoners.[62]

In March 1646, in the face of certain defeat, Royalists were also confident God would eventually prevail for their side. *Mercurius Belgicus* reported that:

> His Majesty two Armyes defeated in lesse then a fortnight, yet we are confident when Almighty God hath sufficiently punisht the sins of this Nation, he will in his good time restore a pious King to his just rights, and his bleeding Kingdomes to peace and union in despight of all Sectaries and Opponents.[63]

The disruption and destruction of constant sieges inevitably took its toll on the residents of both counties. In late January 1648, the Justices of the Peace, Grand Jury and Gentlemen of Hereford sent a petition to the House of Commons that expressed the sheer desperation felt by the people after years of conflict. The language used by the petitioners made it clear that the people were desperate for the wars to end as they used words including 'Misery', 'Total Ruin' and 'Poor, almost wasted Kingdom'.[64] They were undoubtedly war-weary, and the language expressed the desire for a return to peace and stability. This petition received a response from Lord Fairfax and the Council of War:

> Blessed Patriots; for you have been blessed ... we cannot but send you our Acclamations to strengthen and quicken your hands in that mighty work. ... Proceed, therefore, vigorously, and thoroughly in the name of the Lord, and you will eternize your own, while we subscribe ours.[65]

This was unlikely to be the response that the people of Hereford were seeking. A reward in the afterlife was not going to help repair the damage to the city and county of Herefordshire or deliver them from their earthly misery. Equally, surviving records show the damage caused by a decade of war in Worcester to numerous homes and to the cathedral.[66] Places of worship were not spared, and buildings were 'burnt and pulled down in the late wars' and 'destroyed in the late warrs'.[67] The continual struggle, bloodshed and destruction had the ability to undermine even the most ardent believer.

Monarchy was a constant, seemingly immoveable, force. There would be conflict and disagreements, but everyday people could not have imagined that in January 1649, King Charles I would be tried and convicted of high treason and then executed on 30 January. Even without a king, the figurehead to rally for or against, the fighting would not end until the Battle of Worcester on 3 September 1651.

Following the final battle of the civil wars, in a pamphlet detailing 'every particular of the fight at Worcester', the victors acknowledged that 'it pleased the Lord after some sharp dispute, ours beat them from hedge to hedge'.[68] Another pamphlet read, 'what shall we return unto the Lord for his great kindnesse, his mercies never faile'.[69] This was a victory that God himself had fashioned. The statement from Parliament read:

> The Parliament being very sensible of the wonderful and seasonable Mercies God hath been pleased to vouchsafe unto this Nation, by his great Blessing upon their Army neer Worcester. ... on the next Lord's Day, give Publique Thanks to Almighty God for this great Mercy.[70]

A letter to Lord General Cromwell stated:

> Oh! My Lord, what are you, that you should be the instrument to translate the nation from oppression to libertie, from the hands of corrupt personas to the saints? And who are we, that we should live to see these dayes, which our fathers longed to see, and reape the harvest of their hopes.[71]

On 5 September 1651, two days after the decisive Parliamentarian victory, an 'eminent officer' at the Battle of Worcester wrote anonymously that:

> In all the engagements that ever hath beene, I think we have not seen a more immediate hand of God appearing than in this; I believe there was never more courage and resolution in an Army, yet lesse done by us as men; that which adds much to the mercy is that the presence of the Lord was so immediate with us, that we may say no flesh hath cause to boast, but we must say it is the Lord hath done all these things.[72]

There was an expectation that innocent people would be killed, or their lives destroyed. Particularly in the garrisoned towns and cities, the day-to-day unrest and instability was devastating. A decade of war would unavoidably have its casualties, both in terms of bloodshed and religious observance.

Chapter 3

The Sparks of Radical Faith

The war-weary people found themselves in a crisis of faith, often encouraged to challenge their longstanding beliefs by radicalised travelling preachers. As a consequence of war, the inescapable instability of the state church in the 1640s left the casual layperson with the freedom to subscribe to new and sometimes radical ideas. The radical movements and sects of the 1640s and 1650s were often led by persuasive, charismatic preachers and leaders who had served on the battlefield.

Censorship fell away during the wars and the printing press was a means of political participation.[1] In the social turmoil, space was created for the development of radical ideas from the bottom up. Access to printing and published material widely expanded during the wars. Pamphlets and newsbooks provided the people with access to political and religious propaganda, not only in terms of Royalists versus Parliamentarians, but also about issues that struck the core of mid-seventeenth-century society: new religious ideas.[2]

As the wars progressed, the soldiers in the New Model Army disseminated the ideas of obscure radical groups that were scattered up and down the kingdom.[3] Camp preachers travelled with the armies and the geographically large scale of the conflict meant that radical elements were trickling into the mainstream. Tub preachers were the subject of a notoriously critical 1647 pamphlet entitled *Tub-Preachers Overturn'd or Independency to be Abandon'd and Abhor'd as Destructive to the Majestracy and Ministery, of the Church and Common-Wealth of England.*[4] These preachers were referred to as 'lay illiterate men and women' who displayed madness in their attempt to 'usurpe the Ministry and audaciously vent their own hereticall opinions'.[5] This pamphlet demonstrated that not everyone was going to accept such disruptive forces in their communities. But, as David Cressy explains, 'the genie was out of the bottle, artisans and shopkeepers had tasted the elixir, and England would never be the same. This was a revolution from which there was no going back.'[6]

The wars provided the basis for these dissenters to pursue purposes quite different from the formal war aims of the military parties. Many of these dissenters advocated living in the present moment and not waiting for an uncertain afterlife. This belief gave people both comfort and freedom – a kind of liberty that made the authorities nervous. These ideas created an atmosphere of anxiety and challenged the fragile government in a way that some dissenters were able to use opportunistically to their advantage.[7]

The civil wars managed to take a dislocated world and connect it and spread ideas. Dissenting groups were able to articulate their views to an audience that was dissatisfied and deeply damaged by the impact of war. Various religious groups sought a captive audience in the years following the wars. While many of these groups were not firmly established in the two counties examined here, all of them were intent on disrupting established religious practices or challenging prevailing social norms.

Many of these groups formed 'gathered churches', congregations formed voluntarily based on their shared faith and doctrine.[8] Independent congregations were highly influential and favoured by Oliver Cromwell and much of the army. These gathered churches advocated independence over religious matters rather than the control of a clerical hierarchy. Although Independents distanced themselves from orthodoxy, they still considered themselves a legitimate part of the national Church.[9] In contrast, Baptists were more intent on challenging the practices of the established Church. General Baptists believed that Christ had died for everyone and repudiated the Calvinist dogma of predestination. They opposed the taking of oaths and were also against the collecting of tithes, but not as virulently as Quakers would later do.[10] John Tombes, the vicar of Leominster, became an 'increasingly radical Baptist' who refused to observe the established rites and ceremonies of the Church after 1640,[11] and founded churches in Herefordshire and Bewdley, Worcestershire, while also maintaining his parish churches at Bewdley and Leominster.[12] In this environment of freedom and with the confidence to express new ideas, clergymen had more evangelical opportunities in a parish church than merely in his gathered church.[13] Other dissenting religious groups were meeting at this time, but in private homes.

More radical groups were taking shape, with more threatening ideas.

Ranterism came into prominence in 1649 and was relatively short-lived, but their radical ideas were viewed as dangerous.[14] The Ranters took the extreme view that if God was present in a person, it was impossible for that individual to commit sin and the law was therefore irrelevant.[15] This was demonstrated in their denial of the authority of the Scriptures as well as their open attitudes towards sex. It is easy to see why the authorities were alarmed by their presence. However, Ranterism was a leaderless, disorganised, and fluid movement, unlike the Fifth Monarchists. Bernard Capp describes the latter as a 'pressure group rather than a new denomination or party', and perhaps because they constantly anticipated the imminent reign of Jesus, they never created any lasting, national organisation.[16] They were a political movement, nonetheless, seeking a Millenarian parliament that could potentially usher in the Second Coming.[17] Their shared core of ideas consisted of opposition to the Church and tithes, the illegality of the Protectorate, and that morality should be upheld by a set of laws modelled on the Old Testament.[18] Socially distinctive, Fifth Monarchists also refused hat honour and used 'thee' and 'thou'.[19] Spiritually, they believed that the 'Saints' needed to clear the way for the millennium; and they linked prophetic symbols in the Bible to contemporary events, particularly in light of the execution of Charles I (God's anointed ruler) and the decade-long series of wars.[20] Elsewhere in England, the Levellers, led by John Lilburne, advocated for equality before the law, popular sovereignty and religious tolerance.[21] Their influence waned by 1649, but their ideas would live on. The Diggers, known as the 'True Levellers' advocated for communal ownership of the land and longed for a society without private property. Led by Gerrard Winstanley, this would also be a short-lived movement, effectively disbanded in 1650.

In the early 1650s there was another movement developing unnoticed in the north of England. People and, most importantly, local authorities may have been aware of Quakerism in 1653 if they had happened to read any early Quaker pamphlets. The earliest Quakers were deeply prolific writers and they wrote in a way that would tap into the fearfulness and anxiety of the day. Some of the early Quaker converts in Herefordshire and Worcestershire began their journey of religious dissent on the battlefields. James Merrick of Ross-on-Wye was in the Hereford militia, fighting for Parliament.[22] Most early Quakers in the two counties were not political radicals like the Fifth Monarchists. However, Morgan Watkins of Eyton, Herefordshire, a cornet (junior officer) in the New Model Army, noted Independent and early Herefordshire Quaker convert, could be considered an exception.

Watkins wrote to Cromwell in 1653 concerning the painful experiences of the past decade, yet expressed optimism and stated that under Cromwell's guidance, 'the great and long desired reformation is neere the birth'.[23] Moreover, Watkins believed that God had bestowed great powers on Cromwell as he had 'called you forth and led you on, not only in the high places of the field, making you a terror to the enemie, but also to the dissolving of the late parliament'. It was, according to Watkins, to be a time of rejoicing and of hope after the calamities of the civil wars.[24]

The status quo was rapidly changing, and radical religious ideas were becoming more widespread. The leadership of these emerging religious movements had to capitalise on this opportunity with swift organisation and the refinement of their message.

Chapter 4

A Plague of Northern Locusts

In the mid-1650s, the environment of uncertainty and ideological freedom helped to make Quakerism a viable religious belief system for those coping with the trauma of war. The Quakers tapped into the dissatisfaction and uncertainty of the period and spread their message with zeal, prolific writing and a gifted travelling ministry.

The desire for a new religious identity was growing in these communities and Quakerism was viewed by some as an attractive alternative to the state church. The Quaker message brought together many of the concepts initiated by other radical groups and was packaged in a way that resonated in these war-torn communities. Quakers would eventually establish meetings in every English county – a tribute to the enthusiasm of the missionaries and to the organisational skill of the first Quakers.[1] These widespread meetings demonstrated the efficacy of their message and acceptance by local groups as well as the effectiveness of the leaders sent to propagate the Quaker message. There were three key influential individuals setting the Quaker foundation at the onset – George Fox, Margaret Fell and James Nayler.

George Fox was born in the village of Drayton-in-the-Clay (now Fenny Drayton), Leicestershire, in July 1624. At the age of 19 in 1643, Fox left his family and began a period of travelling. He wrote that he was plagued by the temptations of sin and despair and found no solution in any of the religious options of the day. He felt most at home amongst the 'dissenting' people (particularly the General Baptists) and as he travelled, he remained within regions controlled by Parliamentary forces. During the late 1640s, Fox had several significant religious experiences and he regarded as divine revelations received through inward encounters with Christ. He believed that 'The Lord would teach his people himself'. The experiences prompted his public ministry, which began in the Midlands and Yorkshire in 1647. During this period, Fox began his practice of entering churches to dispute with the clergy. Unsurprisingly, he was often attacked by mobs of local people when preaching. In 1650, he was imprisoned for blasphemy in Derby. He was offered a captaincy in the army in exchange for his freedom, but he declined, claiming he fought with spiritual weapons, not outward ones.

Fox recruited important early Quaker preachers at the onset, including Nayler. James Nayler was born in Ardsley in Yorkshire. He served in the Parliamentarian army. After experiencing what he described as the voice of God calling him, he gave up his possessions and began seeking a spiritual direction. He met George Fox in Wakefield in 1651. Nayler became the most prominent of the travelling Quaker ministers, attracting many converts, and was considered a skilled theological debater. He led much of the work in London and the south of England, especially when George Fox was sporadically in prison. Margaret Fell was another strategically important, early convert. Her home, Swarthmoor Hall, near Ulverston in Cumbria, was the movement's organising base and refuge, under her husband, Judge Thomas Fell's, protection. Margaret Fell's writings, including letters and pamphlets, contributed to the theological foundation of Quakerism.

George Fox's mission to the north of England from 1651 to 1652 was overwhelmingly successful because his message was acceptable to pre-existing congregations of religious dissenters.[2] There was an early rejection of church hierarchy. Fox and the earliest converts preached that true worship did not require buildings, ostentatious ornaments or ordained ministry. They refused to take oaths because they felt that by always speaking the truth, there was no need, and more importantly, in swearing an oath, they would disobey Christ, who said 'swear not at all' in the Book of Matthew. This tied into the belief that all were equal before God. Quakers observed that when oaths were required before local authorities and in courts, it demonstrated an inequality amongst men. Quakers also refused to remove their hats to social superiors, as was the custom in the seventeenth century. This was another demonstration of social hierarchy they wholeheartedly rejected.

It has been observed that the distinctive Quaker beliefs were already current, but it was the charismatic leaders and ministers that people found inspiring.[3] While Fox's opinions were not distinctive, it was the 'sense of spiritual power, the depth of insight, and the profound conviction of the reality of his own experience' that shaped his compelling argument.[4] Fox, however, was unwilling to acknowledge the influence of other religious radicals he met during his spiritual pilgrimage of the 1640s.[5] His was a policy of adopt and adapt. Those who became disillusioned, especially with the Baptists, often drifted towards the more vaguely defined doctrines of the Quakers.[6]

The Quaker message may have appealed to those who felt excluded in the community, or 'parish malcontents' who were intrigued by the bold and confrontational style of the earliest Quakers.[7] However, its viability as a religious community stemmed not only from the message being conveyed, but also by the way it was introduced. Larry Ingle writes that Fox was a 'spark, lighting the way' and people would abandon their leaders to follow these 'new prophets' who provided a vision of an alternative, seemingly better, future. Fox was aware of the demographics of his audience and was able to tailor his message accordingly.[8] This targeted approach was not only intuitive and effective, but also quite shrewd. Fox was a mastermind of organising and packaging this message in a way that made it irresistible to those looking for an alternative.

The Quaker message resonated with a younger audience perhaps because it was one of hope, possibility and radical change, and relied not only on the spoken word, but on competent literacy as well. As discussed earlier, it was also about recovering from the psychological trauma of a decade of warfare. This was a belief system that valued a deep and personal connection to God and provided a liberating alternative to the state church.

What is clear is that the Quakers were communicating radical biblical ideas that were challenging to the clergy, but they also challenged the religious orthodoxy, the foundations of civic and ecclesiastical authority, and expressed these sentiments with considerable enthusiasm.[9] The Quakers held firm against a paid ministry and as tithes were paid to the clergy, it was a natural opposition to such a financial exaction. Equally, in 1646, Fox declared that formal qualifications from Cambridge or Oxford Universities was 'not enough to make men fit to be ministers of Christ' and he told his family: 'did not the apostle say to the believers, that they needed no man to teach them' and that 'the Lord would teach his people himself'.[10]

There were political radicals, like Morgan Watkins in Herefordshire, who engaged with the earliest message and joined the early Quakers. Quakerism was presented as being open to all, and that would have been appealing. However, some of those who converted to Quakerism were influenced by their experiences in the civil wars and the way in which new social and religious ideas were spread on the battlefield. This idea of liberating the soul from the hands of the clergy became a cornerstone of Quakerism and acted as a focal point for the message being conveyed, both in preaching and in print.

This 'liberation' also leads into another mainstay of the early Quaker message and that is the concept of 'light'. As such, Quakers did not require a priest or other intermediary as they had direct access to God and could also share in Christ's perfection, and that 'their word for this experience was "light"', 'the light in their consciences' that emanated through everyone, providing spiritual equality.[11] Fox strongly emphasised the 'light' in an undated letter he addressed to Worcester Quakers, in which he stated that:

> Every one of you having a light from the son of God wait in the light that you may come to receive the son of God from whence it comes and receive power from him to become the sons of God and have faith in him. ... faith gives the victory over the world.[12]

The idea of a 'light within' each person was a radical notion that everyone had the freedom to communicate with God when and wherever they pleased. The freedom to choose also meant that it was part of a message that needed to be shared as widely as possible.

Quakerism would not have survived without the foresight and capability to take the message further afield. Fox set the precedent at the onset for Quaker missionary activities. Years later, William Penn wrote that Fox:

> left his friends, and visited the most retired and religious people in those parts; and since there were short of few, if any, in this nation, who waited for the consolation of Israel night and day ... to these he was sent, and these he sought out in the neighbouring countries and among them he sojourned till his more ample ministry came upon him.[13]

Fox, like others in the early movement, used his travels and tribulations as a training ground. These had strategic value, and Fox planned his journeys to meet 'potentially useful and sympathetic people and separated church groups'.[14] These groups had already separated themselves from the established church, so if approached by persuasive missionaries with sufficient confidence, they could be gathered into a new religious community. The aims of these early Quaker missionaries were to establish meetings, and offer spiritual leadership and, particularly, fellowship.[15] They took their early message to towns and villages, seeking out hospitable groups and drawing widespread scepticism and hostility: on the road is where their message evolved and developed.

From their administrative centre at Margaret Fell's home, Swarthmoor Hall, the first itinerant preachers travelled widely throughout England and further afield. In 1654, George Fox declared that their work was divinely inspired, which could be witnessed in the multiplication of adherents: 'the heavenly dew the living mercies which nourishes the tender plants which causes them to grow, bud, and bring forth which is blessing'.[16]

There was no shortage in finding willing missionaries to tend to these 'tender plants'; the early Quakers were deeply moved to propagate their message.[17] The correspondence from Swarthmoor Hall between Margaret Fell, George Fox and the Quaker missionaries demonstrates the fervour and dedication of those embarking on their missions. The missionaries served as the natural link between the administrative centre and the growth of the movement. At the onset, missionary activity was highly organised. Thomas Willam and George Taylor were appointed treasurers for the Kendal Fund, which was set up in 1654 to support the Quaker mission.[18] They were responsible for reporting activities to Fox and Fell, and financial maintenance of the whole endeavour – for ensuring that the itinerant preachers also had basic necessities. In June 1655, they reported that over £27 was received from local meetings in the north of England.[19] In August that year, Taylor wrote to Margaret Fell to advise that money was dispersed to missionaries for clothing and shoes.[20] The missionaries were provided with the things that they needed to ensure their success, within reason, as there was always the expectation that their expenses would not be excessive.[21] They sent regular correspondence to Fell to advise her of news and provide inventories of books and travel expenses distributed to the travelling Quakers.

On the ground, the missionaries gave notice of their impending visit, if possible, to let word of mouth generate interest, which would draw a crowd for a meeting. In most cases, these meetings were held in a local residence. The Worcester Quakers first met in 1655 at the home of Sarah Drew, a widow, who lived in Darke Alley near Worcester Cathedral.[22] During the Protectorate, Oliver Cromwell was tolerant of religious groups, but the Quaker mass meetings, which were becoming more and more frequent in many places, seemed likely to provoke public unrest.[23] The Quakers were travelling around the country with a radical message that was strongly expressed by the missionaries. With this in mind, the Vagrancy Act was passed in 1656. The intention of this Act was to prohibit travelling without cause, and this was used against the early Quaker missionaries. It was a precursor of legislation to come.

The fact that many of the early Quaker missionaries were northerners helps to account for the opposition they met with in the south and west, where they were judged to be 'men of a strang humor'.[24] In Wiltshire, these missionaries from the north were viewed as 'troublesome outsiders' and described as 'Northern locusts'.[25] However, rather than their regional dialect, they were more likely unwelcome due to their actions and their message. The Quakers were well aware of their reputation and the derision they faced. As early as 1652, this was apparent in the frontispiece to *A Discovery of Truth and Falsehood*, written by Richard Farnworth of Tickhill, Yorkshire, in which he stated:

> Written from the Spirit of the Lord, by one whom the people of the world calls a Quaker, but is of the Divine nature made partaker: whom the world knows not, that are in their old nature, and so mock and deride: but wo to the wicked, it shall be ill with them.[26]

Farnworth's earliest tracts often contained warnings to those who mocked or challenged them. His tone, like that of the other early Quaker writers, swings on the apocalyptic scale, perhaps demonstrating the influence of Fifth Monarchists. In his tract *Light Risen out of Darkness* (1654), he warned:

> Now in these latter days shewing the dark way and worships of the Ministry of Antichrist now in these Apostated Times, which is perilous, as is foretold of often by the Holy Ghost that spoke through Paul, and now is fulfilled in these latter days.[27]

The early Quaker tracts were bursting with biblical references, not only in the text itself, but the published tracts featured marginalia or annotations containing the copiously referenced Scripture. The Bible provided 'not just the grammar in which to frame ideas, but a source for those ideas as well'.[28]

The printed marginalia in their published tracts would demonstrate to the people that the Quaker message was not heretical; it was based on the word of God.

Another reason why their message would resonate is that, for the most part, the Quakers consciously wrote on behalf of the movement rather than as individuals.[29] This was important because at the onset, it gave the impression of organisation and community. Farnworth frequently published as 'A Quaker' or 'one whom the people of the world call a Quaker, whose name is Richard Farneworth' or 'Richard Farnsworth the Quaker'. Richard Farnworth and the term 'Quaker' were interchangeable and synonymous. Farnworth's published tracts from 1652 to 1654 included such provocative titles as *A Discovery of Truth and Falsehood*, *A Briefe Discovery of the Kingdome of Antichrist*, *England's Warning Peece Gone Forth*, *Light Risen out of Darkness*, *A Woman Forbidden to Speak in the Church* and *A Call Out of False Worships* – these tract titles were chosen for impact.[30] Farnworth was not afraid to challenge the status quo.

He was one of the first Quaker leaders to visit Herefordshire and Worcestershire. He was known as a young, energetic, prolific writer and, by all accounts, a gifted preacher. His message was a cautionary tale, a warning of the impending apocalypse. He acknowledged that these were perilous times. Indeed, the Quakers, despite their serious-mindedness and devotion to God, were targeted by a 'hostile clergy' and accused of being 'radical malcontents, possessed by the devil, witches, or mentally unbalanced'.[31] The early missionaries were trying to save as many souls as they possibly could, with an uncertain time remaining. They were searching for an alternative and moving out of the darkness of religious uncertainty with an identity shaped by organisation and missionary activity. Equipped with this message, packaged in an unorthodox manner, it is therefore not surprising that they encountered suspicion and fierce resistance along the way. They could not separate themselves and thus protected themselves from the world because this would have minimised their impact and they needed to be involved in the wider community.[32]

Farnworth's extant correspondence from his time in the counties provides an insight into the life of a missionary and, most importantly, the general atmosphere he encountered in 1654. In a letter to George Fox, he described Hereford as 'dark, one or two pretty hearts there is but herein and some others ... turn enemies to the truth by words'.[33] Thomas Goodaire travelled with him. In May 1654, they were 'moved to go to the steeplehouse' and after causing a disturbance, Farnworth was removed from the church while Goodaire continued his preaching, much to the annoyance of the congregation. Farnworth recorded that they were 'in so great rage that [they intended] to have killed Thomas', and Goodaire was predictably imprisoned the next day.[34] Despite their reception in Herefordshire, they continued to hold meetings throughout the two counties. In Worcester, Farnworth wrote that 'many are convinced but little else, the Crosse is hard to the ground'.[35] Goodaire was arrested for speaking to Richard Baxter at his place of worship in Kidderminster.[36] It is worth noting that Quaker records state he was 'speaking to' Baxter but their usual methods of confronting the clergy were usually more hostile and confrontational. Nevertheless, they were undeterred from their mission. During this initial visit to Worcester, Farnworth wrote that they had a great meeting in the city, which continued for several hours until late at night.[37] However, there was a sense of weariness from such missionary work, even at the onset.

In 1654, Farnworth wrote of his intended travels after his visit to Herefordshire and Worcestershire, and noted that he would be at Tewksbury, near Gloucester, and 'then as ye Lord pleaseth if it be downward into Yorkshire again I am content, but I shall visit friend I do believe I have been long in the wild world'.[38] Even with his enthusiasm and youth, as Farnworth was only in his mid-twenties, it is clear from his letter that fatigue could strike even Fox's most trusted and devoted minsters. Farnworth carried on with his mission, and he continued writing for a much wider audience. Thomas Goodaire and George Scaff, another missionary from the north, visited Herefordshire on a separate occasion later that year. These multiple visits in short succession suggests the importance of converts in this region. Farnworth's presence in the counties is important not only because of his higher profile within the early Quaker structure, but also because he was a very prolific writer, whose work possibly reached open-minded congregations of dissenters prior to his visit. This familiarity may have worked in Farnworth's favour and, in turn, aided the work of his travelling Quaker companions.

Farnworth and John Audland of Westmorland shared a youthful enthusiasm that played a significant role in spreading the early message.[39] Audland was a former Independent preacher and one of the earliest converts, and frequently travelled with George Fox.[40] Audland visited Hereford in 1655 and in his correspondence with his with fellow itinerant preacher, Thomas Airey of Northumberland (d. 1679), wrote, 'we parted, having given up our lives into the hands of the Lord, nor knowing when we should meet, and we had not the least knowledge of anyone in the city.'[41] Writing letters that painted a realistic picture potentially gave Fox the opportunity to send reinforcements to one particular area. Farnworth's presence is significant in the region, not only because of his higher profile within the early Quaker movement, but also because he was one of Fox's key early converts, alongside Margaret Fell and James Nayler.

Quakers wrote about large meetings with eager audiences and ministers, which convinced many to join. This was a carefully crafted narrative that unfurled from the leadership downwards and across the country. One of the consistent themes in the records of early Quakers is that 'no man had made them a Quaker'.[42] It was a divine conversion. However, in 1655, George Fox visited Anthony Cole (d. 1661) in Chadwick, Worcestershire, and witnessed a peculiar convincement conducted by Cole. Fox wrote that Cole had given an Independent preacher 'a meeting place' and the Independent 'came to be convinced'. Fox further recorded that it was such a large meeting, Cole's house 'would not hold the people' so the meeting was moved to the nearby hillside and 'many were turned to the Lord that day'. According to Fox, Cole gave the Independent preacher £100 a year when he was convinced.[43] Quakers were certainly not known for offering such ostentatious financial incentives to potential converts, yet Fox's matter-of-fact account showed no displeasure or surprise at Cole's actions.[44] In fact, the Independent did not remain a Quaker and 'the old Cole took away his hundred pounds a year from him again'.[45] Fox did not specify how long the Independent was a Quaker or how Cole reclaimed his money. This example from Fox's journal nevertheless demonstrates that this kind of transaction was perhaps not a common practice but also not unheard of in the formative years of the movement. At first glance, it does appear that Cole was inducing the Independent preacher to convert, but the £100 may have been offered to him as a travelling minister's maintenance payment. While this may make the transaction slightly less suspicious than the alternative, it remains a very ostentatious amount of money to offer a new convert. At the onset, Fox and the early leadership needed the support of wealthier converts who were willing to support their respective communities. These converts were able to accommodate local meetings, providing burial grounds and, as Anthony Cole demonstrated to George Fox, able to provide economic incentives, for whatever purpose, to potential converts.

In February 1656, Thomas Goodaire and George Scaff held a meeting in Ross-on-Wye[46] and amongst those in attendance was James Merrick, a tanner from the town. He was later described as 'a faithful servant and minister of Christ, and a sufferer for his name and of a good report among all men that feare [*sic*] God'.[47] Merrick would be among the first convinced and helped to settle the Ross meeting. Again, this demonstrates the importance of the critical social and economic connections made by the first itinerant ministers. In their testimony about this initial meeting in Ross, early converts William Fisher and Richard Ingram Sr. wrote that Goodaire and Scaff went to the church for a pre-planned meeting with a group of Seekers. This group was permitted to meet following the divine service to:

> sit in silence and no particular person appointed to speak or preach amongst them, but each of them did speak by way of exhortation ass had freedom, so that ye Lords power was mightily at work in their hearts and great openings there was amongst them.

In their testimony, Fisher and Ingram confirmed that there were 'parish malcontents' in the region and that these people had been separated from the state church for quite some time.[48] This group of people were willing to hear Goodaire and Scaff, and they had already been exposed to what would become the characteristics of a Quaker meeting – sitting in silence with no appointed spiritual leader. This was an ideal setting for these ministers. In Leominster, Morgan Watkins said that in the October 1656 meeting held by Goodaire there was 'gathered a multitude of people out of ye towne and country, there being notice given of ye Meeting beforehand'. At this publicised meeting, Watkins reported that the people gave 'great attention to the Things Declared' and that 'many received the Truth and were convinced'.[49]

Despite examples of a warm reception, like Goodaire's experiences in Ross and Leominster, the life of a Quaker missionary was not an easy one. The early Quaker message was one that almost deliberately antagonised the local authorities. Larry Ingle describes Fox's early message and argues that it was not his charisma that would have endangered the life of the Quaker, but rather the 'social aspect' of his sermons, and his 'forceful way of attracting attention was like waving a red flag' to the authorities who saw him as disrupting the public peace.[50] The evidence that remains, comprising letters, manuscripts and tracts, demonstrates that this was a decision made without regret, despite the likelihood of imprisonment, heavy fines and physical abuse. During their travels, the missionaries would often send correspondence to Fox and Margaret Fell. In 1654, in a letter to Fox, Farnworth wrote:

> Deare Brother, In whome I am; I have not had way to write to thee since but thou art written in my heart table, we eat together & drink together, when thou Rejoyceth I Rejoyce, & so pertakes of thy Joy & sufferings.[51]

Similarly, to Fell, he wrote:

> Deare Sister, In & with whome I Am, in the eternal dwell & Abide & go not out from it any time, neither to seek Relief nor to Relief, but wait Low, & the door will open in the eternal, & let in the heavenly treasurer to fill & Refresh thee, that with it thou mayest be as A Brest & Purse to give out milke & treasurer, Lie low & in the Life I Live with thee & all the Babes & lambes & ye Almighty Power of ye Lord be with you & Amongst you Bless Preserve & keep you now & for ever in that which is eternal Amen.[52]

Quakers frequently used exalted language when addressing Fox and Fell but Fox was addressed in a way qualitatively different from anything addressed to anyone else.[53] This was not isolated to the earliest missionaries. As late as 1664, the travelling minister Daniel Baker (*fl.* 1650–64) of London wrote to Fox from Worcester City gaol and addressed him in language befitting a deity. In the opening paragraphs of two separate letters, Baker wrote:

> Deare George, My very Deare & tender love of Blessed Remembrance is to thee, & with thee, whom my soule unexpressibly loveth, glad should I be, yea I even long to heare some what from thee & how its with thee, tho: I believe its not otherwise but well in thy Blessed life, & Dominion of god eternal for which my Living Soule together with many Brethren travels, even for its unspeakable inlargement over all in

ye beloved Election, to whom with ye father be glory & immortal living endless prayers & Dominion everlasting Amen.[54]

Deare George, My precious love & life of blessed Remembrance springs well & Fresh in ye Deare Kindness of my hart, unto thee. ... I am present with thee, as A babe with its mother of right deare tenderness, oh my very hart cryeth, & my soule ceaseth not to travel that I may be preserved to ye end & finishing of that holy & unalterable testimony that has blessed, & upheld & preserved me, ever since I believed.[55]

There is no evidence to suggest that Fox or even Fell courted such over-effusive adoration and devotion. They saw themselves as providing paternal or maternal care and guidance, but over time, this evolved from a nurturing relationship into one that was more centralised and less personal. Rosemary Moore states that a number of the surviving letters show that the recipient was addressed 'in the language of popular devotion as Christ would be' and that it is probable that later on, Fox attempted to delete these sorts of passages from the letters.[56] In the throes of enthusiastic excitement, it is not surprising that the language used was lavish and unrestrained. It is also equally unsurprising that Fox may have found these grandiose words of affection to be a point of contention, against the principles of Quakerism and possibly embarrassing.

These ministers all possessed the drive to preach, to proselytise, to encounter those who opposed their message, and to convince those who were receptive to their words – it was a multi-faceted role. Proselytising was imperative at the onset. These ministers needed to make a statement, one that would resonate beyond the written word; they needed to show the people something tangible. They needed to demonstrate their passion and the urgency of their message in a way that would be meaningful to God, themselves, and to potential converts. These meetings demonstrated one of their core tenets, that God did not require worship in a specified church building. On their travels, early ministers also spread their message in print, but tracts and pamphlets could only take the message so far at the start. These committed supporters of Fox and the early leadership were driven to propagate this message and recruit more members.[57]

The first followers were inspired by this and saw themselves as disciples of Christ. It is not surprising that young people, looking for a greater purpose after the wars, were receptive to this message and that they were willing to uproot their lives and put their personal safety at risk by preaching throughout England. There was a spread of ideas led by vociferous, literate and active preachers, but ultimately, who were they trying to convince? In any fledgling movement, strength lies in the number of new adherents. Well-placed converts and the influence of these converts meant that the ideas could flourish within that community. The itinerant preachers, including Farnworth and Audland, did not linger in Herefordshire and Worcestershire; they visited their predetermined destinations, and tried to make as great an impact as possible by converting as many as possible before they moved on to the next town or county. Daniel Baker visited Worcestershire twice and was arrested both times. In 1660, he wrote *Yet One Warning More, To Thee O England* from Worcester gaol, a tract filled with violent, apocalyptic warnings against 'antichrist, the Whore, the Great Whore, the Woman, the false Church, Mysterie Babylon the Great, the Mother of Harlots, and Abominations of the whole Earth'.[58] His letter to Fox in 1664 from Worcester gaol had a much more muted tone. Baker wrote:

> [Worcester City and County Friends] are universally well preserved & ye blessed thuth prospers in its good Savor & liveliness & Dominion through the exercise of sufferings & Consolations which together in order have Abounded.[59]

The hope for the travelling ministers was that indigenous Quakers would then carry on the message and the movement would grow and multiply within that community and beyond. This was the only way they would succeed.

Chapter 5

An Organised Grassroots Effort

In the seventeenth century, there were local Quakers who proselytised but stayed within the confines of their respective counties. These regional roles had a distinctive and important place in the formative years of Quakerism. Meetings needed to be established to further legitimise their religious beliefs and provide structure and pastoral care for their members. Once local meetings were established, the local or county-based spokespeople had different objectives to their travelling counterparts. In Herefordshire and Worcestershire, James Merrick and Edward Bourne served their local meetings as well as in a countywide capacity, and the meeting minutes and sufferings records show that Merrick largely stayed within the county borders, whereas Bourne and Morgan Watkins travelled more widely in England to spread the message.

In their roles as missionaries, Bourne and Watkins suffered great hardships and were imprisoned outside of their respective counties. Bourne was imprisoned in Marlborough, Wiltshire, for refusing to swear an oath and, in March 1656, he was sent to Bridewell gaol in London for three days and two nights.[1] In 1660, he was imprisoned in Warwickshire under the Vagrancy Act and 'put into the dungeon with locks of iron on his legs'.[2] Even his punishment in this instance was significant, for by chaining his legs he was literally being stopped from moving and preaching. In July 1664, Bourne wrote a letter to Charles II from Hereford gaol and this letter was signed 'From him who suffers imprisonment with others here for the testimony of a good conscience towards God & for no harm done unto thee or unto any person'.[3] In writing to the king, this action demonstrates Bourne's confidence, both as a writer and as an activist.

These missionaries also witnessed tumultuous events. For example, in the summer of 1665, London was swept with a fierce plague. Morgan Watkins was imprisoned in the Gatehouse near Westminster in August, during the peak of the disease – the death rate reached a high of over 6,000 per week in August alone. On 31 August 1665, the diarist Samuel Pepys recorded:

> Thus this month ends with great sadness upon the publick, through the greatness of the plague everywhere through the kingdom almost. Every day sadder and sadder news of its encrease. In the City died this week 6,102 of the plague. But it is feared that the true number of the dead, this week is near 10,000; partly from the poor that cannot be taken notice of, through the greatness of the number, and partly from the Quakers and others that will not have any bell ring for them.[4]

Watkins echoed these sentiments in a letter to Mary Penington on 18 September 1665 and observed that:

> There is a terrible cry and indeed the miseries that are upon many here, are hardly to be uttered and yet wickedness is little abated in the persecutors but they are rather worse in cruelty; for they have found a new way to murder the innocent and others that they account enemies, by thronging them into infected prisons and so their cruelty executes them in a short time.[5]

For authorities, this was an effective punishment, yet early Quaker missionaries were aware of the risks they took on their travels and continued regardless. Missionary work was critical to the early success of Quakers in Herefordshire and Worcestershire. However, without local organisation, the message of the early Quakers would have had no lasting impact.

In Herefordshire, meetings were first established in Leominster in 1655, and in Ross and Hereford a year later.[6] A meeting was established in Bromyard in 1668 and at Almeley in 1672.[7] In Worcestershire, meetings were established in 1655 in Worcester, Chadwick, Evesham, Droitwich, Bromsgrove, Stourbridge, Dudley, Shipston-on-Stour, and Bengeworth.[8] By 1661, there was a meeting in King's Norton, and in Pershore by 1662.[9] A meeting in Grafton Flyford was established by 1670 and Armscott around 1673.[10] The Herefordshire meetings were relatively equidistant and were situated in the central and north-east of the county. In Worcestershire, the meetings were predominantly in the central and eastern side of the county. Within the area, meetings like Bromyard in Herefordshire would have accommodated Quakers from the western side of Worcestershire. County organisation began in 1657 and 1658, but the main reorganisation came in 1667 and 1668, after George Fox was released from his imprisonment in Scarborough Castle.[11] Fox used the phrase 'Gospel Order' to describe this period of reorganisation from 1666 to 1668, when the county meetings began to be called Quarterly Meetings or Quarterly Meetings for Business.[12] Elsewhere, the Quarterly Meeting for Somerset began in 1667, whereas Gloucestershire, North Wales (which included Shropshire) and Worcestershire, Quarterly Meetings began in 1668. Prior to this development and formalisation of regional meetings, the Quakers in Herefordshire had already established a Quarterly Meeting.

The earliest meeting minutes demonstrate that the Herefordshire Quakers were following the traditional pattern of parish meetings. These meetings were not the more formalised Quarterly Meetings for Business that would follow two years later. The Quarterly Meeting minutes show entries for financial considerations or disbursements to those in need. This follows the same format as parochial administration for relief. The first recorded minutes also show that local meetings had reliable members to attend Quarterly Meetings; the same names appear meeting after meeting and in many cases, the children of these members would also begin to attend meetings before the end of the century. The Herefordshire Quarterly Meeting for Business would officially commence in September 1667, but these early minutes demonstrate the pioneering organisational strategies of the early members.

The Herefordshire Quarterly Meeting largely focused on issues of general organisation, discipline, and financial assistance. By time the Herefordshire Quarterly Meeting was established, Morgan Watkins was a reliable ally of Fox. In the foreword written in the Quarterly Meeting minute book, Fox makes numerous references to Watkins – advising others that Watkins was a point of reference and contact for the county, especially for those in need.[13] The Quakers certainly distinguished themselves in providing poor relief. This was important to them.

Poverty was seen as a threat to spiritual well-being and had to be prevented if possible.[14] In addition to combatting this spiritual threat, poor relief was also a way of solidifying the benevolent identity of Quakers.[15] The Herefordshire Quarterly Meeting also looked after their own community by setting aside money to aid poor local members.[16] Quakers would come to the aid of those imprisoned 'for the testimony of Truth', like David Edwards, to whom the

Herefordshire Quarterly Meeting paid 20 shillings 'towards relief in his necessities'.[17] In January 1675, a member was 'appointed to take the care to enquire after Thomas Phillips he continuing a prisoner that his necessities might be supplied if there be occasion'.[18] The main purpose of the Quaker meetings was to discover who was in need and determine if they could be assisted by the local meeting.[19] The Herefordshire Quarterly Meeting would often come to the aid of struggling Quakers in the region beyond the Herefordshire borders. In 1676, James Merrick was asked to start a collection to help members in Northampton, whose meeting house was damaged by fire. The collection for the Northampton Quakers from the Monthly Meetings in the county was received in May 1677.[20] In his will, James Merrick left £10 to the poor of the Pant Meeting in Monmouthshire and 40 shillings to the poor of the Adderbury Meeting in Oxfordshire, demonstrating his own responsibility to help needy Quakers outside of his own local meeting.[21] In July 1686, the Herefordshire Quarterly Meeting ordered that 40 shillings be distributed to poor Quakers in nearby Brecknockshire.[22] In December 1686, the Leominster meeting collected £2 4s. 9d. and the Almeley meeting collected £1 for 'the redemption of Quakers in captivity beyond the seas'.[23] In March 1687, Herefordshire meeting members collectively sent £6 5s. 6d. for the Quakers in Algiers.[24] They had been taken by the Barbary Corsairs, who had captured seamen and travellers since 1625, held them to ransom or enslaved them in Morocco and in the Ottoman regencies of Algeria, Tunisia and Tripoli.[25] Eight years earlier, money was raised to pay the Barbary Corsairs' ransom in Buckinghamshire and Somersetshire, and there was another request to come to the aid of Quakers in Algiers in 1684.[26] There was no further correspondence on this matter in the Herefordshire Quarterly Meeting so it is unknown if the ransom for the Quakers in Algiers was successfully paid. Closer to home, the Quakers also provided poor relief to their own membership and the wider community in their wills. James Merrick left £40 for the poor Quakers in Ross and £3 'to the poor of Ross'.[27]

Another aspect of Quaker organisation was the construction of purpose-built meeting houses throughout the second half of the century, often thanks to the generosity of the early local leaders and despite the persecution that was taking place during this intolerant period. Equally important were the homes of leading Quakers. The Ross Monthly Meeting was held at James Merrick's home for twenty years and, in 1678, he left a legacy in his will for land, timber and money for the construction of a meeting house in Ross.[28] In 1672, Roger Prichard built a house on his land and donated it to be used as the Almeley meeting house.[29] Edward Pitway, another early Worcestershire Quaker, was the landlord of the Red Lion Inn in Waterside and hosted the Evesham meeting. He was central in the organisation and maintenance of this meeting and, after his death in 1676, he bequeathed land for a burial ground.[30] The property is described as a small piece of garden ground in Bengeworth, adjoining 'the Parsonage Close' and behind Edward Pitway's home.[31] In 1677, the Bromyard Quakers collectively raised funds to build their meeting house.[32] As the first generation passed on, their legacies ensured that future generations would have a more solid financial foundation with which to flourish, alongside a strong network, and structure to maintain their religious community.[33]

The Herefordshire Quarterly Meeting was the regional meeting that covered Hereford, Bromyard, Almeley, Ross and Leominster, which was the centre of county activity. Monthly Meetings usually sent two representatives to the Quarterly Meeting with an average of eight members present from 1665 to 1688. In spite of his travels and incarcerations, Morgan Watkins was present at every Quarterly Meeting in Hereford until December 1682; these meetings were often held in his home, again, demonstrating the importance of local and devoted members.[34] Indeed, Roger Prichard, the leading Almeley Quaker, was convinced at a meeting at Watkins' home.[35] It can be estimated that Watkins died within the next two years as he was last mentioned in the Quarterly Meeting minutes on 30 September 1684.[36] In Herefordshire, the Ross and Leominster Monthly Meetings were established in 1668, while the Worcester Monthly and Quarterly Meetings were established in the same year.[37]

The Monthly Meetings handled lifecycle events including burials and marriages. It was important for Quakers to establish their own burial grounds as they sought to demonstrate their distinctiveness from the established Church and other dissenting communities. In 1669, Fox urged them to 'speedily provide themselves Burying places Convenient that thereby a testament may stand against the Superstitious Idolizing of those places Cal[l]ed holy grownd, formerly used to that purpose'.[38] Without the need for consecrations, any 'convenient' land was acceptable for burial.[39]

Once the land was designated as a burial ground, the funeral itself could bring its own problems with the local authorities. Joan, the mother of James and Thomas Merrick, was buried on 8 May 1658 in Kings Caple, Herefordshire.[40] Later that year, the Merricks were questioned by the coroner as to why they did not bury her in the parish church and why she was buried in Kings Caple instead. A jury was appointed and witnesses testified that she died a natural death; the coroner asked James and Thomas Merrick, and Walter, their cousin, to take an oath, knowing they would refuse to do so because they were known Quakers to the local authorities. The Merricks were subsequently fined an unspecified amount for refusing to swear the oath and were sent to the Quarter Sessions in Hereford.[41] Private interment, lay burial, and improvised ceremonies that flourished alongside more traditional ecclesiastical practices during the 1640s and 1650s were once again outlawed with the passage of the Act of Uniformity in 1662, but dissenters and Roman Catholics continued to hold their own ceremonies.[42] The authorities knew this was happening but they were usually unable to prevent such events from occurring.

The Quakers in Herefordshire were establishing their burial grounds long before Fox's above-referenced statement in 1669. In 1660, Henry Bedford, a Leominster glover, sold a piece of land for £16 on South Street in the town to Peter Young, Morgan Watkins, Thomas Holte, Thomas Bach, Hugh Powle Sr. and Charles Barnett, and this became the site of a meeting place and burial ground. The transaction recorded that this was for the use of the 'Church of the first borne and begotten unto God of the seed Immortall heires of Life and inheritors with the Saints in Light gathered by the Eternall Spirit meeting in and about Leomynster who are of the world scorned and in reproach called Quakers'.[43] Even the wording of this land transaction was tinged with bitterness towards the outside world. In his will, written in 1675, James Merrick provided a burial ground for the Quakers located in Kings Caple.[44] From his earlier dispute with the local authorities about his mother's final resting place and his prominent role in the movement in Herefordshire, Merrick was keenly aware of the importance of an appropriate burial ground.

The recorded minutes concerning burials and the maintenance of burial grounds in Herefordshire illustrate the regular, disciplined and increasingly centralised processes that were being developed by Quakers. This centralising process is evident in July 1673 when the Herefordshire Quarterly Meeting requested that all gravestones be 'removed immediately'.[45] The Herefordshire Quarterly Meeting was one of the earliest meetings demanding the removal of memorial stones; this was common practice in Herefordshire forty-five years before the London Yearly Meeting advised the removal of gravestones from Quaker burial grounds.[46] In 1675, John Cater and Thomas Merrick were ordered to 'look to Friends burying place and what is wanting it is left to their discretion to put it in order'.[47] Four years later, Cater and Thomas Taylor were asked to speak to 'Widow Smith to let her know Friends minds about the stone that she have brought in our burying ground and who gave her leave to bring it thither'.[48] Even grieving widows were interrogated for practices that, up until their conversion to Quakerism, were a societal norm. In 1680, Cater, William Fisher and Henry Powell were ordered to speak to Elizabeth Cowles, a member of the Leominster Meeting, because she wanted to erect a doorway from her garden to the burying ground.[49] There is no further documentation or correspondence to show why Cowles needed the doorway, but a month later, Thomas Merrick and William Fisher were asked to speak with her again. Cowles had to 'give under her hand and soul before witness' that she had no claim or interest and then Friends would give her a 'loan' and if any Friends were not satisfied with this arrangement at any point, they could 'stop it up'.[50] A month later, Henry Powell was given a bond of £5 to build the walls of the burying ground.[51] Cowles and her doorway were never mentioned again. Any resolution to the matter was not recorded in future meeting minutes. These were issues that were important enough to be recorded, even if there was no documented resolution or satisfactory explanation. What is being established here is organisation and a keen eye on how they were being viewed by their neighbours.

Establishing burial practices was a foremost concern for the early Quakers, but when examining the dynamics of the Quaker family, three factors must be considered: construction, maintenance and purpose. The Quakers reverted to the medieval practice of unsolemnised matrimony by common consent.[52] The Interregnum government made provision for civil marriages before a magistrate, but many of the Quakers were still unhappy with that arrangement.[53] Moreover, when Fox replaced the sacrament of marriage in the presence of a priest, he nevertheless ensured that intended Quaker marriages were approved with adequate public notice. As such, Quakers could demonstrate that these marriages were not conducted in a hasty manner that might otherwise bring commendation in the wider community.[54] While there is no evidence of arranged marriages, increasingly the Quakers were expected to marry within their community, as it was a vital way to secure the future of their respective meetings.[55] The couple seeking permission to marry would attend the Monthly Meeting where they wanted the marriage to take place, while appointed members would investigate if their parents approved and if the 'parties were of good conversation'. If consent was given, and if all other matters were resolved, then the Monthly Meeting granted permission to the couple.[56] Thus, when Jonah Cater and Sarah Browne of Ross sought the approbation of their marriage in 1686, members took 'deliberate consideration' of their request before allowing them to proceed.[57] The marriage certificates followed the prescribed format outlined by Fox as they were signed by the couple and all who were present at the event.

The Ross Monthly Meeting minutes of the 1680s nevertheless show that they were concerned with members and their children 'going to the priest to be married'.[58] In September 1681, William Fisher and Thomas Taylor were 'ordered to speak with John Barber about his daughter' who was married by a priest.[59] For Taylor this was a common practice as he was often responsible for approaching his fellow members concerning any disciplinary infractions.[60] In order for Quakers to feel confident that a marriage was God's will, permission was not always immediately granted. Once established, though, the family unit was an important way of maintaining the Quaker community. The earliest leading Quaker family of Ross was the Merrick family. James Merrick and Elizabeth Merrick married late in life and it is likely that any children from a previous marriage died young, as James's will only left bequests for his daughter-in-law.[61] As noted earlier, James Merrick's brother and cousin, Thomas and Walter, were also Quakers, while Thomas's daughter, Elizabeth, was married at the Ross Meeting House in 1686.[62] Another significant Quaker family in the region were the Prichards of Almeley, including Roger and Mary, his wife, and their son, Edward, and daughter, Elizabeth, who in 1679 married John Eckley, a Leominster Quaker.[63] Marriages were not only between local Quaker families, as they married beyond county borders, providing evidence that they were not restricted to marriage partners in their own meetings or localities.

The life of a Quaker family was not always harmonious or without controversy. In 1677, David Prichard of Ross was noted as exhibiting 'unkindness in him towards his wife'.[64] Domestic violence as a 'means of demonstrating dominance' was not tolerated by Quakers and the action taken against Prichard demonstrated that this sort of behaviour brought dishonour. Such actions were quickly condemned in Quaker meetings, especially as such behaviour had the potential to damage their reputation in the wider community. Indeed, the Quakers were expected to reject these displays of worldly masculinity and thereby demonstrate both self-control and the well-being of their households and meetings.[65] Significantly, the Ross Monthly Meeting felt a responsibility to protect Prichard's wife and children as well as the reputation of their meeting members.

From an examination of the Quarterly and Monthly Meeting records, it is evident that the Quakers were acutely aware of maintaining the integrity of their community. In November 1656, the Epistle from the Elders of Balby established a code of conduct to adhere to.[66] Matters of discipline were addressed in the third clause of the Epistle; if the offending member would not reform after a verbal warning, the case would be referred, in writing, to an elder. Other clauses instructed Quakers not to disparage each other or interfere in the affairs of others.[67] In the second Quarterly Meeting in Herefordshire, each Monthly Meeting was designated two members to speak to 'disorderly' Quakers. Morgan Watkins and Nathaniel Smith were the responsible members in Leominster, William Fisher and James Merrick in Ross, and John Barber and John Carver in Hereford.[68] They believed that if misconduct was not condemned quickly within their meetings such actions would lead them open to charges of immorality in the wider community.[69] The appointed members, as with their marriage procedures, were often asked to investigate the behaviour of Quakers who were allegedly engaging in unseemly conduct, and thereby demonstrating an eagerness to deal with them as quickly and efficiently as possible. It was standard practice for two or more of them to visit the offending Quaker and offer advice as the local meeting saw fit.[70] The minutes show that this could be as gentle as 'speak with William Grindall and encourage him to come to the Men's Monthly Meeting', or as forceful as asking absent members why they were not attending meetings and 'not living answerable to truth'.[71] In March 1688, the Ross Quakers were asked to enquire into Robert Turner's 'disorderly life'.[72] The term 'disorderly' could mean swearing, gossiping, and general delinquency, but it is uncertain how Turner was living. In other regions, namely Bristol, meetings would warn the disorderly Quakers of their possible expulsion, but this does not seem to be commonplace in Herefordshire and Worcestershire.[73] The wayward members were mentioned in the meeting minutes, but these incidents never escalated nor were they mentioned again in subsequent meeting minutes, suggesting that their measures were effective.

Quakers were buried together, practised their religion together, and their paths often crossed outside of the 'meeting house' – in marriage and business. In this region, Hereford gloves were highly regarded, and the trade was lucrative in the second half of the seventeenth century.[74] Indeed, during this period, nearly half of the boys who entered into apprenticeships were bound to glovers, while a quarter of the Quakers in Herefordshire were employed in the glove trade.[75] It can therefore be assumed that they worked alongside non-Quakers. More significant is that their religious convictions may have influenced the economic activities of the Quakers outside of their meetings.[76] Wills demonstrated the relationships that they had with non-Quaker family members, neighbours and the wider community more generally, while such financial provisions helped to secure the future of their respective meetings. Roger Prichard and Edward, his son, amassed a modest portfolio of property, and while these land purchases are documented, not a strip of land is mentioned in Roger's will, written in 1678, a year before his death. Indeed, his bequests mainly consisted of cash and silver to his family and closest friends.[77] The likelihood is that he used the land for the construction of the Almeley meeting house. The production of wills can also demonstrate a reproachment between the Quakers and non-Quakers in wider society. For example, David Jones, a Ross victualler, was not a Quaker, but his will dated in 1676 was witnessed by two prominent Herefordshire members, Thomas Taylor and William Fisher.[78] However, having a will proved by the courts was not straightforward for Quakers because in order to have probate granted, they were required to swear an oath before the Affirmation Act of 1697.[79] Under normal circumstances, this would have been viewed as unacceptable. Jones's will stated that it was 'signed, sealed, and published in the presence' of Taylor and Fisher.[80] However, Quakers did not appear to object to the practice of having wills proven by the courts; it was deemed an acceptable practice by local meetings and also confirms that Quakers in this region from the 1670s onwards were the recipients of some local toleration.[81]

James Merrick died in June 1678 and his will was strictly a business transaction to secure the future of the Ross Meeting and his large family, both immediate and extended. He left the land surrounding his 'new house' and 'free passage and liberty' through the 'entry' of the 'new house and court' to Roger Prichard of Almeley, James Exton of Hereford, and Thomas Merrick, John Cater, William Fisher and Thomas Taylor of Ross for the use of 'people of God called Quakers at all times and seasons'. Merrick's wealth is evident in his numerous bequests to family, friends, fellow Quakers, and servants; most of his bequests were in cash, but his occupation as a tanner was also in evidence by his bequest to a fellow Ross Quaker, William Fisher, of a 'dither of good leather'.[82] In this context, Merrick's will supports Adrian Davies's findings that Quakers did not discriminate in their bequests and included non-Quakers in their wills.[83] Merrick distributed his property holdings amongst his wife, two brothers and four cousins, as well as one undefined relation. The overseers of Merrick's will, the Quakers James Exton and Roger Prichard, were also given a half-crown each to purchase gloves. Merrick's will was witnessed by William Goffe, William Poulton, John Long and Christopher Barrett, none of whom were known Quakers.[84] This shows that Merrick, while an integral part of the Ross Quaker community, also had networks outside of his local meeting and non-Quakers were prepared to endorse such transactions.

Quakers would come to be renowned for their financial responsibility in the later eighteenth century. This behaviour was, however, publicly encouraged by the Herefordshire Meeting at an early stage in their development. In July 1676, when approached by the nearby Radnorshire Meeting to come to the aid of a Quaker who had debts, the Herefordshire Quarterly Meeting responded that if a member fell into debt by 'sloth or negligence or unadvisedly making rash and wilful ventures and undertakings without or against counsel' then they were not obliged to provide assistance. They felt that this would be seen as mutually 'assisting on endeavours by contributing to them'. The Herefordshire Quarterly Meeting believed that in such cases, denunciation was the preferred response because these actions would be deemed 'contrary to the holy Truth and out of the Counsel of God'.[85] The Herefordshire Quakers also criticised the irresponsibility of their own members. In March 1678, John Cater and William Fisher were ordered by the Ross Monthly Meeting to speak with Thomas Turner to discuss his debts. Accruing debt could certainly go against the Quaker principles if Turner was lavishly spending his money. It was not specified how or to whom the money was owed, but this willingness to discuss matters was met with patience by the meeting.[86] In this, as in so many other cases, Quakers had to cooperate with each other and with the outside world to ensure due probity.

Quakers in Herefordshire and Worcestershire were by no means isolated as there were close networks, both economic and personal, throughout these counties. The challenge of being a dissenter could nevertheless mean ostracism by family members and peers within these networks. Moreover, as they were judged, quite harshly, for the misdeeds of members of their community, it is not surprising that they began to show greater care for their outward image.[87] This outward image included the higher profile of women in the movement, not only as pastoral figures, or as support for men, but they also found themselves as active participants in the Quaker ministry. Women certainly played an important role in early Quakerism.

Prior to the establishment of the women's meeting in 1676, notable women in Herefordshire signed the '7000 Handmaids of the Lord' petition. This document was a petition against tithes and was submitted to Parliament in 1659.[88] Stephen Kent notes that the petition of 1659 provided 'an opportunity for Quaker women and their female neighbours to register their objections to the practice, just as others did from shires across the country'.[89] The signatories in Herefordshire included the relations of prominent local Quakers, including Mary Merrick, Mary Prichard and Elizabeth Prichard.[90] Outside of activism, the Quaker women also had more gender-conforming roles. Lucy Wyatt of Worcestershire was an early convert who was known for travelling throughout the country visiting imprisoned Quakers, making and mending their clothing, as well as spending time with the families of those imprisoned.[91] It was common for women to take on more of a 'domestic ministry' or pastoral role. In many cases, this would have been the most helpful form of ministry, particularly in the turbulent 1660s. In *Piety Promoted*, it was acknowledged that she was raised, in part, by her Puritan uncle who 'cautioned her to shun idle company, never to learn to dance or to read ballads, nor to wear lace or ribbons on her clothes; but to go and hear the best men that preached at that time'.[92] With this advice, it is not surprising that she found solace with the Quakers after listening to Humphrey Smith's preaching.

As found in Patricia Griffith's study of the early Quakers in Cornwall, women in the two counties were rarely mentioned outside of marriage records in this early period (1652–88), and there is no extant evidence that any woman held an identifiable occupation.[93] Most women in the marriage records were identified as either widows or spinsters. This also correlates with Kay Taylor's findings in Wiltshire.[94] Despite a lack of identifiable occupations, there is evidence that some women had some control of money and land, if only on a temporary basis. In Roger Prichard's will, he left £100 to his 'loving wife', Mary Prichard, £250 to his daughter, Hannah, and £50 to his granddaughter, Elizabeth.[95] This is a significant shift from the sixteenth century, when women were seldom mentioned in probates and the fiscal responsibilities fell on the shoulders of the eldest son. Moreover, the Quaker women were often named as executrixes of their husband's estates. Thus, Elizabeth Merrick was named as a co-executor of her husband James's will in 1675.[96] This financial trust displayed by Merrick in his wife demonstrates the equality sought by the Quaker wives and daughters but one that was not always given. Christine Trevett addresses the discrimination faced by early modern women and the opportunity provided by Quakerism, adding that the Quaker theology was 'restorationist and positive', unlike the state church which had stressed the 'Eve-like susceptibility' to transgressions, weak moral character, a 'God-given subjection to men', and no right to speak or teach in the Church.[97] The Quaker emphasis on Acts 2:17 'And it shall come to pass in the last days, saith God, I will pour out my Spirit upon all flesh: and your sons and daughters shall prophesy' demonstrated the justification of women's speaking.[98] The open and consistent promotion of women's public activities within the Quaker community assured unprecedented opportunities for them; this was radical change for this time.[99]

This justification led to the creation of women's meetings – meetings that were separate from the men. In Herefordshire, there is no evidence to suggest that there was any opposition to the creation of a women's meeting as was found elsewhere. John Wilkinson and John Story of Wiltshire objected to the establishment of women's meetings as being of no use in country areas, but they admitted that areas like London might benefit as women could administer poor relief.[100] George Fox encouraged the establishment of women's meetings everywhere, and in an open letter to Quakers in 1676, he asked them to:

> encourage all the women of families that are convinced and minds virtue and love the truth and walks in it, that they may come up into god's service, that they may be serviceable in their generation ... and therefore train up your young women to know their duty in this thing: that they may be in their services and places for all businesses.[101]

He first suggested a women's meeting in 1671,[102] yet the 1676 letter was a stronger recommendation that women ought to have a more visible and tangible involvement in the running of their local meetings. In this way, they would contribute to the stability of their community, ensure 'a lasting and significant role' for themselves and be on an equal footing with their menfolk.[103] On the subject of equality and the need for the greater involvement of women in the Quaker community, Fox wrote in 1676 that:

> I say to all you that be against womens meetings, or the mens, and sees no service for the womens meetings, ye are out of the power of the God and his spirit ye live not in. For God saw a service for the Assemblies of the women in ye time of ye Law about those things that appertained to his worship and service and the holy things of his Tabernacle. And so doth ye same spirit see now their service in ye Gospel.[104]

He saw women as having spiritual equanimity and this measure provided them with the opportunity to join the ministry. This can certainly be compared with his views given in *The Woman Learning in Silence*, published twenty years earlier in 1656, where his commentary on the role of women was not progressive. In this tract, Fox wrote, 'Wives, submit yourselves to your husbands as to the Lord,' but he did, at least, concede that women could preach.[105] His reassessment of the role of women in the Quaker community is more clearly defined in his 1676 statement that 'many things in those meetings which are more proper for the women to see into then ye men'.[106] This strongly suggests that he believed that women were more suited to pastoral responsibilities. He was not alone in such beliefs. Mary Penington explained the importance of the women's meetings in September 1678:

> Our meetings apart from the men in point of business is both comely & advantageous, & that which we have found virtue in & is honest, & of good report amongst those that have proved it as to do those services that are more proper for us than for the men & to do some other services that are mean, & of less concern than is convenient to engage the men in. Those more proper to the women are.[107]

Whilst women were able to strive for spiritual equality in the Quaker meetings, there is no evidence to suggest that the daughters and wives of the Herefordshire and Worcestershire Quakers enjoyed any such equality in the home. Generally speaking, women in this period held traditional roles in the household, including maintaining the family home and the upbringing of children. Seventeenth-century families were still 'held together by deference and obedience to superiors, in much the same way that society at large functioned at the time'.[108]

It is important not to idealise the early Quaker attitude towards women, but also equally important not to underestimate the Quaker contribution to the history of women and religion.[109] The first women Quakers took an active role in the establishment of the movement, and the high profile of Margaret Fell fully demonstrates the importance of women in early Quakerism.[110] It has been argued that the concept of idealising the Quaker women as 'proto-feminists' is nullified by the requirement to abide by the rule of plainness in the code of discipline, which was primarily directed towards them.[111] Nevertheless, it has been observed that:

> no Quaker woman or girl was to be regarded simply as an appendage or property of a husband or father. … the tenet about the spiritual equality of the sexes … retained enough of its vigour to ensure that the worst excesses of other churches were avoided.[112]

There were opportunities for women to take on missionary roles that were previously exclusive to men. They were able to be fully engaged in the proliferation of their faith in ways that contravened seventeenth-century society norms. Hilary Hinds highlights that the women who challenged social conventions, those who devoted their lives to complete their 'divine mission', often sacrificed their familial responsibilities in the process.[113]

Women were integral to the early development of Quakerism; however, in Herefordshire and Worcestershire, there were few high-profile female Quakers in this period. This hypothesis may change in time, but there are scant surviving records of women's meetings, and those records are available only from the mid-eighteenth century onwards. Indeed, the earliest extant women's meeting minutes in Herefordshire are from 1754 onwards; in Worcestershire, from 1793 onwards. The evidence of women's involvement in the early period in the two counties thereby comes from the records of the Herefordshire Men's Quarterly Meeting minutes rather than from their own meetings. The women of Herefordshire were approached to set up a women's meeting in April 1674, two years before Fox's strong recommendation, where it was advised that:

> Friends do order at this meeting that all the older and faithful women in the Truth have notice by Friends to come to the next mens monthly meetings for this County for the setting up of womens meetings in this County.[114]

Women in Herefordshire were encouraged but the formation of women's meetings was more controversial elsewhere. It appears that Herefordshire avoided the disputes found in Bristol, Buckinghamshire, Westmorland and Wiltshire.[115] Nevertheless, the first mention of a fully functioning women's meeting in the county did not take place until October 1676 at the home of James Exton, after Fox's letter had been sent to the constituent meetings and after the 1675 London Yearly Meeting had sanctioned such meetings.[116] However, even with the limited evidence provided by the Herefordshire Quarterly Meeting, details of the location and leadership of the earliest women's meetings can be determined because in June 1681, the Quarterly Meeting was referred to as the 'Men's Quarterly Meeting'.[117]

The establishment of meetings (for men and women) led to the growth of the Quaker community in the two counties, but who attended these gatherings? Herefordshire and Worcestershire were (and remain) predominantly agricultural areas; this is exemplified by the number of farmers and yeomen in the region. There was also a thriving textile industry in this period, including textile treatment facilities known as 'fulling mills' found along the Wye, Lugg and Severn, while retail traders were plentiful.[118] Many of the towns and villages throughout the counties were easily accessible to Bristol and other trading centres via the road network. The same roads that enabled the dissemination of the Quaker message also created prosperity for those who were able to trade. Comparisons and tentative conclusions on the wealth, occupation and business transactions of Quakers can be made by examining their meeting minutes, probate records, marriage records, marriage settlements, land leases and deeds, as well as the tax records.[119] The Quakers in the two counties were therefore primarily of the 'middling sort'. These people found a ready home in Quakerism as they were able to exercise religious freedom, thanks in part to growing literacy and greater economic independence.[120]

They were employed in a variety of occupations, but primarily in agriculture and the retail trade. This is reflective of the geographical landscape. Commercial ties, especially those in the cloth trade, were easily converted into 'channels of evangelism' and those on such journeys were exposed to new ideas due to the travel required for their businesses.[121] Roger Prichard, his son, Edward, and his son-in-law, John Eckley of Leominster, all worked in the profitable Herefordshire glove trade.[122] A quarter of the Herefordshire Quakers with identifiable occupations were employed as glovers. The early converts in this area were primarily men of moderate means and influence. The evidence confirms that these local meetings were fostered by members who used their economic resources to lay the foundations of the movement. Business acumen and the pursuit of economic success were not always valued by Quakers, and some saw this desire for 'outward goods' to be a sign of spiritual weakness. Herefordshire Quaker Humphrey Smith wrote a tract detailing his life before his convincement that essentially condemned his father and his former self for yearning for financial success.[123] Unlike Smith, most of the early Quaker members in these counties could see that financial support and especially land ownership were vital to sustaining this nascent movement.

The skilled occupations and levels of wealth among the Quakers in these counties implies a grasp of basic literacy. Richard Vann has suggested that there had to be a connection between the ability to sign one's name and the ability to read as writing was 'a skill for which ordinary people had little use, and it was even thought to be unsuitable to the poor'.[124] There is some evidence that the Quaker women in this area were at least nominally educated.

Edward Prichard's mother Mary signed a 1685 document transferring part ownership of property in Almeley to Edward. In the various Prichard family documents, there is a visible improvement over several years in the signature of Roger Prichard, the son of Edward Prichard.[125] This would suggest that Roger was being educated throughout this time. In land deeds, marriage settlements, and often, meeting minutes, original signatures can be found, with a minority of the Quakers signing with a mark. Margaret Spufford suggested that the ability to read was more widespread than the ability to write and given the prolific production of Quaker printed materials, it can be assumed that literacy was high amongst many of the Quakers.[126] Indeed, some regional meetings certainly encouraged literacy.[127] Books published by Quakers in London were a *de facto* requirement of the local meetings. In December 1678, the Ross Quakers were advised that William Sparry would 'retain friends books and to be accountable to the printer for them'.[128] The Quarterly Meeting was expected to purchase the books from London and distribute them to the local meetings. Usually, someone in the meeting was appointed to distribute the books upon receipt and the meetings were then expected to make contributions towards their payment. There are numerous references in the Herefordshire Quarterly Meeting minutes in reference to these transactions.[129] In September 1673, it was ordered that any books sent to the county from London be divided, with two books going to Ross meeting, one to Hereford, two to Leominster, and two to the Almeley meeting.[130] In 1676, Francis Howgill's books were to be divided as aforementioned but with an additional book going to Bodenham.[131] Quakers saw the value in continuing spiritual education. The books they wrote served as guides, and a connection to their co-religionists outside of their own local meetings further strengthened this wider sense of community.

Early Quakers established a structure to disseminate their message via missionary activity and a structure to ensure that the movement's momentum was maintained via centralised meetings. Even though the missionary activity decelerated by the mid-1660s, it was important at the start to spread the message to a wider audience. By the middle of the seventeenth century, Foxian centralisation was at work. In conjunction with this, Quakers were increasingly outgrowing missionary activity and sought to consolidate their local and regional meetings. It could be viewed as a natural progression from an amorphous movement to a sect. The missionary activity became less important, and possibly not viewed as worthy of the risk as many early itinerant ministers died either from imprisonment or on their missionary tours, like Edward Burrough and Richard Farnworth, respectively. The recognition of the need for centralisation and organisation was critical to the longevity of Quakerism. The early leadership were able to read the political landscape and react accordingly. However, all of the Quakers, including those in Herefordshire and Worcestershire, would still face suspicion from their neighbours and local authorities. Indeed, there is little evidence to suggest that the wider community were by any means sympathetic to the Quaker plight.

Chapter 6

Early Quakers and their Fierce Opponents

The enthusiasm of the early Quakers inspired not only spirited disputations, but also direct confrontation from those opposed to their beliefs and their often-incendiary behaviour. Their adversaries believed that the Quakers were intent on disrupting social order and they responded in a manner that they felt was appropriate to combat the threat posed. In 1655, Thomas Thurston of Gloucestershire was 'moved by the Lord' to go to Evesham and was imprisoned for 'speaking to the people in the graveyard as they were passing from the steeplehouse and exhorting them to repent and fear the Lord'.[1] It has been argued that the punishment of the Quakers in the seventeenth century was more personal and more severe, possibly because their enthusiasm, zealous words and eccentric behaviour were more challenging to accept.[2] The disruptive behaviour, both actual and alleged, encouraged virulent opposition to Quakers. The hostility generated by both the provocative and peaceful actions of the Quakers in Herefordshire and Worcestershire was exhibited by Richard Baxter, the Puritan vicar of St Mary and All Saints' Church in Kidderminster, from 1647 until 1660.

While at St Mary's, Baxter's congregation grew, and he estimated that 600 out of a possible 1,800 were regular communicants of the church.[3] He was also a hugely prolific writer who transcended regional boundaries and his work was read by a nationwide audience. From his place of authority, Baxter rallied against the Quakers and used his popularity to address a broad, engaged and captivated audience. He believed that the Quakers were enemies of scripture, the clergy and sobriety, who spoke in allegories and instead of an ordered system of belief, provided 'incoherent scraps'.[4] While in Kidderminster he wrote three tracts specifically dealing with the Quakers, which garnered responses from leading Quakers, including Edward Burrough of Westmorland, who referred to Baxter as 'a corrupt tree which brings not forth good fruit'.[5] It is also important to note that with Baxter's reputation and stature, it was unlikely to be the responsibility of the local members to engage him in written disputations. That was indeed a role fulfilled by the leading spokespeople of the 1650s like Burrough, James Nayler, Richard Hubberthorne, and Richard Farnworth, but Worcester Quakers also rose to the challenge of sending Baxter written enquiries.[6]

Baxter was naturally a significant target of the earliest Quakers in Kidderminster. While he was confronted in print by the early Quaker leaders, the local and visiting Quakers in Worcestershire were a nuisance to him in person. In 1655, Thomas Goodaire accompanied Thomas Chandler of Chadwick, Worcestershire, to St Mary's Church, where they questioned Baxter following his sermon; they were imprisoned for disrupting him and his congregation although Goodaire and Chandler claimed that they were attempting to engage him in a dispute on theological issues.[7] It is highly unlikely these two men were trying to have a civilised conversation – the earliest Quakers were known for enthusiastically and aggressively confronting their opponents. Nevertheless, Baxter requested an audience with the Quakers to answer their queries in person but was refused. In his frustration, Baxter wrote:

> But have you not betrayed your deceitfulness in refusing to consent that I should come and answer your questions? Why would you send me queries which you would not give me leave to answer by speech? What was it that you feared?[8]

Baxter was will willing to meet them for a discussion, so his questions are valid. Rather than allow him to attend their meeting, on 25 March 1655 the Quakers attended Baxter's service in Kidderminster with the intention to 'make a disturbance'. Baxter accused them of trying their 'rhetoric on the minds of people in this place; whereupon it pleased the magistrate to bind one of you to the good behaviour, for the public disturbance, and railing at the magistrate'. The Quakers then accused him of being a persecutor, to which Baxter responded that he was 'not concerned in the business, and when indeed no man did so much as once ask my advice in it'.[9] Baxter's frustration with the Quakers was understandable. In response to this incident, in the spring of 1655, Baxter wrote *The Quakers Catechism*, a fifty-five-page tract that included a thirty-two-page response entitled *An Answer to the Quaker Queries*.[10] This was written as a rebuttal to twenty-four queries posed by the

Worcestershire Quakers Jane Hicks, Thomas Chandler and Edward Neway, and also Richard Farnworth and Thomas Goodaire.[11] Baxter's annoyance with them was palpable from the onset, as he lamented:

> I find that they do so challenge and brag and triumph, if we say nothing to them, and that too many simple people expect that we should answer them. ... if I say nothing they will insult; if I write to them they will print it; being therefore so far called to speak, I chose rather to print my own papers, how mean soever, than let them do it.[12]

Baxter felt that he just could not win against them. He was essentially damned if he did or damned if he did not. In *An Answer to the Quaker Queries*, Baxter addressed them as 'miserable creatures' and immediately addressed the 'dunghill heaps of false accusations', writing:

> Having received in your first letters almost nothing but some sheets of 'thou serpent, viper, thou child of the devil, thou son of perdition, thou dumb dog, thou false hireling, thou false liar, deceiver, greedy dog, thou ravening wolf, thou cursed hypocrite', with much more of the like, I returned you no reply, as confessing myself not so well skilled in that language and learning as you are. ... For if I be a dumb dog, you cannot expect that I should equal you in snarling, or barking, or howling.[13]

His tone throughout the letter was one of exasperation. That feeling was understandable. Quakers were accusing him of being a liar, a hypocrite and the spawn of Satan. He equated them with the Ranters and asked for clarification of these misdeeds, demanding proof, and concluded that:

> The Quakers (all that yet have wrote to me or spoke to me) pour out the greatest abundance of most impudent lies, and spew their filthy railings in the faces of almost all they come near, so that I know not whether ever the sun saw a more hardened, shameless, abominable generation than they (with their brethren the Ranters) are; and yet with all this filth upon their lips, they confidently profess that they are infallible and without sin. You may well excuse us that we be not hasty in believing you till we see more reason for it.[14]

In addition to his claims that the Quakers were 'shameless' and 'abominable', Baxter also claimed that they professed their own perfection. To him, the Quakers were heretics. Elsewhere in the tract, Baxter directly addressed the March incident, writing that Thomas Goodaire chastised him because he studied and that studying made him 'empty of spirit'. In his own words, Baxter responded, 'I the less marvel at his nonsense.' Quakers were steadfast in their belief that such ministers were contributing to the moral decay of the country and Goodaire suggested that Baxter would not preach unless he was paid. Baxter deeply cared about his ministry and was eager to defend his position and his livelihood. He responded that he had 'long preached already without pay and been glad of liberty', and 'would labor with my hands as far as my languishing body would bear, to supply my necessities, as Paul did to stop the mouths of your predecessors, rather than I would give over preaching the gospel'.[15] He was also frustrated with being asked the same queries repeatedly, writing, 'have you soberly read what I have there wrote already? If not, to what purpose should I write more to you of the same subject,' and:

> Your fourth, fifth, sixth, seventh, eighth and ninth queries are all about tithes, the substance of which I had answered long ago to some of your leading brethren, in a book called *The Worcestershire Petition Defended*, to which book I refer you, to spare the labor of speaking one thing twice; and modesty should have taught you to take notice of that which I have done already before you call for the same things again.[16]

In his conclusion, he asked:

> Are not the ministers whom these men despise, of the same calling and practice as those were that suffered death in the flames in Q. Mary's days? Such as Bradford, Hooper, Latimer, Ridley, Cranmer, Saunders, Philpot, and the rest. Were not these called Masters? Did they not preach in pulpits and take tithes or money for preaching as their due maintenance, and the other things that the Quakers accuse us for? And do not these men justify the bloody opposers of them, and condemn God's saints afresh?[17]

Baxter then stated that when Quakers had answered these questions:

I require you to have no more to do with me nor any of this church. For we renounce you as heretics after a first and second admonition and will have no fellowship with such self-condemned persons, nor receive you into our houses, or bid you Godspeed, lest we partake of your wicked deeds.[18]

His most detailed arguments in *Quakers Catechism* centred on the Quakers' attitude towards the state church. He accused them of being a 'company of carnal hypocrites', having 'more zeal than knowledge', and compared them to men who lost their way on a dark night, one who has lost his guide in the wilderness, or 'like a dog that hath lost his master and therefore will be ready to follow anybody that first whistleth to him'. He felt that the Quakers were attempting to destroy the church with the help of Catholic subversives,[19] and commented that:

> these papists have begotten this present sect of Quakers, first pretending to strange revelations, visions and trances, such as are commonly mentioned in the lives of their saints in the legends. And so you have here and there a papist lurking to be the chief speaker among them, and these have fashioned many others to their turns, to supply their rooms, who yet know not their own fathers.[20]

Baxter saw the Quakers as heretics, associated with popery and the devil. He was also making an appeal to the youth because he feared that the Quakers could lead them astray from the church. He felt that they were especially audacious in their damnation of orthodox religious beliefs.[21] In contrast, Quakers were adamant that they held the truth of God alone, suggesting that Christians in the last 1,600 years, including the Protestant martyrs executed by Mary I in the previous century, had been misguided in their beliefs. It is not surprising therefore that Baxter accused them of 'unmatchable pride and impious infidelity', further observing:

> and is not that man either an infidel and enemy to Christ, or stark mad with pride, that can believe that Christ had no church till now, and that all the ministers of the gospel for 1600 years were the ministers of the devil (as they say of us that tread in their steps), and that all the Christians of that 1600 years are damned (as now they dare denounce

against those that succeed them), and that God made the world, and Christ died for it, with a purpose to save none but a few Quakers that the world never knew till a few years ago; or at least a few heretics that were their predecessors of old.[22]

Quakers declared that they had the spirit of God, but Baxter and his congregants had not seen any evidence of this. Why should these disruptive and unpleasant Quakers be believed? Consequently, Baxter and his contemporaries frequently equated the Quakers with the Ranters, who were visualised as 'the true anarchists' who blurred the lines between good and evil. As Charles Cherry pointed out, there was no difference between free will and the 'voice of the Spirit' for the Ranters – if it felt right, that meant that it was correct.[23] The Quakers and Ranters were more alike than Quakers would have liked to admit, but they were mindful of avoiding swearing and drunkenness, as both were associated with Ranterism.[24]

In 1654, Richard Farnworth wrote a pamphlet defending Quakers against such accusations, entitled *The Ranters Principles and Deceits Discovered and Declared Against, Denied and Disowned by Us Whom the World calls Quakers*.[25] It goes without saying that the Ranters were 'regularly demonised as a lustful, ungodly crew given to all manner of wickedness'.[26] Indeed, Baxter accused the Quakers of acting:

> as if they were sent from heaven to persuade men to wear no lace, or cuffs, or points, and that damn so many ministers for being called masters. But alas do you not know that pride of inward qualifications commonly called spiritual pride is the most killing and abominable! the better the thing is that you are proud of, the worse is your pride.[27]

Despite believing that their beliefs and methods were full of unjust pride – the 'very master sin in them' and ignorance, he took the Quaker threat to the church and harmonious community relations seriously.[28] He was not alone as the diarist John Evelyn was more pronounced in his judgements, writing in 1656 that the Quakers were 'a new phanatic sect of dangerous Principles, [they do not] show respect to any man, magistrate or other and seem a melancholy proud sort of people'.[29]

This danger was on full display in Bristol in the autumn of 1656.

On 24 October 1656, James Nayler and his companions staged a demonstration that proved disastrous: they re-enacted the arrival of Christ in Jerusalem. Nayler rode on horseback into Bedminster in Bristol attended by followers who sang 'Holy, holy, holy' and strewed the muddy path with garments. This was certainly a provocative act that would have caused a scene. Predictably, Nayler was arrested and charged with blasphemy. Though Nayler denied that he was impersonating Jesus and said rather that 'Christ was in him', he refused to explain his actions, and the ecstatic devotion of his followers convinced many that he was the Messiah. Nayler had attracted a loyal personal following, which troubled some other Quakers. George Fox often expressed concern that Nayler was becoming over-enthusiastic and erratic, and by 1656 they were hardly on speaking terms.

Nayler's case was tried in Parliament, despite its lack of legal jurisdiction. Nayler's trial dominated the sessions. The testimony of some of his followers was, unsurprisingly, deeply damaging to his case, and it was exploited to the full by those who wanted to use the incident to attack Quakers more generally. When asked during the trial if she believed Nayler was the 'Prince of Peace', Martha Simmonds declared, 'He is a perfect man; and he that is a perfect man is the Prince of Peace.' When pressed further, she said that Nayler had been anointed by a prophet but refused to name said prophet.[30] Timothy Wedlock stated that he did 'own him [Nayler] to be the son of God' and Thomas Stranger confessed that he 'called James Nayler Jesus'.[31] Dorcas Erbery testified that Nayler was 'the only begotten Son of God' and she knew 'no other Jesus' and 'no other Saviour'. Their testimonies were extremely unhelpful.

Nayler's character witnesses solidified the widely held belief that Quakers were indeed dangerous and perhaps more threatening than previously thought. This incident encouraged challenges to the Protectorate's policy of religious toleration. Nayler was used by the Puritan majority in Parliament as an example to justify increased persecution and suppression of the troublesome Quaker sect. Whereas Parliament wanted to undermine religious toleration for radical sects, Cromwell used the case to convince the army that he should have more effective control of Parliament.

In the end, Parliament declared Nayler guilty of 'horrid blasphemy' and said he was a 'grand impostor and a great seducer of the people'. He was sentenced first to be pilloried (put up in the stocks) and whipped through the streets of London, then pilloried again and then to have his forehead branded with a letter B for blasphemer and his tongue bored through with a hot iron. Then he would be indefinitely imprisoned. The first round saw Nayler so badly injured from 310 lashes that petitions were presented to postpone the second round. At his second pillorying, the three women grouped themselves around him in a way that evoked pictures of the three Marys at the cross. If Nayler was used as an example of the dangers of where unfettered religious toleration would lead, it might also be argued that he was made a scapegoat by a Quaker movement that was just beginning a process of transition.

Many argued that the 'Nayler affair' revealed critical organisational weakness in terms of corporate discernment and discipline. This incident occurred at the start of a period of significant change for the Quaker movement and served to accelerate this transition. To the Quaker leadership, Nayler stood for everything they were trying to leave behind. George Fox was inevitably linked to Nayler during this trial. Ralph Farmer wrote about the incident in *Satan Enthroned in his Chair of Pestilence* and in his conclusion, he wrote, 'if Nayler be under the devil's power, Fox is not much behind him. Both are bold blasphemers.'[32] The case validated all of the concerns and fears of their staunchest opponents, like Richard Baxter.

Wider society viewed religious minority behaviour, like Nayler's, as 'enthusiastic' or 'fanatical'. In 1662, Dr Henry More published *A Brief Discourse of The Nature, Causes, Kindes, and Cure of Enthusiasm*, an appendix of 1656's *Enthusiasmus Triumphatus*.[33] In this appendix, More equated enthusiasm or an 'overbearing phancy' to atheism and stated that 'the enthusiasts' had lost the use of their 'more noble faculties of Reason and Understanding'.[34] Quakers had to 'steer a delicate line between being perceived as fanatical enthusiasts and rigid if secret papists'.[35] Specifically targeting Quakers in *The Fanatick History*, Richard Blome immediately referred to Quaker behaviour as 'blasphemous', 'dangerous' and 'malitious endevours to subvert church and state'.[36] He added that:

> They [Quakers] are of the synagogues of Satan, and know nothing of God but are enemies of God, being guided by the Spirit of error. ... they are Heathens, wallowing in the mire and filth of the flesh, on whom all the plagues of God are to be poured.[37]

The descriptive language used by Blome painted a picture of a very dangerous group of people. It is therefore not surprising that the Quakers were viewed as a universal threat and their opponents took action with legal sanctions, physical violence, and intimidation.

There is a distinction to be made between public disorder offences and popular hostility. Popular hostility was recorded by Humphrey Smith in 1656 in his publication entitled *Something Further Laid Open of the Cruel Persecution of the People Called Quakers by the Magistrates and People of Evesham*.

Smith wrote that on 17 November 1655, Margaret Newby and Elizabeth Courten from Westmorland visited Evesham 'in obedience to the Lord' and, after the meeting at Edward Pitway's home, visited Quaker prisoners, including Smith. Smith then claimed that after they left, Mayor Edmund Young 'laid violent hands on them himself' and sent for officers to place the two women in the stocks. On the surface, because the mayor was involved, it appears that the Quakers were guilty of public disorder. Alternatively, it can be argued that the mayor was exhibiting extreme behaviour and not the Quakers. Smith nevertheless observed that Mayor Young was determined to punish the women by placing them in the stocks, and he graphically described this punishment. He noted that the holes for their hands were too small and that they would be forced to have their legs apart.[38] To add to their humiliation, Young then requested the constable bring a block for them to sit on and 'thrust it between their legs, & said they should not have them between their legs which they would have, & other uncivil words he used, and locked the prison door, and went his way'. The mayor made a spectacle of these two women and was graphic in his sexual references. This was an extreme case of vicious sexual politics, and the implication of this incident is that Young believed that the women had overstepped social conventions by challenging both his position as mayor and presumably his legal jurisdiction. Moreover, these women were challenging patriarchal rule and were punished with severe physical torment in public. The women were forced to endure their punishment for fifteen hours in what Smith called the 'most barbarous and cruel manner'.[39] This public spectacle would have served as a warning to others, and especially women, that the Quakers were unwelcome in Evesham. Smith's account is an extreme example of social control and the determination to uphold the patriarchal values against the challenge of the Quakers, and in this case, particularly those women who dared to challenge his power.

In 1657, Baxter published *One Sheet Against the Quakers*, which highlighted the actions of the Quakers and suggested that they were dangerous and bordered on the sacrilegious in their actions and publications. He remarked that their delusions were more odious and wicked because they believed their actions were inspired by God, noting that they often stated: 'thus saith the Lord and the Spirit of God within me'.[40] Their provocative conduct and public disorder was exemplified by the Worcester Quaker Edward Bourne, who regularly was imprisoned for his confrontational style of preaching. For example, in 1657 he spent thirteen weeks in confinement for 'speaking the truth' to a local church congregation. While incarcerated, he wrote about his arrest and imprisonment. He claimed to be innocent of any offence as he 'stood there peaceably, yet suffered violence from some, who struck off my Hat, and pluck't it off from my head, and threatened me with words; but I bore these things'. By attending the parish church in the first place was one thing, but to wear his hat on his head while there was, to the gathered congregation, a provocation too far. Later on in the tract, he stated that he asked the people to repent for their sins. Unsurprisingly, the people then pushed him into the graveyard, where Richard Moore and William Collins, 'a Parliament-Man, laid hands on me', and Collins claimed that the Quaker had orchestrated a 'tumult'.[41] In his commentary of the incident, Bourne made a point of highlighting Collins's political background as a 'Parliament-Man' and perhaps of the impression that Collins should have been more forgiving and understanding of the Quaker's dissenting behaviour.

In the Interregnum period, there were still lingering suspicions of a Royalist uprising. However, the ideals of many of those who supported Parliament made them receptive to radical preachers during and after the civil wars.[42] Naturally, the authorities were less inclined to sympathise with the Quakers, no matter what their allegiances had been in the 1640s.

Bourne responded that he simply sought the repentance of the population. This implied that the clergyman was misleading the congregation and, thereby, not performing his duties. As such, he was displacing the clergyman in his own church. Bourne provoked the clergyman, and yet he argued that this gathering of people was an ideal opportunity for him to speak. Not only that, but he stated that the 'Lord required' him to do so.[43] He suggested that God was with him rather than the clergyman or the congregation. His methods of proselytising confirmed one of Baxter's arguments – that the Quakers' virulent attacks on the clergy and their congregations were contrary to God's will and English legal practices.[44]

Baxter believed that the Quakers were unable to fully grasp the consequences of their actions. Indeed, the Quakers did not consider that these congregations might find their actions offensive, or that their perception that the clergyman was a 'false teacher' was provocative.[45] Bourne's actions demonstrate the urgency the Quakers felt when proselytising, regardless of the potential offence it may have caused the congregants. Quakers, particularly the earliest adherents, felt that it was their duty to speak and warn others, despite the significant risks of being mobbed or arrested. They refused to see that they were widely viewed as a threat to social order.

Chapter 7

The Blasphemous Susanna Pierson

Early Quakers recognised a divine presence in their encounters with authorities and the unconvinced, and also recognised God's vengeance when their adversaries succumbed to the divine, so a power to cure and perform miracles was accepted by Quakers and was not viewed as more supernatural than other recognised phenomena.[1] Miracles were equated with inspiration and the earliest Quakers knew that they needed miracles to support their claim that theirs was the true church.[2] They needed evidence to show that God was working through them in tangible ways.

George Fox knew that they needed miracles, too. Fox documented over 150 of them in his *Book of Miracles*, written alongside his journal. His journal was edited and published in 1694, three years after his death. The *Book of Miracles*, however, was very much edited out of public record. By the end of the century, Quakerism looked very different to its origins in the 1650s. Fox's editors arguably felt it best to distance themselves from 'miracles' while protecting the legacy of their much-loved founder. The miracles described in what remains of the *Book of Miracles* are predominantly those of a 'healing' nature; there are many records of people being healed by touch – 'and as I laid my hands upon him the Lord's power went through him'.[3] There was also healing by tincture – Edward Bourne of Worcester was a trusted Quaker doctor and sent 'healing water' to Fox in 1675.[4] The idea of being able to perform miracles was important to the early movement.

Richard Baxter vehemently expressed his concerns about Quakers, their beliefs, and their modus operandi. His arguments were supported by a strange incident in 1657 in Claines, Worcestershire, that was audacious enough to be reported in the national press.[5] This case provided those sceptical of Quakers and their proclamations with evidence of their extreme actions. On Friday, 20 February 1657, William Pool, a young apprentice to a clothier, left his employer's house in Worcester and did not return. This behaviour was very much out of character and his employer, George Knight, grew quite concerned. On Sunday morning, Pool's clothes were found on the banks of the Severn River and his naked corpse was found floating in the river later that day.

There was no foul play involved. It was suggested that Pool had committed suicide, and he was buried the next day in Claines, just north of the city centre.[6] Pool and Knight were known Quakers and there is no evidence to suggest that either of them were outspoken or troublesome individuals before this incident, but Pool's Quakerism was immediately seized on by the press.[7] His reported actions on the day he disappeared suggest that he was experiencing a spiritual epiphany of sorts (or a fit of insanity). It was recorded that he:

> did walk forth from his master's house into the Garden, where having made some stay longer than ordinary he was demanded where he had [been], he made answer that he had [been] with Christ, and that Christ had taken him by the hand, and that he had appointed him to come to him again, and that he must go unto him.[8]

Christ himself had requested Pool's presence. Christ himself compelled Pool to undress at the riverbank and step into the icy Severn. As the cold water rushed over his body and filled his lungs, William was on his way to his eternal home.

It is well documented that the Quakers were willing to abandon their families and livelihoods when compelled by a gospel calling. This was commonplace for the earliest travelling Quakers, but as Pool died barely a few hours later, it is unknown what he intended to accomplish. Did he simply mean to commit suicide? This might be confirmed by the statement that he was alleged to have made that he was 'going with Christ'. Indeed, the coroner announced a verdict of suicide, which was:

> so full of pitty as to exempt the dead body from that sentence to which those who do destroy themselves are lyable [liable], for he was not buried in the High-way, he had no stake placed with Iron thrust through his body to terrifie all passengers from committing such a black and desperate act, but on the Monday following about four of the clock in the morning he was civily buried in the Parish of Clains.[9]

While the coroner was 'full of pitty', a suicide was a suicide and those who committed this act were expected to be punished for going against God's law. In the early modern period, suicide was the worst way to die. It was a result of giving way to the diabolical temptation of despair, where the desperate, abandoning all hope of God's mercy, condemned themselves.[10] Furthermore, in 1653, Baxter wrote that suicide was a 'very act of gross sinne' and asked:

> How can you think then that he [God] will take pleasure in your consuming and destroying your own bodies? It is as unreasonable as to imagine that he delights to have men cut their own throats or hang themselves.[11]

If suicide was a heinous crime, why was Pool, who was guilty of such an offence, buried in the churchyard? The policies for burying perpetrators of suicide were not universally applied and burials under the cover of darkness were commonplace.[12] The family and friends of the dead in these situations made 'strenuous efforts to circumvent the ban by nocturnal interment'.[13] The anonymous author of *A Sad Caveat to All Quakers* suggests that there was considerable sympathy for Pool and his family because he was buried without the stigma of a suicide.[14] In the *Publick Intelligencer*, the author wrote that Pool's mother was an honest and godly woman, which may have aided the Pool family's pleas for a dignified burial.[15] In addition to the issues that arose with the burial of a suicide, Pool was a known Quaker and thereby readily despised by the authorities. While it is likely that his family persuaded the church to allow for his burial to take place, his interment in a churchyard went against the principles of Quakers. In this matter, it is also highly likely that his family made this decision quickly without respecting or even acknowledging the wishes of Pool's Quaker meeting.

Following his early morning burial in Claines, Pool's grieving mother was approached by a local Quaker, Susanna Pierson. Pierson offered to perform a miracle and bring her son back to life. In what must have been a moment of desperation, Mrs Pool accepted Pierson's unusual offer of divine intervention. Pierson saw herself as a conduit between the divine and the human. She was confident, persuasive, and believed that the Holy Spirit was working through her and that she had the ability to act as the intermediary. This is also an example of 'sign performance', defined by Richard Bauman as 'public performance of shocking, dramatic actions, intended to convey, by nonverbal means, an expression of moral reproof and/or prophecy'.[16] In suitably dramatic fashion, Pierson's unnamed accomplices continued with the performance, opened the fresh grave, and removed William's body. This was sacrilegious, unacceptable behaviour. Pool was buried in consecrated ground and to be disturbed was in violation of all conventions.

Pool's corpse was taken out from the grave and placed on the ground. The shroud covering his body was removed, and:

> Mistress Pearson [sic] drawing nigh unto it, did rub his face and his breast with her hand, and laying her face upon his face, and her hands upon his hands, she did command him to arise.

This description immediately provided the reader with a disturbing visual image of Pierson frantically desecrating Pool's bloated decomposing corpse. The report continued:

> The eyes of the multitude, at those words, were all fixed upon the dead body, being intent to observe what the event would be; it came also into their minds ... that our Saviour Christ has raised Lazarus four days buried which made them the more earnest to press near unto her, and with a curious diligence to observe what passed. But the Body not moving at all, and neither voice nor sneezing being observed to proceed from it, she kneeled down and prayed over it, and did command him in the Name of the Living God, to rise up and walk ... but the body not stirring at all, and neither life, nor any hope of life appearing, Mistress Pearson commanded them to put it into the Grave again, excusing herself, that it had not been buried four days, and speaking those words, she departed.[17]

After her failed attempt to resurrect Pool, she simply left the scene of the sacrilegious act.

There was no statement from Pool's anguished mother, no statements of support from Pierson's accomplices. The statement above highlights Pierson's self-delusion, but the commentary is remarkably unbiased, allowing the reader to make their own conclusions, despite the author's likely astonishment that the incident had taken place.

In *One Sheet Against Quakers*, Baxter stated that the Quakers 'must prove that Authority, and their Revelations and Divine Mission by Miracles, or such supernatural means, before any reasonable man can believe them: Unless you will believe every man that saith, he is sent of God.'[18] In the attempt to raise Pool from the dead, Pierson was seeking to perform a miracle. In the earliest years of Quakerism, they believed that miracles added substance to their ideology; they were a supposed sign of the true Church.

Significantly, the incident in Claines took place two months after James Nayler was tried for blasphemy following his notorious ride into Bristol. Dorcas Erbery, as his character witness, claimed that Nayler had performed a miracle and raised her from the dead while she was imprisoned in Exeter. During Nayler's trial, Erbery was asked to clarify her statement that Nayler 'raised' her; she responded: 'He laid his hand on my head, after I had been dead two days, and said, "Dorcas arise" and I arose, and live as thou seest.'[19] The Nayler incident had deep ramifications on the early movement, as it brought to light the deep concerns of less provocative Quakers who witnessed and feared the actions and consequences of the more 'disorderly' members with characteristics of the Ranters.[20] Nayler's blasphemous actions created a public relations disaster and Fox was eager to distance himself from Nayler's behaviour. He advised Nayler that it would be more difficult to subdue 'thy Rude Company' than it was to 'set them up (if ever thou come to know and owne christ) whose Impudence doth spurt & blaspheme ye truth'.[21]

Another failed resurrection allegedly occurred in Colchester in 1656. James Parnell of Nottinghamshire was 15 years old when he converted to Quakerism and 19 when he died, hence he was referred to as the 'Boy Martyr'. Described as a minister of great ability, he travelled widely throughout England until he was arrested and imprisoned in Colchester, Essex.[22] After ten months, Parnell died in prison – his death was attributed to fasting but Fox, in his journal, wrote that he had fallen and 'broke his head'.[23] Fasting was mentioned in Fox's journal; it was practised by the earliest Quakers, including Fox and Nayler. In 1652, Fox wrote that Nayler 'was under a fast fourteen days'.[24] In Parnell's case, fasting was weaponised against him and 'to cover their guilt and shame, they spread among the people, that by immoderate fasting, and afterwards with too greedy eating, he had shortened his days. But this was a wicked lie.'[25] By refusing to eat, Parnell's death was entirely preventable and thus, his own fault. The diarist

John Evelyn visited Colchester in 1656 and likely referencing Parnell, wrote: 'one of these was said to have fasted twenty days; but another, endeavouring to do the like, perished on the 10th, when he would have eaten, but could not.'[26] In the provocatively titled *Hell Broke Loose*, it was reported that after Parnell was laid to rest, 'a man Quaker (how many more than one I cannot say) waited by his Grace untill the end of three dayes, expecting his Resurrection; but James not rising, the poor man ran mad upon it, and so continued many weeks, but at last got loose both from his madness and Quaking, through Gods mercy to him.'[27] Reverend Ralph Josselin of Earles Colne, Essex, also recorded this in his diary, writing that it was reported that Quakers went to Colchester 'to see his resurrection again'.[28] There was an expectation that Parnell would live again. While Parnell's case lacked the desecration of a corpse, there was still the belief that resurrection – the most remarkable miracle – was possible.

The radical fringe, with its provocative tendencies, was exposed with nationally reported events like Nayler's and Parnell's and, to a much more limited extent, Pierson's. Consequently, the actions of radical members needed to be curtailed, or else the whole movement would be placed in jeopardy and subject to widespread ridicule and legal sanctions. However, in the case of Pierson, it is notable that she was never officially censured or disowned by the Quaker establishment for this grievous error in judgement in trying to perform this miracle.

Susanna Pierson fully believed that she was the conduit, the intermediary between heaven and earth, and could 'raise the dead' with the guidance and intervention of the Holy Spirit – that light inside that could and did awaken the living could also raise the dead. The fact that she failed to raise Pool from the dead did not undermine her belief that she could do so with divine help. Acts like these were an embarrassment to those Quakers, particularly George Fox, who wanted peace and acceptance.[29] Pierson's actions also demonstrated what could be viewed as the error of allowing women to take a role in spiritual matters – in *A Sad Caveat to All Quakers*, the author made clear that these evangelical women 'of note' made their 'utmost indeavours to seduce others'.[30] This incident, despite taking place after a private burial in a small parish church, did not go unnoticed. The damning story was published in the *Mercurius Politicus* and the *Publick Intelligencer* within a fortnight.[31] It was reported that Susan Pierson:

having formerly been a pretended lover of, and a Zealous contender for Christ, Scriptures, Ordinances, Ministers, Members, etc. But all being but (as the end concludes it) meerly pretended, she since hath proved an apostate form, and been (as I may say) halfe madd against the former, and at length she imbarqued [embarked] among the idle Sect called the Quakers.

The carefully chosen terms 'apostate', 'halfe madd' and 'idle' are appropriately damning to both Pierson and the Quakers. They were asserting that Pierson zealously renounced her Christian faith – doubting that she was a true believer in the first place and had joined the Quakers so that she could rail against 'Christ, Scriptures, Ordinances, and Ministers'.[32]

Baxter had vociferously argued that the Quakers were disparate and divorced from reality, and he stated that their beliefs consisted of 'notorious wickedness, injustice and uncharitableness'.[33] In *A Sad Caveat to All Quakers*, the anonymous author concurred and reported that Pierson 'undertook to raise him again to life' and used words 'the like whereof never heard in Christendom'.[34] It was further suggested that Quakers and Pierson had become 'the daily discourse and laughter of the City of Worcester, and of all the Country round about it'.[35] By undermining the Quakers and highlighting their inadequacies, the author suggested that the state church was the correct church.

Thomas Willam, a well-respected Quaker correspondent, wrote to Margaret Fell at this time to advise her of what was happening in Worcester. Willam observed that Pool's mind had become unbalanced and he had committed suicide ('destroyed in the water'). His letter serves as the only piece of Quaker evidence pertaining to Pool's involvement with them. However, Willam was only made aware of the incident from newsbooks. It can be gathered from Willam's words that Pool was convinced and had spoken in meetings, but ultimately was unwell, or as he phrased it, his 'mind run out'.[36] Choosing Quakerism was not without its risks and Pool may have had difficulty reconciling his new beliefs with the reality of his everyday life and possible ostracism in the wider community. For him, it may have been too much to bear. The sad fact remained that a young man was found in the Severn River on a February day and his distraught mother was persuaded by Pierson to attempt the greatest possible miracle. Willam wrote that Pierson and another woman went 'to the grave and took him forth, and imitated the prophet, and that not doing went to prayer, and nothing prevailing they buried him again and so the enemy got advantage'.[37]

Willam recognised that Pierson 'imitated the prophet' by attempting to raise Pool as Christ had raised Lazarus. It is noteworthy that Willam continued by stating 'nothing prevailing they buried him again' – as if there was a slight chance that Pierson could have performed this miracle. The wording strongly suggests that a successful revival was within the realms of possibility. Willam also referenced 'the enemy' – in this case, Baxter, and all non-believers. The readiness of the press to cover this incident demonstrates a wider determination to suggest that all Quakers behaved in this manner. When editing the Swarthmore letters around 1676, George Fox endorsed the letter with the words 'mad whimsy'.[38] Fox certainly distanced himself from Pierson and her actions. This is not surprising as at the time of Nayler's trial, his name was very strongly associated with Nayler's folly. Shortly after that trial, a tract was published entitled *The Quakers Quaking: or, The Most Just and Deserved Punishment Inflicted on the Person of James Naylor ... to which is added The Several Damnable Opinions of the said Quakers*, which stated that 'the names of George Fox and James Nayler have been famous with many deluded people in this City'.[39] This publication also warned that there would be more who claimed to be Christ or were 'false prophets' who 'shall shew signs and wonders, in so much that if it were possible, they shall deceive the elect'.[40] The Quakers were not only being viewed as disruptive, but there was also a palpable fear that they were dangerous and engaging in diabolic acts.

Aside from Fox's brief comment concerning Willam's letter years later, there is no evidence to show whether Pierson was reprimanded or not by the Quakers for her actions. There is no mention of the incident in other Quaker sources, suggesting that it did not merit attention amongst them. The records show that Pierson made no further attempts to raise anyone from the dead or perform any other miracles, and thereby this was an isolated incident. Pierson was not punished by authorities for her actions, nor is there any evidence to show that she was cautioned by Quakers about her behaviour. This leads to a possibility that Quakers, and certainly those in leadership positions, did not believe the incident took place at all. Fox's 'mad whimsy' comment may have not been directed towards Pierson, but towards the whole episode.

Quakers were willing to disown members if they were embroiled in a public scandal. For example, in 1655 Christopher Atkinson of Westmorland had confessed to engaging in a sexual relationship with a servant of Thomas Symonds and was promptly disowned.[41] Regardless of the reliability of the reporting of Pierson's actions, it helped to demonstrate how dangerous the Quakers could be. Pierson's actions provided further ammunition for Baxter, who stated that the Quakers were 'malignant enemies to the very *cause*, and *Church*, and *Gospel*, and *Servants* of Jesus Christ' based on their favoured methods of operation.[42] Moreover, Quakers were at risk of alienating the wider population, the very people they were trying to save, with their disorderly activity, while their opponents sought to highlight such behaviour and to force the authorities to punish them.

Chapter 8

Persecution or Prosecution?

In May 1657, James, Walter and Thomas Merrick were verbally abused and arrested at the Ross-on-Wye meeting by 'a rude rabble … with dogs and staves … whooping, halloeing [sic], pushing their Staves at the windows, and throwing sticks and dirt'. Another Quaker present at that meeting, Giles Milton, was physically attacked by the unruly crowd, resulting in his arm being injured.[1] In the same year, Rice Morgan of Weobley, Herefordshire, disrupted the service at St Peter and St Paul's parish church and requested the clergyman to 'prove his doctrine by Scripture'. Incensed by this behaviour, the minister is alleged to have encouraged his congregation to attack Morgan. Consequently, they knocked him over and plucked the hairs from his head.[2] It is not that surprising that the clergy would encourage such demeaning, violent and un-Christian behaviour when an individual was deemed to be a threat to the Church. This humiliation would have certainly served as a warning to other Quakers to think twice before confronting clergymen in front of their parishioners or behaving in a manner that could upset public order.

Elsewhere, William Simpson of Lancaster was charged with public indecency after he walked naked through streets of Evesham 'in a prophetic manner' in 1659.[3] Simpson had a reputation for public indecency throughout England as 'he was moved of the Lord to go at several times, for three years, naked and barefoot through cities, towns, marketplaces and into priests' houses, as a sign that they should be stripped as he was'.[4] He, like many other early Quakers, saw himself as a prophet. In 1659 he defended his actions, writing that the prophets walked in sackcloth and naked 'as I had done'.[5] Quaker behaviour was 'virtually an intrinsic philosophical part of Quaker belief … heavy with symbolism … offending many and intriguing some'.[6] Simpson reappraised scriptural warnings and turned them into dramatic performance to draw an audience. He defended his indecency by presenting it as a heavy metaphor for the times to come:

Oh, Church of England, this is unto thee, who livest in oppression and cruelty, pride and covetousness, a day of misery is coming upon thee, thy nakednesse and shame is coming upon thee as an armed Man, from which no Man can hide thee.[7]

The late 1650s were a challenging period for Quakers, as they had to cope with intense periods of persecution as well as having to self-censor members of their own community. John Miller referred to 1659 and 1660 as the 'zenith of popular anti-Quakerism', yet the difference between those two years, in terms of legislation, was vast.[8] The years 1659 and 1660 certainly should not be conflated for statistical purposes because of the drastic changes in government; however, Quakers played a major role in the widespread political disruption and apocalyptic hopes in these years. The provocative behaviours of Quakers – going naked as a sign, confronting townspeople in the marketplace for their wickedness and denouncing ministers in front of their congregations seemed to 'court violence'.[9] In comparison with the outlandish activities of Simpson in 1659 in Worcestershire, Quakers were similarly charged with public indecency and disturbances, disrupting church services, and breaking the Sabbath. In Herefordshire, nevertheless, there were no recorded incidents of suffering, but this changed in 1660.

Following the restoration of Charles II in May 1660, the relationship between the Quakers and the authorities became strained, at best. In his Declaration of Breda, Charles had promised religious toleration and although his intentions were almost certainly genuine, tolerance would not last. It became increasingly clear that it was arguably in Parliament's best interest to act against radical dissenters.

The Cavalier Parliament was thereby determined to establish the supremacy of the Church of England and admit no other as well as severely punish former republicans and religious fanatics.[10] After Charles's restoration to the throne there was a rapid adoption of legislation that greatly impacted the early Quaker movement. Charles, along with Edward Hyde, the Earl of Clarendon and chief minister at the beginning of his reign, needed to control this situation. The series of legislation that followed is unfairly known as the Clarendon Code. Clarendon was not in favour of all of the legislation that bears his name – it was the work of the Cavalier Parliament from the summer of 1661 onwards.

The Quakers were thought to be intent on the destruction of the state church as well as social and political upheaval. Their refusal to remove their hats, their use of thee and thou, and their general behaviour marked them out as restless troublemakers.[11] Perhaps most damaging was that they were associated with their extremism of the 1650s, and their allegiance to the state was considered questionable. Quakers' refusal to pay tithes, church rates and other levies to the state church and their unwillingness to swear the Oath of Allegiance exacerbated suspicions that they did not support the restored monarchy.

By not abiding to the law and refusing to swear allegiance to the restored monarch, they were viewed as traitorous. To the restoration authorities, any resistance to conform would have suggested that they were the radical deviant republicans who had provoked the civil wars. In the two counties, the offences committed by Quakers in 1660, during the aforementioned 'zenith of Anti-Quakerism', were for refusal to swear. It was an effective method to arrest Quakers; if the authorities could not find an alternative indictment, their outright refusal to swear was a guaranteed offence.

The authorities were efficient in their punishment – 97 per cent of the Quakers in Herefordshire arrested in 1660 were imprisoned, while 96 per cent were imprisoned in Worcestershire. They were regularly arrested in both counties for attending unlawful meetings, closely followed by their refusal to swear.[12] The authorities were clearly suspicious of the increasingly large, often clandestine, gatherings and moved swiftly to extinguish these defiant radical sparks, possibly because they believed that they could proliferate to an uncontrollable level. From 1662 onwards, Quakers continued to be charged with the same offences, although in Worcestershire, they were charged with 'disturbing the realm', non-payment of tithes, and absence from state church services.

From 16 to 18 July 1662, several Quakers were brought before the Assize Court in Worcester.[13] This trial is of importance because it brings together Edward Bourne, Susanna Pierson and George Knight from the William Pool controversy. It shows the characteristic way in which the Quakers addressed local authorities, especially their distrust of the judicial process. This included their belief that judges and witnesses were partisan, but it also exemplifies the patience of the judges and the balanced approach that they could take with the Quakers. Attitudes from local authorities varied considerably, and certainly not all judges were outwardly hostile to them.

This map captures a nation reshaped by crisis, where Herefordshire and Worcestershire truly felt the tremors of civil war and radical reform. These counties became contested spaces, their market towns and rural manors swept into networks of dissent, loyalty and shifting power. England, though familiar in form, was a country transformed after the civil wars. (*Courtesy of the Norman B. Leventhal Map & Education Center at the Boston Public Library*)

Crowned in splendour, Charles I (1600–49) ruled with conviction, but clashed fatally with Parliament over power and faith. Captured, tried and executed in 1649, his death marked the first regicide of a reigning monarch and changed the course of British history. (*Kunsthistorisches Museum Wien. Public domain image*

This image reflects the climactic struggle of the civil wars, fought in Worcester in September 1651. Once loyal royalist stronghold, the city became a strategic crossroads – where Charles II's hopes for restoration met Oliver Cromwell's disciplined advance. The battle's brutal conclusion shattered monarchic resistance and sealed Worcester's place as the site of the final conflict of the civil wars. (*Original painting by Paul Stanley, 2025. Courtesy of the Battle of Worcester Society*)

Rising from modest gentry to lead the New Model Army, Oliver Cromwell (1599–1658) steered the nation through regicide and revolution. His rule as Lord Protector marked a brief experiment in republicanism – rooted in both religious conviction and military discipline. A figure both revered and reviled, Cromwell remains central to the story of a kingdom turned upside down. (*Wellcome Collection. Public domain image*)

George Fox (1624–91), for all intents and purposes, was the leader of the Religious Society of Friends otherwise known as the Quakers. Fox rejected institutional religion and preached direct spiritual experience. His itinerant ministry defied social hierarchies and his message sparked a radical movement that challenged both Church and state. He was frequently imprisoned, yet remained steadfast, guiding the early Quakers through fierce persecution and a process of organisation and centralisation. (*Library of Congress. Public domain image*)

James Nayler (1618–60), one of the most radical, controversial and enigmatic figures of the early Quaker movement. Born in Ardsley, Yorkshire, Nayler served as a Parliamentarian soldier during the civil wars before embracing Quakerism under George Fox's influence. His charismatic preaching electrified audiences but it was his infamous 1656 entry into Bristol that ignited scandal. Arrested and tried for blasphemy, Nayler endured severe physical punishment and was imprisoned. He died in 1660 near Huntingdon, Cambridgeshire, and while his death did not mark the end of ecstatic Quaker behaviour, it certainly served as a cautionary tale. (*Yale Center for British Art; Yale University Art Gallery Collection. Public domain image*)

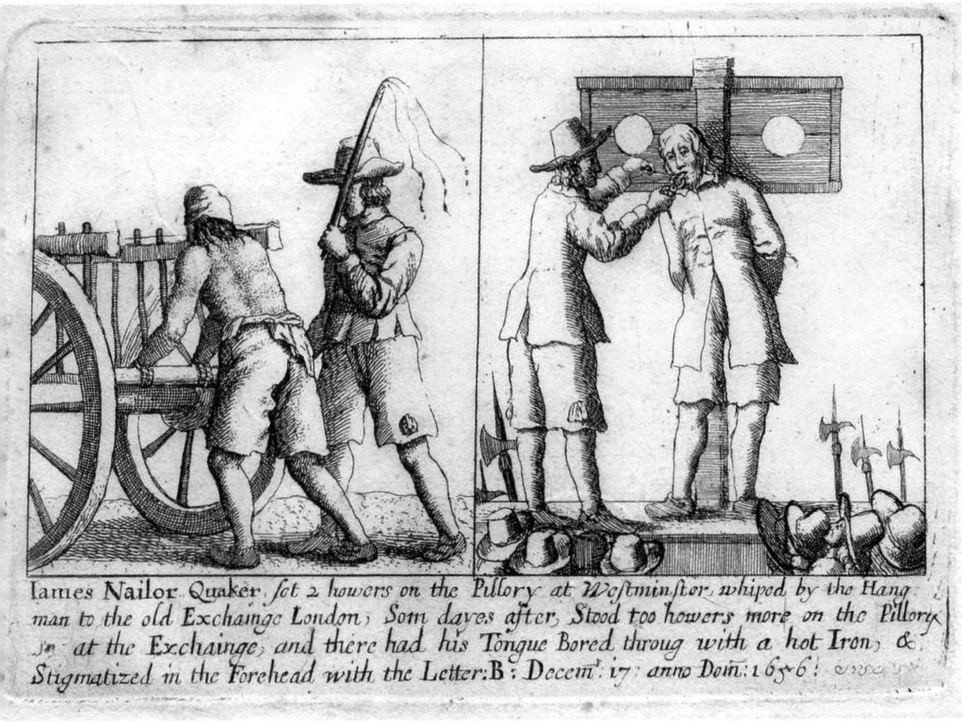

This contemporary engraving depicts James Nayler being severely whipped and having his tongue bored with a hot iron – a brutal punishment handed down by Parliament in 1656 after his controversial re-enactment of Christ's entry into Jerusalem. His public humiliation also included his forehead being branded with a letter B for blasphemer. This event marked a turning point in Quaker history, prompting a shift towards inward discipline. (*Wikimedia Commons. Public domain image*)

Richard Baxter (1615–91), the outspoken Puritan minister whose turbulent relationship with the emerging Quaker movement mirrored the religious fragmentation of England after the civil wars. Baxter rose to prominence in Kidderminster, Worcestershire, preaching reform and unity amid chaos. His zeal met fierce resistance from early Quakers, whose unmediated spirituality and confrontational style clashed with his ordered theology. Through pamphlets and polemics, Baxter sparred with George Fox and other early Quakers. (*Llyfrgell Genedlaethol Cymru – The National Library of Wales. Public domain image*)

One Sheet against the Quakers, printed in London in 1657, showcased Richard Baxter's fierce opposition to the rising Quaker movement. Within its pages, Baxter denounced the Quakers as heretical, unstable and dangerously enthusiastic. He accused them of rejecting scripture, undermining Church authority, and promoting spiritual delusion. This pamphlet stands as a vivid example of how print became a battleground for theological control and public persuasion. (*Courtesy of Haverford College Quaker & Special Collections*)

Charles II (1630–85) had a complex relationship with the Quakers. Restored to the throne in 1660, Charles presided over a period of intense persecution, enacting laws like the Quaker Act of 1662 that criminalised their meetings and demanded oaths they refused on religious grounds yet he also responded to Quaker appeals. In 1661, early Quakers presented their famous Peace Declaration, distancing themselves from violent radicals and affirming their commitment to nonviolence. Charles's reign marked both the harshest suppression and the earliest recognitions of Quaker distinctiveness. (*Wikimedia Commons Royal Collection Trust. Public domain image*)

Lamentation Over England, written by Quaker minister Morgan Watkins (d. 1682) in 1664, was a searing indictment of England's rulers, priests and people who, in his view, had strayed from divine truth. Written in the wake of relentless persecution, Watkins appeals to conscience and scripture, urging oppressors to reflect on their actions and the spiritual consequences of cruelty. His voice, both mournful and defiant, embodied the early Quaker commitment to truth and resistance through the printed word. (*Courtesy of Haverford College Quaker & Special Collections*)

The word cloud highlights the most commonly used words in the posthumous testimonies of Humphrey Smith. The words appearing most frequently include 'God', 'Lord', 'Faithful', 'Truth', 'Suffer' and 'Prison', which is expected. The word cloud also highlights other keywords, including 'Innocent', 'Love' and 'Servant', which are more frequently used than words of a negative connotation, for example, 'Wicked', 'Cruel' and 'Fear'. (*Courtesy of the author*)

On 8 June 1662, Bourne, Pierson, Knight and other Quakers, including Gervase Pierson,[14] were arrested for attending an unlawful meeting at the home of Robert Smith in Worcester. They were promptly imprisoned and were not granted trial until the Assizes, starting on 16 July. The group of Quakers were requested to plead their case in front of Judge Hide and Judge Terrill. The defendants' immediate concern was about entangling themselves in their own arguments, but the unnamed judge tried to reassure Gervase Pierson by saying, 'I doe not go about to ensnare you by your own words.' In addition to their unlawful assembly, their collective refusal to swear the Oath of Allegiance, Smith presented himself to the court wearing a hat. When questioned about the law, the judge replied that it was 'custom in England to show their subjection to Authorities by putting off their hatts', but as Smith continued to argue on this point, the judge fined him £5 and demanded that the gaoler remove the offending item. This pattern of calm reasoning by the judge followed by frustrated, defensive remarks from the defendants continued throughout their trial. When Smith stated, 'I am not here only ready to suffer but also to seal those truths with my blood if thereunto be required,' the judge responded, 'God forbid I should seek your blood.'

Again and again, the presiding judge showed patience and restraint, although his frustration was becoming clearly visible. Indeed, after repeatedly asking Smith for his plea, he finally called on the Quaker to be 'speedy in your Answers, you will not be permitted to weary the Court'.[15]

Bourne, Pierson and Knight would not simply plead 'guilty or not guilty', much to the clear exasperation of the judge, but he remained composed. In her defence, Pierson said that the Quakers were innocent and that they had 'dirt thrown on us and, in our faces, going to and coming from the meetings without lifting up our hands against any'.[16] This did not alter the fact that they were attending an unlawful meeting.

Bourne later asked the judge, 'suppose that if Christ and his apostles were here at this time and if they should meet together would not this Law take hold of them?' to which the judge responded, 'Yes, that it would… you are not apostles.'[17]

The Quakers further questioned the validity of the witness statements. Pierson accused a witness of providing a false statement because he was not a 'competent witness' and 'he had enmity in his heart against them'.[18] Knight added that a witness 'swore carelessly' because he said that he could prove that he was at his father's business at the specific hour the witness swore he was at Robert Smith's house.[19] One of the witnesses claimed that there were forty-six people taking part in the meeting, and when asked by defendant Robert Fidoe if he heard anyone 'pray or speak or see any book opened amongst them', the witness replied, 'No.' Fidoe later explained that they met at Smith's house because they cared for 'three or four fatherless children' so that the parishes would not be financially responsible for them. He added that it was the responsibility of the authorities to prove that they were meeting for another reason. The Quakers were unable to prove that they were all attending an inexplicably silent meeting to discuss the fatherless children in their care and were fined £5 each, or, on non-payment, they would be imprisoned and 'put to hard Labor for three months'.[20]

The authorities did not discriminate in their retribution; the young and old were just as likely to be punished. In 1662, Frances Thomas, a 70-year-old woman in poor health from Herefordshire, was excommunicated for absence from divine services and, as a further punishment, the prosecutor seized her bedding. Furthermore, it was recorded that she suffered much from the cold, so this seizure could be viewed as particularly harsh.[21] On 31 December 1662, Richard Walker of Broadway, Worcestershire, was arrested for unspecified charges by Major John Wilde. It was recorded in the Great Book of Sufferings the following February that Walker was over 60 years old and referred to as a 'sickly', 'weakly', 'harmless' and an 'innocent' man who was:

> of good report among his neighbours and relations and friends that were well acquainted with his conversation and behaviour, of which they testify was a good innocent and sweet savory life and also upright fearing God and loving righteousness and hating evil.

Immediately following his arrest, while en route by foot to Worcester gaol, Walker was unable to keep up with the pace, so was dragged by force. It was reported that the Major Wilde 'beat him down with his horse' and threatened to 'pistol him'. This abuse by Wilde is cited as a factor in the death of the elderly Quaker shortly thereafter.[22] Quakers often wrote that their oppressors would be judged and harshly so by God. Following Wilde's death, Quaker Daniel Baker wrote that he was now:

> at rest with the Lord, free from all oppression and cruelty and hard heartedness of Men of Sin who shall die and come to Judgement and

he shall have Judgement without Mercy – who showed no mercy the Mouth of the Lord hath spoken it through his servant.[23]

Walker was a well-respected member of his community but, even so, was punished in an undignified manner without compassion. Similarly, John Waite and five other Quakers were required by the Mayor of Worcester and Major Wilde, the magistrate, to pay 4 shillings for a month's absence from church and, upon refusal, coats were removed from all the defendants. It was likely that their coats were needed to keep warm as the court hearing was held on 31 January 1664.[24] The authorities were willing to cause members of the Quaker community, even the most vulnerable, intentional physical discomfort to prove their point. This cruelty by the authorities played into the 'theology of suffering', or the idea that these hardships were part of God's plan.[25] Major Wilde was well known for his ferocity in prosecuting the Quakers. From 1660 until 1664, he charged twenty-seven Quakers with various crimes, and his zealotry against the Quakers was based on one significant factor.[26] Wilde was in his seventies during this decade, nearing the end of his life, and had dedicated his life to public service in the county. An active former Member of Parliament, it was his experiences, especially his involvement in the civil wars and first-hand awareness of the chaos these years caused, that shaped his intolerance towards the Quakers, their disruption of the peace, and their often blatant disregard of the laws during the delicate Restoration period.

To the delight of Wilde and other local authorities, legal measures also took their toll on Quakers. The Quaker Act of 1662 punished those who refused to comply to the strictures of the law by rendering Quaker meetings illegal, while persistent offenders were liable to transportation overseas.[27] To make matters worse for the Quakers, the Conventicle Act of 1664 forbade conventicles (otherwise known as unauthorised Meetings for Worship), from being held. No more than five people could gather unless they were from the same family and, upon a third conviction, the sentence of banishment could again be issued.[28] Comparatively wealthy members provided the premises for meetings and bore the brunt of the fines imposed by the Conventicle Acts.[29] The Five Mile Act of 1665 forbade itinerant dissenting preachers from coming within 5 miles of incorporated towns or their former livings; the measure also restricted their right to teach.[30] These legal impositions were designed to be punitive, and many dissenters were persecuted between 1660 and 1688. In relation to each Act, the itinerant Quaker preachers and those attending their meetings were not only acting against the state church, but they were also challenging the state itself and monarchical governance. The first upsurge in prosecution demonstrates the public outcry against radicalism following Thomas Venner's Fifth Monarchist revolt in January 1661. The last was at the time of the Rye House Plot in 1683, a failed attempt by extremists to assassinate Charles II and James, Duke of York.[31]

Other periods of intolerance and persecution show the impact of the Quaker Act in 1662 and the First Conventicle Act in 1664, and then reported incidents subside until the Second Conventicle Act in 1670.[32] The introduction of this measure brought about another wave of arrests and convictions in both counties. On 19 June 1670, John Alford, John Hunt, Richard Fidoe and Richard Stevens were arrested on Cooking Street, Worcester, for a 'riotous and tumultuous meeting' in the town and their refusal to disperse.[33] Quakers flagrantly held their meetings out in the open, not under the guise of peacefully gathering to worship in an enclosed space. This blatant disregard for public order, as the authorities saw it, was demonstrated again a week later when, on 26 June, Thomas Bourne, Henry Smart and Edward Reynolds were imprisoned in Worcester for holding a 'riotous and tumultuous conventicle'.[34] The authorities were very quick to label the gatherings in well-defined terms, demonstrating that the Quakers were quite hostile and clearly breaking the law. After 1670, 72 per cent of the arrests in Worcestershire and 49 per cent in Herefordshire were as a result of violating the Conventicle Acts. In 1670, Charles Barnet, a baker, was charged with two counts of public preaching in Leominster. He was fined £60 in total for both offences, and it was reported that the authorities took 'all the goods from his house and all the wood'. When advised that they had taken everything from the house except the Quaker's bread, which would spoil before it could be sold, the judge replied, 'if you can't sell it, you may bring it to me and give it to my horses.'[35] The authorities carried out these punishments, often with relish, and, in doing so, attempted to scar their opponents physically and mentally.

In 1676, there was considerable abuse of Quakers in Hereford. In August of that year, Henry Caldicott, the outgoing mayor, issued a warning to them, advising against holding further meetings and stated that if they met again, 'let it be at their peril', as he believed that their meetings threatened the peace and harmony of the town.[36] He may have felt that these quiet and clandestine meetings were simply subversive. His threat was a form of preservation – a way to keep the peace, which was initially ignored by the Quakers in Hereford and countywide until the latter quarter of the century. It was not in their nature to bend to threats and the Quakers continued to meet in Hereford while being subjected to violence. In light of the increasing arrests and convictions, as well as general abuse, in February 1677 the Herefordshire Quarterly Meeting suggested that a new paper book should be ordered to record all of the attacks and persecutions taking place in the county.[37] In another demonstration of popular hostility, the meeting house was mobbed numerous times by local townspeople and 'rude boys' who threw stones and dirt at the building, broke windows and their frames, and attempted to bring a pig inside, possibly suggesting that their meeting house was a pigsty.[38] The 'rude boys' included pupils from the free school and choristers from Hereford Cathedral. In a rare display of sympathy, the schoolmaster apologised to the Quakers for his pupils' destructive behaviour.[39]

Not only were locals vandalising the meeting house, but they were also physically abusing them in acts of popular hostility. In 1676, it was common for Quakers to be chased by stone-throwing mobs or be attacked by stave-waving opponents knocking the hats off of their heads. There were also several cases of excrement and urine being hurled at them. In September 1676, Abraham Seward, the Hereford mayor-elect, nevertheless continued Caldicott's legacy of inciting and encouraging abuse. His officers commanded the crowds to 'knock out the Quakers Brains if they did not depart', and later it was claimed that they threatened to 'fire the meeting house and broil them in it'. This incident further supports the prevailing belief that the Quakers were subversive, and that the local population were encouraged by the authorities to act in any way that would restrict the ability of the Quakers to have a meaningful presence in the town.

Walter Rogers, a clergyman from Mordiford, a village 4 miles from Hereford, saw the ruins of the Quaker meeting house and stated, 'they who did it were very good boys and had done their work better than he thought for.'[40] This testimony of 1676 confirms that anti-Quaker sentiments were strongly encouraged by the clergy and local administrators. As with any 'mob' activity, it is possible that the local 'boys' merely saw it as an excuse for unmitigated violence without consequence, whipped up by the authorities, rather than a profound moral responsibility to the state church.

When documenting their punishments, it is peculiar that Quakers would account for seized bedding yet not record the name of the prosecuting officer or others responsible for their misfortune.[41] In Worcestershire, 59 per cent of incidents recorded were listed without a named arresting official. In Herefordshire, that figure rises to 80 per cent. Barry Reay notes that the Quakers only referred to their opponents 'in the vaguest of terms'.[42] It is possible that by not naming or even describing the public officials, the Quakers were able to gain greater control of their narrative – the brave and pious Quakers against a non-descript enemy. As many of the punishments were economic, the local authorities may have believed this action would destabilise the local meetings. Historians Barry Reay, Stephen K. Roberts and Alan Anderson have suggested that wealth may have also played a part in anti-Quaker activities.[43] According to the Hearth Tax records, many of the Quakers recorded in the Great Book of Sufferings had homes of substantial size, including Edward Bourne, Francis Fincher, James Merrick, Humphrey Smith, and Richard Dolphin of Leominster.[44] This suggests that the local authorities were targeting the more affluent members as they and, more importantly, their financial resources and connections were critical to the movement's growth and success in the region. These members naturally had more to lose, both financially and within the wider community. Reay also suggests that outsiders were attacked more frequently than those who were native to the community and that the Quakers who hosted 'outsiders' were particularly targeted.[45] They were scapegoated as unwelcome intruders or deviants in many communities.[46] There were no incidents involving confirmed 'outsiders' in Herefordshire.[47] In Worcestershire, from 1655 to 1690, there were only six incidents involving 'outsiders'.[48]

George Fox was one of them.

After attending a 'large and precious meeting' in Adderbury, Oxfordshire, Fox attended a meeting the following day (17 December 1673) at John Halford's home in Tredington, Worcestershire (now in Warwickshire).[49] In his journal, Fox wrote that he was in the parlour after the meeting, when Rowland Haines, a Warwickshire clergyman, and Henry Parker, a Justice of the Peace, arrived and sought to break up the meeting.[50] In what must have been quite a coup for Haines and Parker, Fox was sent to Worcester gaol by a 'Mittimus of an extraordinary nature'.[51] Parker's mittimus was as follows:

> *To the Constables of Tredington in the said County of Worcester, and to all Constables and Tithingmen of the several Townships and Villages within the said Parish of Tredington: And to the Keeper of the Goal for the County of Worcester.*

> Complaint being made to me, being one of his Majesty's Justices of the Peace for the said County of *Worcester*, there has of late been several Meetings of divers Persons, to the Number of four Hundred Persons and upwards at a Time, upon Pretence of Exercise of Religion, otherwise than what is established by the Laws of *England:* And many of the said Persons, some of them were Teachers, and came from the *North*, and others from the remote Parts of the Kingdom, which tends to the Prejudice of the reformed and established Religion, and may prove prejudicial to the publick Peace.

This wording, and particularly Parker's specification 'from the North', suggests that Reay's 'outsider theory' is correct. They were viewed as alien and contaminating society and disrupting the public peace. Parker's mittimus continued and requested that Fox, and his son-in-law, Thomas Lower, who had accompanied Fox on his travels, be sent to Worcester gaol until 'they shall be from thence delivered by due Course of Law'. Fox and Lower responded to the Lord Lieutenant and accused Parker of treating them 'unchristianly and inhumanly' and pleaded their innocence, stating that they 'were not in any Meeting, but were discoursing together when they came in'.[52] Fox explained to the Lord Lieutenant that they were en route to visit his dying mother in Leicestershire who had 'earnestly desired to see him before she died'. Fox claimed that he had explained the situation to Parker and asked him to consider whether this was 'doing as he would be done by', to which Parker said that he 'would do it'.[53] This unsympathetic response from Parker would not have been unexpected, but Fox's recording of the conversation for posterity demonstrates that Quakers, in many cases, were not viewed with the same compassion as others would have been. Again, as Fox likely expected, this letter did not have the effect he would have desired and they remained prisoners until the Quarter Sessions in late January, when they were charged with holding an unlawful conventicle; this was compounded with their refusal to take the Oaths of Allegiance and Supremacy.[54] When Fox declared that he would not take any oath, he was sent back to the gaol, while Lower was released; after which Lower asked the magistrates why he had been released and Fox had not. Justice Simpson replied, 'if you be not content, we will tender you the Oath also, and send you to your Father.' After a heated discussion, Lower left the magistrates' chambers.[55]

Fox was sent to appear at the Worcester Assizes in April 1674, where Parker insisted that the Quaker was a threat, 'a Ringleader, that many of the Nation followed him, and that he knew not what it might come to'. Consequently, Fox remained imprisoned until the next Quarter Sessions three weeks later. At the Quarter Sessions, the Quaker refused to take the Oaths and was initially sent back to Worcester gaol, but he was released for a short period until his appearance at the next Quarter Sessions in July. Here he was found guilty under the Statute of Praemunire, which meant that all his goods were to be forfeited and he was sentenced to life imprisonment. Soon after his sentence was issued, he became very ill, and it was later recorded that the Quaker was 'weak and low in Body and his Recovery appeared doubtful'. Quakers pleaded with Justice Parker to release him on compassionate grounds and, surprisingly, Parker responded, 'what lawful Favour you can do, for the Benefit of Air, for his Health, pray shew him.' Fox refused to be pardoned because he felt that he was innocent and accepting a pardon would be an acknowledgement of guilt. Consequently, he preferred to stay in gaol 'all his Days, than come out in any Way dishonourable to the Truth he made Profession of'.[56] The procurement of a writ of habeas corpus demonstrated that he was being held unlawfully, and Fox was finally released after spending fourteen months in prison in Worcester.[57] Quakers exhibited fortitude during these periods of increased persecution. They sought to work within the law to address what they saw as wrongful convictions. From the start, Fox had led by example.

While the Quakers did endure physical, property and financial distress, there is a case to be made that the persecution served as powerful recruitment propaganda. When the attacks became more frequent, they began to develop strategies for minimising the effects of the attacks as well as maximising the publicity of their cases. These strategic actions helped to convey a positive image of Quakerism and aimed to gain sympathy or, at least, awareness of their predicament from the wider public.[58]

However, in Herefordshire and Worcestershire, because of their clear aggressive and disrespectful attitude towards authority figures, there is little evidence of outward sympathy. Their publications and the Great Book of Sufferings often described the cruel treatment and persecution they suffered at the hands of the authorities and the inhumane nature in which local and church officials treated them.[59] The publications printed at the time naturally describe the worst aspects of the actions taken against them. John Miller notes that the collating of cases of persecution was to aid recruitment by promoting their beliefs and subsequent punishment by the authorities as akin to the early Christians. He added that Quakers 'invariably referred to themselves in the third person "as if in press release and ... having no choice but to act as they did'".⁶⁰ They were often open about their experiences, especially the grim prison conditions, while powerfully conveying their message. The testimonies, written under the duress of imprisonment, served as evidence that God was ever-present and would deliver them safely from their predicament. In 1682, while imprisoned in Worcester, Edward Bourne published *An Epistle to Friends*, which addressed God's role in their 'suffering'. He wrote:

> It is an Honour which the Lord doth Honour you withal, in that he accords you worthy thereof; wherefore rejoyce therein, because God hath Honoured you with so high a calling that it hath been His good pleasure to call you thereunto, which is for your good, yeah, for your best good ... you may be made more precious than Gold.⁶¹

This published 'fearlessness' in the face of adversity was a testimony to their strong convictions and willingness to die for their faith. After Thomas Languell, a Leominster Quaker, died in gaol in 1661, the gaoler refused to give over his body without receiving payment of the coroner's fees. The gaoler gave authorisation for Languell to have an undignified burial and remarked that he 'died like a hog and should be buried like a dog'. It was unusual for the Quakers to die in prisons in Herefordshire and Worcestershire. In Herefordshire, two of Thomas Languell's fellow Leominster meeting members, Charles Jones and John Smith, died in the gaol in the town – all three in April 1661, likely from gaol fever (typhus).⁶² These are the only three recorded deaths during imprisonment in the county. In Worcestershire, there were two: Richard Walker and Anne Heming of Chadwick.⁶³ Heming was imprisoned in 1656 for non-payment of tithes, in 1660 for refusal to swear, and again in 1668 for non-payment of tithes – her final imprisonment ending with her death in Worcester prison on 16 February 1672.⁶⁴ These deaths were recorded in the Great Book of Sufferings, but there was no follow-up and certainly no investigation. Death under these circumstances was expected.

The martyrdom of the earliest Quakers, whether intentional or not, was cause for alarm to the local authorities. The evidence suggests that Richard Baxter's criticisms were justified because in the 1650s the Quakers in the two counties often went out of their way to disrupt the peace and challenge figures of authority. Baxter immediately recognised the need to suffocate what he saw as a threat to his ministry, his livelihood and wider society. His anti-Quaker pamphlets were more moderate in tone than other contemporary opponents of Quakers. For example, in 1659, Thomas Danson, a Presbyterian minister from Sandwich, Kent, referred to Quakerism as a 'deformed monster'.[65] Through his position of authority, Baxter was able to exploit the threat that the earliest Quakers posed to his advantage and to advance the position of the state church during his tenure in Kidderminster. He used his publications to deter his audience from joining the Quakers and attempted to expose their flawed beliefs and actions. His demonisation of the Quakers was an easy way to strengthen community solidarity and, in turn, the Quakers used similar tactics against clergymen and the authorities to strengthen their own positions. Quakers speaking and acting on behalf of God was unacceptable to Baxter, but they were insistent that their actions were God's will. In a 1666 letter to Fox, Daniel Baker wrote that Quakers 'in faithfulness are well preserved in ye savor of immortal life ... ye lord abide in ye measure of that which my God has blest, upheld, and preserved to this moment'.[66]

They believed that God was driving forward their actions, yet Baxter dismissed such views, recording, 'tis an evident judgement of God upon those people that turn Quakers; and a punishment for their former sin', and repeatedly questioned the personal traits of those who became Quakers.[67] Baxter was concerned that those convinced by Quakers did not know to whom or what they were declaring their allegiance. Not only were the Quaker recruitment methods questioned, but he also suggested that they were satanic, adding that:

> I should suppose that their proud, scornful, railing language should put it out of doubt what spirit they are of, to any that are acquainted with the language of Christ's Spirit, and of Satan, and are able to judge of spirits by the most palpable effects, and to know darkness from light.

He was fiercely opposed to their zealousness and challenged their belief system, claiming that the Quakers did not understand their own religion and despite this, were zealous and forceful in their evangelism.[68]

An overarching theme in this period of Quaker history is that they saw themselves as apostles and prophets – it was referenced in their writings, in court records and, in the case of Susanna Pierson, physically manifested. The early Quakers self-identified as victims, but the outside world saw them very differently. Their behaviour was easily viewed as disruptive, sometimes bizarre, and occasionally blasphemous. In 1662, Edward Burrough defended their actions, writing:

> What would you have called the Apostles and Ministers of Christ? who had left their Families and Callings, and went up and down, and had no certain dweling Place, but went from City to City, and cared not for the World; nor what to eat, nor what to drink, nor wherewith to be clothed; this they did, and yet were no Vagabonds, nor idle, nor careless Persons, but abode in the Doctrine of Christ: they were hated by your Generation. ... And they said, *They were Troublers of their Cities*, as you do now call us false Prophets and Deceivers. I do declare this Generation to be the same which persecuted the Prophets, Christ, and his Apostles, as it doth persecute us.[69]

The evidence firmly suggests that Quakers were a close-knit group due, in part, to the siege mentality created out of this persecution, but they were not isolated from the outside world. As they became increasingly aware of how they presented themselves and their message to the wider world to gain acceptance, there was recognition that there was very little room for mistakes. They needed to uphold their reputations so that they were viewed positively and not as troublemaking radicals.

Clearly, however, Quakers in these two counties began to retreat from their religious fanaticism of the 1650s. The Nayler affair in 1656 forced the Quakers to reappraise their activities on a national level. The Pierson case a few months later confirmed the suspicions of diabolical Quaker actions. The Pierson episode illustrated how local, regional and national Quakers distanced themselves from this type of conduct. They began to realise that their disruptive behaviour was counter-productive to their message and to their very survival, especially when faced with the measures imposed in the penal code after the restoration of the monarchy. The Quakers had courted controversy with their provocative methods. In many instances, their methods only served to reinforce Baxter's warnings that they should not be trusted and were not God's elected spokespeople. Baxter warned that 'Christ will deal justly with you [Quakers] though you deal unjustly with him and his'.[70] Quakers were able to counter these warnings and used well-documented examples of persecution to strengthen their resolve. In many cases, Quakerism was aided by the martyrdom of its first members, and, in the face of adversity, Quakers were able to take control of their narrative.

Chapter 9

The Evil Multitudes

In *Lamentation Over England*, published in 1664, Morgan Watkins of Herefordshire, as with many of his co-religionists, wrote about the 'wickedness' of the Church and state authorities in England. Watkins wrote with the intention to caution the wider population; his intention was to help. He observed that political and religious leaders had 'erred and strayed from the way of God and were being led by their own desires'.[1] Watkins believed that the authorities were unjust in their pursuit of persecuting the Quakers. Although he addressed them as his 'Friends', he warned:

> You knew not what you did, when you began to meddle with us, and make laws against us, and persecute us because we could not submit to your wills; for had you known us, you would not have begun such an ill work, wherein you should have lost so much labour, and gained so much dishonour, and also incurr'd the wrath of God.[2]

Watkins was direct in his assessment of mid-seventeenth-century English society. He expressed frustration with what was acceptable behaviour, and, in this tract, he made numerous references to those who were blasphemous, licentious, drunken or quarrelsome.[3] Expressing such views in writing was a key component of early Quaker persuasion and the region was well represented by Edward Bourne in Worcestershire and Watkins in Herefordshire. Early Quakers like Bourne and Watkins found the nature of English society abhorrent, and their writing reflected their personal journeys and world around them, or at least the world that they saw.

Some historians argue that with their increased persecution, Quakers found sympathy amongst their neighbours.[4] However, others argue that their alleged disruptive behaviour was deplored by the wider community who believed that Quakers were 'guilty of failing to satisfy the duties of charity and good neighbourliness'.[5] To understand such differing views, it is first important to examine the society in which the Quakers lived, how it was composed and how it operated.

In their publications, the Quakers painted a bleak picture of a world that resembled Sodom and Gomorrah and they warned of God's imminent retribution. They were offended by popular culture that was at odds with their beliefs. Watkins admitted that Quaker 'manners and behaviour' were not 'after the fashion of this world' and that their detractors would 'laugh us to scorn, like as the old world did at Noah's salvation'.[6] This negative attitude towards 'the world' is one of the themes of early Quaker writing and, as such, Watkins was unforgiving in his assessment of seventeenth-century society.[7] Watkins expressed frustration with what was acceptable behaviour, asking:

> Can nothing satisfy you but our destruction? Because our lives are not squared by your wisdom, must we therefore lose them? Because we cannot run with others, in the same excess of riot, must we not therefore live in the moderation? Because our liberty stands not in the flesh, must we therefore be imprisoned? Because we cannot meet in Taverns and Alehouses, to be drunk, whore, and blaspheme the name of God, must we not therefore meet to speak good of his name? Because we cannot disobey the Lord, to obey man, therefore we must be banished out of the land of our Nativity?[8]

By using drunkenness, promiscuity and blasphemy as examples, he was providing the reader with a litany of easily identifiable sins. Watkins was deeply critical of this immoral society and criticised the levels of depravity displayed on a regular basis. It was argued that seventeenth-century English society resembled biblical tales of dancing in the wilderness, singing and other frivolities that amounted to 'vain delights' rather than any religious observance or indication of good behaviour.[9] Throughout his writing, Watkins' most prevalent theme was that the world was engulfed in wickedness and pleaded with the Quakers not to 'follow the multitude to do evil'.[10] To him, the prevalence of indulgent popular pastimes and the 'fashion of this world' caused widespread immorality.

Popular culture was all-encompassing.[11] This included everyday practices such as eating, drinking, speaking and socialising, which were shared by all people, albeit in different forms.[12] However, these practices were never static;

they were ever evolving.[13] There were different elements at play in the second half of the seventeenth century that impacted on traditions and pastimes.

As we know, it was a time of rapid change and radical thought. Communities throughout England saw many cultural practices being challenged and changed during this period.[14] The term 'community', although meant to describe cohesion, naturally implies exclusion.[15] Participation in the local community was transactional and there would always be outsiders whose beliefs and actions set them apart.[16] The early Quakers certainly saw themselves as distant spectators, and from their perspective, they witnessed practices that needed reform. Morgan Watkins described cases of 'beastliness and debauchery, cursed speakers, swearers, drunkards, whoremongers, adulterers, and fornicators'.[17] The Quakers viewed society outside their meetings as vice-ridden, repugnant and at risk of contaminating all of God's creation. Critics, such as Watkins, thereby saw mid-seventeenth-century popular pastimes as the core of this contamination.

In seventeenth-century society, people understood how they differed in wealth and social status, but that these inequalities could be transcended by the ties of the common experience of the church calendar and the agricultural year – a 'comforting rhythmic certainty, marking the annual cycle of birth, death, and resurrection'.[18] Popular pastimes and festivals filled the calendar of the working year and reaffirmed neighbourliness and collective identity, which could be vitally important to the physical and emotional well-being of individuals and families.[19] In 1654, Oliver Cromwell had threatened these time-honoured traditions, for example, with ordinances against cockfights and temporary horse racing bans because of their cruelty.[20] The ban on horse racing was reinstated in April 1658 because of 'wicked and secret plots' by suspected Royalists taking place.[21]

Furthermore, May Day festivities were banned and people believed that these reforms were an assault on seasonal festivals and customs.[22] May Day and maypole dancing were targeted for their fertility symbolism, as these early summer rituals were allegedly a period of sexual incontinence and heavy drinking; dancing was popular with young people and provided convenient courting opportunities.[23] With an overindulgence in alcohol and sex, it is therefore not surprising that riots frequently occurred during these breaks in the working calendar.[24] Most public holidays involved over-indulgence, even on Ascension Day, a particularly holy day, where it was customary to meet neighbours for a community feast and engage in binge drinking.[25] The consumption of alcohol was structured by a number of rituals, including:

> toasting, drinking contests, games and gambling, songs and by a series of behavioural conventions that encouraged liberal spending, heavy but controlled drinking, and the maintenance of a 'merry' disposition and atmosphere. These rituals and conventions expressed a number of values: courage, self-control, loyalty, financial prosperity and independence, a pride in hard work, a bold defiance of dominant gender norms.[26]

Equally, other customary events posed a threat to the well-being of communities as marketplaces and fairs were notorious.

There were four annual fairs in Worcester and markets were held three times a week, serving as a link in trade between north and south-west England, Bristol and the upper Severn region, London and the Midlands, and Wales.[27] Markets were relied upon for food and raw materials for trade, and to attract customers for local businesses.[28] Despite their economic importance, these fairs and markets had to be closely monitored. For example, in Dorset, magistrates had customary policies of regulating these markets, fearing that grain supplies could be diverted into the brewing trade.[29] In Herefordshire, and to a lesser extent Worcestershire, there would have been concerns of apples being diverted into excess cider production. The seventeenth century was known as the 'Golden Age of Apples in England' and the orchards in Herefordshire, Gloucestershire and Worcestershire were becoming well established in the trade.[30] Cider was also given to servants and labourers as part of their wages, while more wealthy farmers had the resources to experiment with techniques in attempts to match or surpass the quality of imported wines.[31] In this context, cider was becoming a valuable commodity, economically and for pleasure. Certainly, drinking culture was embedded in early modern tradition and alehouses were central to the social lives of the wider community.[32] Alehouses were the hive of neighbourly conversation and these informal contacts helped to create a communal feeling.[33] To many, the value of the services alehouses provided outweighed the problem of occasional disorders.[34] Samuel Pepys often drank to excess during festivals and recorded these incidents and his subsequent hangovers in his diary.[35] It is therefore not surprising that the consumption of alcohol played a significant role in a majority of brawls; the alehouse was a central gathering place where many conversations and quarrels between men took place and because of the effect of alcohol on behaviour.[36]

The struggle to reform behaviour and to curtail the activities in alehouses was contentious and legislation was put in place to control drunkenness in the 1650s.[37] Although it was assumed that regulating alehouses would bring an automatic reduction in drunkenness, it merely led to an increase in the consumption of alcohol in private houses.[38] When the Chester Assizes issued an order against unlicensed alehouses in 1654, it justified this action by forcefully claiming that alehouses and the disorders associated with them were dishonourable to God, a scandal of good government, encouraged wicked and licentious people, and endangered the public peace.[39] It was the role of the authorities, particularly the magistrates, to control alehouses and to enforce discipline on those who had escaped the usual regulatory controls.[40] The legislation continued, and in June 1657, measures were passed banning the performing of music in taverns and alehouses, and gambling. Cromwellian legislation, although ambitious with being centred on a determination to affect a reformation of many of these deeply rooted customs, and thereby bring about a wholesale cultural revolution, was ultimately unsuccessful.[41]

In the post-Restoration period, George Fox commented on the debauched behaviours he witnessed, writing in 1660 that he 'never saw the like drunkenness as then in the towns' as he was travelling from Evesham to Worcester.[42] On 30 May 1660, a proclamation was ordered in Worcester against 'vicious and debauched persons' as 'men of dissolute temper were now discrediting his majesty's cause more than any other'.[43] Quakers nevertheless continued to oppose the 'debauched' people who escaped prosecution while their fellow members languished in gaols.

Watkins complained that those that:

> meet together in Taverns and Alehouses, who swear, drink till they be drunk, and whore to the great dishonour of God, and the Government of the Nation, yet these can be let alone in their wicked meetings, and go unpunished, when Honest, Innocent, Harmless people are fined and sent to prison.[44]

Quakers felt justified in their anxiety that many could not change their ways. They were all too aware that popular activities and rituals often conflicted with good behaviour and consequently led to a decline in moral standards and religious observance. Historians have conventionally thought of Puritans, and in this case the Quakers, as the 'enemies of popular culture rather than elements of it', but they were very much a part of these communities even if they served as a barometer for moral behaviour.[45] Indeed, as David Underdown has suggested, 'adherents of one set of beliefs stressed the values of good neighbourhood and cooperation; adherents of the other, those of individual piety and sobriety and the duty of the godly to reform their less enlightened neighbours.'[46] The Quakers clearly saw corruption in their own communities and they felt that they had to respond. In 1660, while imprisoned in Worcester gaol, Daniel Baker expressed dismay that 'fountains of filthiness, have flowed and streamed forth throughout the Land, and woefully defiled thy Neighbouring Towns and Cities, who have drunk deep of thy unclean, filthy, whorish abominations'.[47] Quakers, like Baker, urgently sought to spiritually re-educate the population. They could trace the root cause of this broken society to a lack of spiritual education. As Quakers saw it, these people lived without fear of God's condemnation, and with reckless abandon.

In the same year, George Fox attended a meeting in Worcester and recorded in his journal that many had asked him what he thought of 'times and things', to which he responded, 'the Lord's light shined over all and his power was set over all.'[48] However, the Worcestershire Quarter Sessions show numerous accusations of theft among the wider population, suggesting a lack of trustworthiness.[49] Neighbours also testified against others in their communities and accused them of unchristian behaviour. In 1660, Francis Steed of Pershore was called a 'whoremaster' who was 'taken in bed with Nan Harbidge and the street was in uproar'.[50] Two years later, Anne Durham and Joan Willis of Great Comberton accused Elizabeth Ranford of witchcraft, while in 1665, Anne Golde and Elinor Dipple testified that they saw John Cale in Alice Lymicombe's chamber, 'treading together upon her bare belly'.[51] What is striking is that the Quakers felt that clergymen were to blame for this breakdown in morality.

A fundamental issue Quakers argued against was the need for a paid ministry. Quakers viewed these paid officials as unwholesome, men who were corrupt and corrupting. Richard Farnworth called them evil beasts and liars whose mouths needed to be stopped,[52] while Watkins referred to them as 'blind guides that lead the blind people into the ditch'.[53] Their constant attacks against the clergy were a struggle for the soul of the nation. Simply stated, Quakers felt a responsibility to save their unconvinced neighbours from the established church and the clergy.[54] They believed that there was a scarcity in good religious observance and this is reflective of Puritan assessments from the previous century.[55] It was commonplace for early Puritan ministers to insist on impossibly high standards for their congregants, only to deem them unteachable and be convinced of their own unworthiness.[56] Clergymen had a tendency to denounce their parishioners as ignorant and ungodly, but by the second half of the seventeenth century, parishioners had begun to argue that ministers themselves were 'uncivil' or 'heathen'.[57]

The Quakers were confident that their beliefs and practices were divinely inspired and felt an obligation to warn the people of the risk they faced by listening to these clergymen. The issues of a paid ministry and spiritual ignorance was addressed elsewhere by the Quakers, who observed that even if parishioners were regular attenders, they were never going to be better Christians. Rather, it was suggested that they would 'grow worse and worse, ever learning, laden with sin, and led away with divers lusts, but never able to come to the true knowledge of God'.[58] Quaker writing often reflected this sadness, frustration and anger. The Quaker message was usually quite judgemental, and this is distinctly evident, particularly in Watkins' catalogue of written work.[59]

Watkins observed that the clerical opponents of the Quakers were worse than atheists, and argued that 'you will show yourselves more unreasonable than a Heathen, more blinder than those that knew not God'.[60] This was made worse by what Watkins referred to as a 'changeable, time-serving Priesthood', a 'ministry made by man' that changes 'as the Governments and Powers of the Earth Change'.[61] His deliberate choice of those words to describe the clergy is important. In choosing this language, he was suggesting that there was a level of inconsistency within the state church that was reliant on the whim of the government. For a population who lived through more than two decades of political upheaval, it was a just argument for Watkins to raise. In fact, it was a surprisingly gentle attack on the nature of paid ministry, but as Watkins continued his critique, his distrust for the clergy grew more evident. Indeed, Watkins went as far as to suggest that many parishioners were being seduced by the Antichrist. He suggested that the paid clergy were intentionally keeping their congregations in a state of perpetual ignorance, writing that they were 'keeping people ever learning, that they may be ever paid for teaching'.[62] He then asked the reader to acknowledge why the Quakers had to take such a forceful stand against the clergy and authorities, for 'we had good cause to be bold and valiant, knowing our leader is not to be overcome, nor those that follow him, who are called, and chosen, and faithful'.[63] Despite the risk of stoking the indignation of the local authorities, Watkins used particularly pointed language towards the clergy:

> Oh blood thirsty, bloody minded men, destroyers of souls and bodies, for your bellies, who never have enough: woe, woe from the Lord is your portion, that ever you were born, to live to exceed the false prophets of old, and yet profess Christianity.[64]

He accused them of 'swearing, and cursing, and lying, drunkenness, and whoredom, and all manner of notorious wickedness'.[65] Other contemporary observers also noted how self-righteous the clergy were, commenting that 'they are hated and laughed at by everybody', and that the parishioners were 'so acquainted with the pride and debauchery of the present clergy'.[66] Such claims support Watkins' assessment that the clergy were no better than the deviant people Quakers witnessed in the markets, fairs and alehouses. He compounded his argument by not only questioning their moral character but also their effectiveness as spiritual leaders, complaining that parishioners were compelled to pay them for their message 'although they abhor your work'.[67]

In 1663, Samuel Pepys echoed Watkins' argument as he objected to a Cambridge-educated priest's sermon, stating, 'though a great scholar, he made the most flat, dead, sermon, both for matter and manner of delivery, that ever I heard; and very long beyond his hour, which made it worse.'[68] In contrast to Pepys's complaint of overdrawn and tiresome sermons, Watkins took the view that the clergy were paid for 'deceiving the people, keeping them from ever learning, and never able to bring them to the knowledge of the truth, but ever would be paid, though never do the work'.[69] The Quaker also frequently condemned the priests educated at Oxford and Cambridge whom he refers to as 'beneath' and from a 'corrupt nature'.[70] Richard Baxter nevertheless argued that Quakers wanted to 'separate the people from their pastors, and so assault the people alone, or with weak and unlearned teachers only' so that they could 'easily bear down all before them'.[71] It is no surprise therefore that Watkins stressed that it was impossible for the clergy to claim any moral high ground, as they were:

> not sent of God, and cannot profit the people at all, and are but intruders into that you understand not, and cannot do the Lords work, but are making a trade of selling the Apostles words, being ignorant of the word of faith, in the heart, and in the mouth.[72]

He reiterated his initial argument with increased animosity, writing that they benefitted from being sponsored by:

> the Ministry of the powers of the Nation, who give them their Wages; so the National Ministry are but the servants of the national power, as it doth appear; for when the powers changed, the Ministry changed, except they turn with the time, as for the most part they do, and lick up their own vomit again, as it is clear to most people they have done of late.[73]

These Quaker writers exposed the complex structure of state religion and showed the local population that there was a better way.

Across the border, in mid-Wales, Richard Davies wrote about the desire for a religious alternative when recounting his Quaker conversion experience. Davies openly wrote about feeling adrift from those in the Church and was deeply critical of the clergy for not providing him with spiritual direction and sought religious meaning in his life at a young age.[74] Davies' story of how he grew disillusioned with the state church was a common one. Watkins never wavered from his assessment that the clergy and the state church were altogether unsuitable for the needs of the people. In a particularly damning accusation, Watkins observed that the owls and bats 'love the Light Natural' as much as the clergy loved the spiritual light, implying dark and sinister undertones to their motives.[75] In a later tract, Watkins added that they would never be able to 'bring them to the knowledge of Truth' because they themselves were 'astray from that which gives the Infallible Knowledge of it'.[76] To Watkins, the clergy was irredeemable. Their sins were too numerous, their motivations too insincere. The Quakers had a responsibility to try to convince the wider population that the clergy were untrustworthy. In his description of the Church, he called it 'the False Church, or Whore, that brings forth by an Evil Seed, the Cursed Birth, that never could please God'.[77]

In addition to the messages the Quakers felt obligated to convey, this style of writing was also performance art. In the earliest period, they wrote copiously, openly assailing their opponents and defending themselves from claims that they were heretics and blasphemers. However, after the Nayler incident in 1656, the Quakers temporarily tempered their writing and combative style so that they could avoid the claim that they were Ranters or other dangerous radical groups.[78] In December 1657, Edward Bourne wrote *The Truth of God Cleared* while in Worcester gaol. He tried to comfort his readers by reminding them that:

> Christ said to his Disciples, if the world hate you, you know it hated me before it hated you, if you were of the world the world would love his own, but because you are not of the world, but I have chosen you out of the world, therefore the world hateth you.[79]

This theme of being loathed by the world is repeated throughout the next three decades by both Bourne and Watkins. Quakers were in control of a narrative that, at its core, implied that justice would prevail for the righteous. Bourne, however, recognised that this conflict was not unique to them as the subtitle of this tract is *and above the Deceit Advanced; Which is proved to be the same that ever was in all Generations*. This subtitle suggests that Bourne believed that the issues faced by Quakers and the 'deceit' referenced were not exclusive to the Quakers, or even the seventeenth century. The problems of a corrupt clergy and a deviant society were ones that they had inherited. In Bourne's early writing, there was a sense of urgency, as shown by its apocalyptic style. In *The Truth of God Cleared*, Bourne triumphantly declared that those who would not listen to Christ's word or receive the Light would 'be destroyed from amongst the people'.[80] Bourne referred to Quakers as the 'sober-minded' and also longed for a purified society, proclaiming that his soul longed 'to see righteousness established in the Earth, that Justice and Equity might stream forth as a River'.[81] He questioned Quaker opponents and their virtue, asking how they could identify as Christians but not do the things the Lord commanded. How could their congregants persecute non-violent Quakers with such severity?[82] Bourne referred to this as being 'out of the life of him whom you profess' and compared them to Cain murdering Abel.[83]

From the uncertainty and forced introspection brought on by James Nayler's trial, it was a challenging time for Quakers trying to navigate the political landscape. This was a period of both broad political transition and evolution within the Quaker movement as well as within England itself. Oliver Cromwell's death in September 1658 did not immediately result in the end of the republic and despite his son Richard's lack of authority and leadership, there was considerable opposition to a return to monarchical rule. Politically, there was chaos, and amongst the uncertainty, there was a growing awareness of an uncivilised society that was unravelling. In the spring of 1659, Richard Cromwell's Parliamentarians acknowledged the failure of the Puritan campaign for moral reformation as there had actually been an increase in 'gross ignorance, atheism, and profaneness of all sorts; such as vain swearing and cursing, profanation of the Lord's Day, drunkenness, uncleanness, and other ungodly courses'.[84] By April 1659, he had resigned and amidst the turmoil, there was growing hostility towards Quakers, as reflected in increased Quaker persecution.[85]

In early 1660, it was becoming increasing clear that Prince Charles Stuart would return as king of England, Scotland and Ireland. For the entire population, their communities would be forced to accept this return to monarchical rule.

Even as early as 1660, Bourne's language was becoming more restrained in comparison to Watkins, who maintained his antagonistic approach. Bourne was perhaps reflecting the uncertainty of how the Quakers would be received by the newly restored king. In the same year, Quaker Richard Hubberthorne expressed the view that they did not want their enemies to be destroyed; rather, they wanted their enemies to repent and ask for forgiveness.[86] Bourne stated in *A Warning from the Lord God… unto the Inhabitants of the City of Worcester* (1660) that 'the Light teacheth to love Enemies; the Light teacheth to blesse them that curse; the Light will teach you, to pray for them that despitefully use and intreat you'.[87] His message was developing into one of tolerance, but he remained cautious, warning his readers:

Oh do not that thing which you know by the Light of Christ in your own Consciences, to be contrary to the Mind and Will of the Lord; for now you cannot plead Ignorance in the Day of the Lord, and say, Lord, if we had known thy Mind, and if thy Will had been declared unto us, we would not have done contrary thereunto.[88]

He stated that at the time of Judgement, non-believers could not claim that they had not been warned. It can be debated whether Bourne was calling for non-believers to repent or if this was an invitation to join Quakers to help save their wayward brethren. In his *Warning*, he accused the authorities of 'slaying and stoning' the prophets (thereby meaning Quaker missionaries) God had sent to save humanity.[89] Within this year of great uncertainty, Quakers were negotiating their eventual place in Charles II's England. Morgan Watkins felt confident that the Lord's vengeful return was imminent and predicted that God would:

render vengeance against all that obey not the truth, even the Gospel of everlasting salvation, which is now sounded forth in England, and is passing, and to pass through all nations … for the hour of judgement is come.[90]

Watkins was satisfied in his belief that Christ was returning soon and would do so suddenly.[91] They saw depravity all around them. Yet while they saw a world that needed to be reformed, Watkins made no suggestion about how this could be accomplished. His message was to reprove and forewarn, and, as such, they sought to identify to communicate their 'moral condemnation of the current sinful actions or conditions of others' and warn of the consequences to those who would not repent or change their ways.[92]

Chapter 10

Writing Like the World is Ending

Whilst imprisoned at St Albans in Hertfordshire in 1660, Morgan Watkins wrote to George Fox and confidently declared that they had 'dominion over the powers of darkness, to trample upon the head of him who hath the power of death', but he was also aware that they were 'accounted as sheep for the slaughter'. In the letter, he commented that he had been asked to write 'something to the nation concerning swearing' and that he sent a copy to Fox for review. He requested it to be printed quickly and noted that if Fox needed to make any alterations, he could do so. Watkins' reason for urgency was that he had a dispute with a priest 'doing the devil's work' and when he would not swear the oath, the priest accused him of being a Catholic and called for the gaoler to keep the Quaker under close surveillance and punish him if necessary.[1] The tract referenced by Watkins in his letter to Fox was *Swearing Denyed in the New Covenant*. Within its pages, Watkins declared that 'all swearers, and false swearers, and lyars, fighters, plotters, and persecutors, who are in the strife against the Son of God must bow and submit or be broken to pieces'. He further observed that all those who were, according to his perception, of loose morals would face divine retribution.[2]

In *The Day Manifesting the Night*, also published in 1660, Watkins stated that he had hoped that the non-believers would 'take warning before it be too late, lest they be taken alive in their wickedness and cast into the lake of fire'.[3] *The Day Manifesting the Night* was his unrelenting criticism of popular culture. He positioned the Quakers as faithful, Christ-centred martyrs who faced the barbarous sanctions of the ecclesiastical and state authorities. He saw this as unjustified and that the hearts of these adversaries were 'adulterated, gone after other lovers, far from the Lord'.[4] Frustrated by the widespread persecution and the injustice shown to the Quakers, he declared:

> The spirit that in this age leads such who spares the fighters, and swearers, and drunkards, the prophane and abominable, etc, and afflict,

punish and imprison those who are found in the well doing, because they cannot submit to their wills, and break the commands of Jesus.[5]

Taking a similar approach in his commentary on society, Edward Bourne wrote *A Warning from the Lord God to the Inhabitants of Warwick* in 1661. In this tract, rather than condemn society immediately, Bourne asked that those who had:

> lived in Drunkenness, refrain from it, and do so no more; and such as have lived in Malice, and Envy, and Wrath ... and such as Persecuted, and Imprisoned the Servants of the Lord, let them do so no more.[6]

Bourne, writing with clarity considering the delicate situation the Quakers had found themselves in, was pleading for mercy. Legislation, which led to increased bouts of persecution against the Quakers and other dissenters, was the result of an entrenched view of the Restoration authorities that these religious radicals were determined to plunge England back into the chaos of the civil wars and Interregnum. This point was certainly made by their enemies after the Fifth Monarchy Uprising in January 1661 and the plot to overthrow the government. It could be argued that this period of tension, suspicion and severe prosecution inspired Watkins' most significant contribution to the Quaker written corpus.

Lamentation Over England, published in 1664, defined Watkins as a Quaker writer. It serves as an example of his most spirited, antagonistic, and apocalyptic writing. Watkins immediately addressed the Quaker persecutors, asking them to 'truly consider what way they are in, and whether it leads, and whose work they are doing and what the Scripture faith will be in the reward of Oppression and Cruelty'.[7] This is followed by the following verses:

> Evil shall hunt the cruel man to destruction.
>
> I know that the Lord will avenge the afflicted, and judg the poor.
>
> Surely the righteous shall praise thy name, and the just shall dwell in the presence.
>
> Psalm, 140, 11, 12, 13

He began the tract with the pious, yet vengeful statement: 'it is not against any man's person, or just authority that I have writ, but in the behalf of the good in all, against the evil in all.'[8] He addressed the 'Impartial Reader', suggesting that this was not written for a Quaker audience. The opening sentences make reasonable requests: 'not to call evil good, nor good evil, nor put light for darkness, nor darkness for light, but to deal justly with all men and walk humbly with thy God'.[9] This beginning served as a gentle opening and lured the 'impartial reader' into a false sense of security that the remainder of the tract would be similar. Watkins' tone quickly changed as later paragraphs stressed the unwarranted persecution by the civil and Church authorities. He accused them of trying to 'frighten us out of our Religion' and 'killing the body'.[10] It is an important distinction and demonstrates why the early Quakers were not afraid to die in disease-ridden prisons – the body could be killed but the soul could not. Watkins was merciless in his condemnation of their persecutors, as demonstrated when he asked:

> How will you be able to stand in the dreadful, terrible day of Gods righteous judgement, that is coming, and speedily hastens upon you? And the woeful, dreadful, terrible day of your destruction draweth nigh, wherein you must suffer punishment for every evil thought, and wicked word and action against the innocent.[11]

Threatening their persecutors was a commonly used tactic to minimise the impact of their persecution and give maximum publicity to their suffering. The Quakers in this period firmly believed that God would intervene to punish these 'evildoers'.[12] When Robert Baylis of Broadway, Worcestershire, was commanded to leave his home after being arrested for holding an unlawful meeting, he refused to leave and so the lieutenant drew his sword.[13] It was reported that Baylis's pregnant wife was so terrified she allegedly miscarried.[14] The bold actions of the Quakers would continue as they believed that they 'must stand witnesses against these things, even to the death, if the Lord require them', adding that if God 'shall farther suffer us to be tried to the laying down of our lives, for his name sake, his will be done'.[15] Those who did suffer were 'blessed of the Lord, as are you his people, that suffer for his name sake' and they would not be forsaken, as Watkins proclaimed that God had given them 'an everlasting kingdom'.[16] In *Lamentation Over*

England, Watkins admitted that he and others suffered from draconian laws and brutality because 'we tell you the truth'.[17] Those responsible for this unwarranted persecution he felt would 'reap [divine] condemnation' as they were following the 'Doctrine of the Devil'.[18] In 1664, Samuel Pepys witnessed the Quakers in London being hauled away for contravening the Conventicle Act. He noted, 'they go like lambs, without any resistance. I would to God they would either conform or be more wise and not be ketched.'[19] The same was happening to the Quakers in Herefordshire and Worcestershire. They attended meetings that were against the law but were prepared to face local hostility and imprisonment.

In *Lamentation Over England*, Watkins clearly expressed that while they knew that their struggle against the authorities was unwinnable, they were willing to die to save the souls of others.[20] In his writings he offered vivid imagery of God's terrible vengeance, writing: 'Wo, wo be unto you spiritual Lords (so called) ... who labour to devour the flock of Christ, and lay waste his little remnant,' and his warning became more threatening as he continued:

> his power is turned against you, and shall pursue you in all your ways, and defeat you in all your devises, till he hath left you neither root nor branch, and your name shall be cast out as an abominable thing and abhorring to all people.[21]

Watkins addressed these matters with severe warnings of divine retribution for the sinful, along with a genuine hope of Christ's imminent return to save the true believers.[22] Like the other early Quaker writers, including Humphrey Smith, Watkins compared the plight of Quakers to the biblical prophets, as they believed that they shared a commonality with the prophets of the Old Testament.[23] These prophets provided commentaries on the degradation of their societies and proposed an alternative future that required a spiritual awakening and societal change. When the early Quaker writers compared themselves to the prophets, or the Apostles of Jesus, they reframed the narrative. Quakers, like Watkins, used scripture to draw the reader's attention to the stark similarities between the challenges iterated in the Bible and the anarchy, as they saw it, of the seventeenth century.

Quakers used language and examples that were known to all Christians. They felt compelled to take this path and early Quaker writing was not only designed to serve warnings, but also to educate and demonstrate their biblical prowess. In the same year *Lamentation Over England* was published, Edward Bourne demonstrated the practical benefit of his scriptural expertise. In a letter to George Fox, Bourne recounted an incident in Hereford where he had to act quickly to defend the Quakers who had been arrested during a meeting. When brought to testify in front of the priest, mayor and aldermen of Hereford, Bourne displayed his knowledge, and with a calm demeanour:

> gave the knowledge of the glory of god in the face of Jesus Christ not in the scriptures which I cleared to them by minding them of the Apostles words to the Corinthians which are these 'God who commanded the light to shine out of darkness hath shined in our hearts, etc.' and so I cleared many things to them which we hold by the scriptures and they were quiet and stayed to hear and many were satisfied and speak well of us afterwards and so the truth was brought over them and things were well ended praised be the Lord.[24]

Bourne's skill as an orator and his familiarity with the Bible impressed his opponents on that day, and this readiness to defend their positions using scripture was found frequently in the Quaker tracts and pamphlets of the seventeenth century. In *Lamentation Over England*, Watkins made fifty-eight scriptural references and, in many cases, used biblical terminology to define the oppression faced by Quakers.[25] Watkins admitted that the authorities were wilfully ignorant and he stated that their efforts against the Quakers were useless as they could not do 'the Lord's work, but are making a trade of selling the Apostles words, and Christ's words, and the Prophets words, being ignorant of the word of faith, in the heart and in the mouth, which they preached'.[26] Watkins equated his opponents with biblical oppressors such as Herod. This was a customary practice used by the Quakers, including Smith and Bourne. Watkins' use of scripture throughout this text was deliberate and measured. He demonstrated his biblical knowledge, placed the Quakers and their hardships within that context and could make direct biblical comparisons.

Watkins would have also been familiar with God's warnings for the apocalypse, as foretold in the Book of Revelations:

> The first angel sounded, and there followed hail and fire mingled with blood, and they were cast upon the earth: and the third part of trees was burnt up, and all green grass was burnt up. And the second angel sounded, and as it were a great mountain burning with fire was cast into the sea: and the third part of the sea became blood; And the third part of the creatures which were in the sea, and had life, died.[27]

The catastrophic events of 1665 and 1666 would have persuaded even a non-believer to suspect that they were all experiencing God's wrath. England was beleaguered by the commencement of the Second Anglo-Dutch War in March 1665, followed by the outbreak of plague that reached its peak in the summer that year, and compounded in September 1666 by the Great Fire of London. It was widely accepted that the terrible misfortune suffered by London, and England more generally, had been self-inflicted, or, as Rebecca Rideal concludes, the 'just desserts for indulging in sin and committing acts of heresy'.[28] It was anonymously recounted that 'as if it were design'd by Divine Providence, that each part should have its punishment'.[29] However, it was not only the Quakers who condemned society. In his account of the events of 1665 and 1666, Thomas Vincent, the Puritan minister, echoed the Quakers' condemnations of a broken society; the people had not changed their ways, and, if anything, they had become worse. When the dangers had passed, 'they dropped asleep faster than before'. Vincent, in his frustration, revealed:

> they that are drunken and drunken still; they that were filthy, are filthy still; and they that were unjust and covetous, do still persevere in their sinful course; cozening and lying, and swearing, and cursing, and Sabbath-breaking, and pride, and envy, and flesh-pleasing, and the like God displeasing and God-provoking sins.[30]

Watkins was convinced that these were all signs of Christ's imminent return, but aware of the wretched state of English society warned of the dire consequences for its citizens. These catastrophic events encouraged Quakers, including Watkins, to emphasise the belief that God had not forgotten them.[31] This belief that they were a separate or chosen people echoes the plight of the Hebrews in the Book of Exodus.

In 1666, Watkins asked, 'is not the Plague begun, and doth not war begin to impoverish the Land? For the day hastens that will suddenly overtake them all, from which there is no escaping.'[32] Watkins' body of written work is a clear indication that he held unwavering apocalyptic beliefs, in addition to the belief that judgement would be made at the time of death. Watkins and many of his co-religionists were concerned with the afterlife and the impact earthly decisions would have.

These beliefs naturally were a catalyst for the dramatic nature of their writing. The Quakers were writing with urgency out of a genuine fear that there was truly little time remaining to save willing souls. Their early message was a 'call to repent' in preparation for the impending apocalypse and that their instinctive reaction when faced with opposition was to 'deliver fierce warnings of coming doom'.[33] Quakers saw these events as signs of God's wrath. The dissenters of this period inherited a 'deeply providential and apocalyptic mentality', meaning that every event from their renewed persecution to the plague was interpreted as God working out his ultimate purpose.[34]

In a letter to Margaret Fell, shortly after the Great Plague swept through London, Watkins wrote that he was 'wonderfully preserved' and that he had several 'battles with death' but even though many people were unable to withstand the pain and weakness, 'the Lord was very merciful to the remnant of his people'.[35] In light of this divine intervention, it is not surprising that he wrote with urgency and with a palpable fear the following year. In 1666, he warned that 'while you have a day, prize it' and that 'the revenger of the innocent blood is on his way'.[36] He wrote that God would 'glorifie himself over all his enemies, either in their Conversion or destruction' and that the 'clusters [of the Vine of Earth] are very ripe and ready to be cast into the great Winepress of the wrath of God'.[37] According to Watkins, this was not a new phenomenon, and he stressed that 'in all ages it hath been the work of the wicked one to keep the people in blindness'.[38] In the same year, he asserted that 'good Rulers are a blessing to the Nation; but bad ones are a curse; for they encourage the evil doers, and are haters of those that are good and evil deeds bring a plague'.[39] He continued that the children of light would 'subdue Armies by their love and patience but also conquer Nations and subdue mighty Kings, who are making war in the spirit of enmity not only against enemies but also against friends'.[40]

Watkins' outpourings could certainly be viewed as a threat to the restored monarchy and aroused suspicion. He tried to reassure their opponents that they were not plotting or 'contriving evil' against the king or his people, and that their meetings had 'not brought forth such fruit yet, nor never will'.[41]

There were simmering political tensions because of the Duke of York's Catholic affiliation. Pepys regularly mentioned the long-standing rumour that Charles II would name the Protestant Duke of Monmouth, thought by some to be his lawful son, as heir to the throne.[42] This uncertainty would have resonated with those alive during the civil wars, therefore anyone considered a Catholic was suspected of being disloyal to the king. In response to allegations that the Quakers were also crypto-papists, in 1667 Edward Bourne wrote a tract entitled *Certain Queries Answered, Which Were Sent by a PAPIST for the People Called QUAKERS to Answer*, with the subheadings *Here are some Questions to the Papists, from the Pope, who is head of them to the foot of them, for them all to Answer* and *With a few Words to those who are Members of the Church of ROME*.[43] The Quakers were often associated with Catholics and there were widespread allegations that they were papists in disguise. As soon as they began to emerge from the north of England, Richard Baxter was convinced of this theory and suggested that the Quakers had been seduced by Catholics.[44] This concern about the Quakers and other dissenters being wolves in sheep's clothing became part of the religious culture of this period and was a result of official and popular intolerance.[45] Bourne's tract was directed to Catholics who lived their lives in 'error'.[46] In this tract, he demonstrated his knowledge of the basic tenets of Catholicism and countered their core beliefs with scriptural evidence. His response to the statement 'we believe the penance is one of the seven sacraments, wherein the priest hath Power under God to absolve the sinner' is simply 'we believe you have no such power' and adds that they 'do not find in the Scripture any mention made of seven sacraments in the Church of God'.[47] Bourne then proceeded to list the Catholic rites and rituals that the Quakers did not accept had any scriptural foundations. Bourne asserted that they did not believe in purgatory, nor that:

> Bread and Wine after Consecrations is the Body and Blood of Christ, but is as other Bread and Wine; we do not believe that the Apostles did use Surplices nor Hoods, nor black Coats, nor Tippets, nor silk Girdles, nor Preach by the Hour-Glass, nor observe Days and Times, neither did they run to Graves for Reliques, nor bow to outward crosses, or images,

neither did they set up Tythes, nor Mortuaries, nor Easter reckonings, or Midsummer dues, nor offerings in their Councils, neither Christ nor the Apostles, for People to pay.[48]

He discussed the idea of bread and wine as the 'Body' and 'Blood of Christ' at length in this tract. He expressed a desire to be convinced by the Catholics of the validity of this sacrament, stating that he could not understand how these items could be transformed into the 'very Body and Blood of Christ'.[49] Elizabethan Protestant reformers had previously maintained that this was the 'worst kind of idolatry' and that the priest performing the ritual was a 'charlatan' who used 'stage tricks and sorcery' to trick his congregation.[50] Bourne then went as far as to ridicule the accepted belief in transubstantiation by asking:

> and is Christ's Body living, when you eat it so, that it can speak? For Christ could speak, who said, this is my Body? Or is it a dead Body? And can a dead Body give life? And so after you have Consecrated the Bread and Wine, is it living, that it can speak?[51]

His commentary on the sacrament of Eucharist was particularly damning and perhaps served as evidence to their Protestant opponents that the Quakers were not papists in disguise. In his argument against Catholicism, he repeatedly used the term the 'Light of Christ in their Consciences' when referring to the 'Truth' and reiterated this by asking the Catholic reader if the 'Members of the Church of Rome differ from the Apostles, who commended themselves to every Man's Conscience'. He chastised 'Members of the Church of Rome' for their cruelty in using 'inquisitions, and racks and tortures' as methods of punishing those who did not consent to their theology. He drew a direct comparison to Christ and the Apostles, and maintained that Christ 'did not teach his followers to persecute and kill' because Christ said 'love your enemies and bless them that curse you'.[52] He concluded his responses to Catholics with 'from a Follower of the Lamb, who am a Member of the true Body, whereof Christ is the Head'.[53]

Bourne's writing, more than Watkins', showed the fluid adaptations Quakers needed to make in their conversations with the outside world. The Quakers were 'encouraged to recognise in themselves the fulfilment of ancient and modern prophecies which proved the day of deliverance was eminent'.[54] The Quakers viewed themselves as 'divinely recreated creatures', 'an army going forth to battle, only the battle was not one of worldly war and violence'.[55]

In 1671, Bourne asked his readers to take an introspective look at themselves and at society in *A Looking-Glass Discovering to all People what Image They Bear*.[56] This tract was also instructional, answering questions that may be posed by new converts or those considering adopting the Quaker faith. He demonstrated a willingness to help Quakers on their spiritual journeys and provide instruction. Bourne's writing suggests that he was more willing to persuade the unconvinced through education, while Watkins relied upon fearmongering to convey his message. Bourne's guidance in *A Looking-Glass* countered the experience many disillusioned people had in the state church. This was his opportunity to illustrate to new converts that the Quakers wanted to share everything they had learned, unlike the clergy who offered this sporadically, if at all. In his answers, he considered the political climate of the early 1670s and the re-emergence of the threat of Catholicism. He addressed idea of purgatory for those who had lived a sinful life on earth, writing, 'but sin is to be purged away here, you must know Christ to free you from your Sins while you are here, else Wo be to you, if you put it off till hereafter.'[57]

Perhaps most telling of the changing times of the later seventeenth century is that the early Quakers were slowly becoming more accepting of other Christian denominations. Raymond Brown and Alan Sell suggested that both the Quakers and their religious opponents may have gradually accepted that they were at an impasse.[58] As early as 1668, it had been recognised by contemporary observers that 'the business of abusing the puritans' had begun to grow tiresome and it was futile because 'they being the people that at last will be found the wisest'.[59] In 1671, Bourne exemplified this tolerance and a desire for peace, declaring:

> Let every man be fully persuaded in his own mind in what he doth, for whatsoever is not of Faith is Sin; now as the Papist would have liberty to worship God in that way which he judges best, so the same liberty he would have, must be given to another. ... lay aside forcing, and compelling, and persecuting about these things ... so long as they

are peaceable, and do nothing that tends to the disturbance of the Commonwealth, nor the injury of any person, but do only worship God as they judge they ought.[60]

The early Quakers had begun to change their message from condemnation to one of acceptance. No longer were they promising hellfire and brimstone to those who opposed their form of worship, although the evidence suggests that Watkins was less willing than his peers to embrace this modified message. In *A Looking-Glass*, Bourne asked for liberty, not just for the Quakers, but for all peaceable faiths.[61] In the postscript of this tract, he reiterated this point, that they were all Christians, and asked for tolerance – 'What? Shall Christians persecute Christians?'[62] This is perhaps the most critical difference from the earliest work of Quakers, demonstrating that they were beginning to close ranks, to protect themselves and their religious communities.

In 1672, Charles II issued the Declaration of Indulgence, which suspended penal restrictions on Catholics and dissenters, and enabled freedom of worship for the latter as long as their places of worship were licensed.[63] This provided the Quakers with relief from what they viewed as government-approved persecution. It was only a temporary respite, as in 1673 the Declaration of Indulgence was abandoned and Parliament passed the Test Act, which excluded Catholics and other non-conformists from public office.[64] Again, the Quakers found themselves in a politically tumultuous environment and they were still on the defensive as they were depicted as a 'worse evil'.[65] Despite Bourne's more tolerant and accepting tone, the long-burning disputes between Quakers and their opponents were not yet ready to be extinguished.

In the 1670s, Watkins remained steadfast in his belief that Christ would imminently return, and it remained a central theme in his writing. In *The Marks of the True Church*, written in 1675, he addressed the non-believers and admonished them, declaring:

> Wo[e] is unto you, that ever you were born, because of the terrible day that is coming upon you, which you can no ways escape, but by coming out of her, in whom is found all the Blood of the Saints and Martyrs, and all that have been slain (for the Testimony of Jesus) upon the Earth.[66]

Watkins recognised that many of the early Quakers had died by this point, often in prisons, and regularly without a dignified burial. Again, echoing the sentiment expressed in the late 1650s, Watkins concluded that 'they that have received his Spirit, are they that the world hates, as he said it should be'.[67] The *Marks of the True Church* would serve as Watkins' final publication and while it maintained his trademark admonishment, there was also a sombre, reflective element for the lives that had been cut short and perhaps a disappointment that the long-awaited Second Coming of Christ had not come to fruition in his lifetime.

In 1682, Bourne wrote a six-page tract to residents of his own parish in Worcester, arguing that the Quakers were merely trying to 'exhort, advise, and persuade people to dwell together in Love', to find peace and obey and fear the Lord.[68] There was a noticeable change in the tone of this tract compared to his 'warning' to Worcester written twenty-two years earlier. The sweeping statements about a fast-approaching end time were replaced by descriptions of their treatment by the parish wardens and he carefully explained why they could not, in good conscience, contribute financially to church repairs.[69] As the Quakers became more organised, their approach to legal matters became more sophisticated, but they were able to find loopholes and impracticalities in the penal code.[70] In 1685, John Bowater of Bromsgrove, Worcestershire, addressed a publication 'To the Bishops and Clergy of England and Wales' and attempted to reason with the members of the clergy, stating that:

> The law was not made against the Righteous, but to punish such Sinners and Evil-Doers as the Apostle speaks of, but not to punish Christians for their Faith and Religion, and for Worshipping, Obeying and Serving Almighty God that made them.[71]

Four years earlier, he had observed that Thomas Willmate, the vicar of Bromsgrove, demanded payment of tithes, but the Quaker had refused and instead proposed that if Willmate:

> could prove himself a Minister of the Gospel, and Tythe a Gospel Maintenance, I would pay him Tythe: But being he neither did, nor could make out to me by the Scripture, I refused to pay him ... I never read in the Scripture of the New Testament, that Christ ever ordained Tythe to be a Maintenance for his Ministers, neither was Tythe established

by his holy Apostles for a Maintenance for Ministers, but rather in the time of Popery.[72]

In *For the Inhabitants of Worcester*, Bourne explained that Quakers were being punished for refusing to pay tithes, with many of them being imprisoned. For Bourne, this was a serious error of judgment by the authorities because this affected the poorest in society. As Bourne saw it, Quakers were then unable to pay taxes to help the poor.[73] In presenting themselves as charitable citizens, the Quakers were increasingly able to shape their position as one of peace, and one of concern for the welfare of wider society. There were elements of self-preservation in their writing but as the century was ending, they were more willing to become a part of wider society. They could not isolate themselves and they realised quickly that it was they who needed to be more open-minded to living in what they had always viewed as a contaminated society. In their writings, Quakers prepared themselves by providing warnings to their own not to backslide into improper behaviour but rather to maintain their moral authority.

In his final epistle, written while imprisoned in Worcester in late December 1682, Bourne emphasised the important of patience and faith. He hoped that others in similar circumstances would 'be purified and made clean from all Impurity and filthiness'. He addressed imprisoned Quakers and reminded them that Christ died for all of them, implying that their suffering was not too much to bear for the Lord. He also added that through this suffering Jesus was made perfect, perhaps suggesting that they too could achieve spiritual maturity. He concluded by writing that he was 'dwelling in the Love and Goodwill of the Almighty towards all people, not desiring the Ruin or Destruction of any of them'. In this statement, which he requested to be read 'in the Assemblies or the Righteous everywhere', he acknowledged the level of persecution, but even though he referred to himself and all the Quakers as the 'called, chosen, and faithful of the Lord', he did not threaten or bemoan their persecutors; he did not threaten them with God's wrath.[74] This epistle was written for them; to comfort them, to encourage them, and to ask them to focus on their heavenly rewards instead. He recognised that society was still contaminated, but he quickly moved the focus to the things within their control – their individual spiritual and moral reformation. National moral reform was the one issue that fostered both collaboration and rivalry between churchmen and dissenters. Both groups wanted to curtail activities that were offensive to God and man, notably drunkenness, sexual transgression, swearing and blasphemy. Both believed that through regulation of external behaviour they might be able to reform the moral character of the communities in which they lived.[75] The Quakers may have felt that it was their divine purpose to save the people from the temptations of society, but their opponents believed that these dissenters were the ones who needed to be reformed.

Throughout this period, Quakers encouraged debate and their publications were provocative.[76] The latter attracted wider attention and their words forced other Quakers to 'prepare, think through, and sharpen their theological positions', as well as challenge the beliefs of their adversaries.[77] This is most evident in Bourne's writing. His ideas were more increasingly finessed and more tolerant while other contemporary Quakers were still producing work with apocalyptic warnings.[78] Watkins' publications support this argument. It can be argued that his views were representative of his personal struggle, but he framed his writing with a generic apocalyptic approach. Both men were not solely writing about their own personal experiences nor writing spiritual autobiographies; they were writing on behalf of all Quakers. Watkins never gave any indication of the origin of his beliefs, nor did he provide any biographical information; he did not write about his personal journey. The publications of these men display little individuality by means of describing a personal struggle, and, in examining their extant catalogue of work, they tend to be rather formulaic. Bourne adapted his arguments and tone in conjunction with current events and the increasingly centralised Quaker movement, while Watkins portrayed his antagonists in overly simplistic terms. He labelled everyone who was not a Quaker as 'wicked', and this is the clearest indication that he was not writing for a wider audience as a means of persuading the undecided. He knew that the life he and his co-religionists had chosen would not be easy, but it can be argued that his words were composed to soothe them; as difficult as life was for an early Quaker, it was infinitely worse for their souls to not be a member of this religious community.

Chapter 11

The Good Argument against Quakerism

From the start, Quakers engaged in disputations and found themselves in positions where they had to defend themselves. These encounters provided Quakers with opportunities to reach a wider audience by debating with those higher profile opponents with a national audience, like Richard Baxter. Their aim was to demonstrate that their opponents were misleading, often unethical, and speaking from a place of ignorance.

In 1675, Edward Bourne wrote *An Answer to Doctor Good (so called) His DIALOGUE against those call'd QUAKERS*, with the subheading *Wherein he hath Forged the QUAKER and Confuted HIMSELF*.[1] This twenty-four-page tract was written in direct response to Doctor Thomas Good of Oxford and his book entitled *FIRMIANUS and DUBITANTIUS, OR Certain DIALOGUES Concerning Atheism, Infidelity, Popery, and the Heresies and Schisme's That Trouble the Peace of the Church, and Are Destructive of Primitive Piety*, written in 1674.[2]

As implied by the title, Good's exasperation was not directly concerned with Quakerism; his arguments against the Quakers comprised only 9 pages of the 166-page book, but these arguments demonstrate how the Quakers were targeted and conflated with Catholics, Baptists and atheists. Good accused all these groups of disrupting and damaging the most basic Protestant Christian values. In the preface, Good wrote that he was purposefully writing in an accessible manner so that his queries could be understood by those who may have struggled to understand or have time to read the more 'elaborate' tracts written on the subjects at hand.[3]

With this intention in mind, Good's book was written in sections and each section was framed as a conversation between two men, Firmianus and Dubitantius. Firmianus was meant to 'personate the sound Believer' and Dubitantius the 'Sceptick Christian'. It was an effective way to discuss controversial and weighty topics of faith and worship. Dubitantius approaches each topic with naivety and an open mind and by the end of the discussion

Firmianus has convinced him of his folly. In 'Dialogue IV Against Quakerism' the conversation opens as follows:

> Firmianus: You have informed me in our last discourse that being sometime a Quaker you had a ready way open to become a Papist. I pray tell me why and how you turned a Quaker.
>
> Dubitantius: You put me hard to it. for I can give you no very good reasons for that change, and those that moved me are so ridiculous, that I am almost ashamed to name them, yet such as they are I shall give you the trouble of hearing them, I am almost persuaded, that the man that perverted me, used some enchantments and Diabolical arts. so that I was rather bewitched. then rationally persuaded, to be of that party, (as I have heard some have been) but because I am not certain of this, I shall wave it, and shew you my reasons.[4]

In these observations, the Quakers were referred to as 'spurious brats' and 'poor deluded souls'.[5] Good, as the character of Firmianus, provided a list of what he contended were the core Quaker beliefs, but before he begins, Dubitantius reassured him that he was 'fully of [his] persuasion that these men hold and practise many things which are contrary to the law of nature, good manners and holy Scripture'.[6] At the close of the discussion, after having swiftly convinced Dubitantius of his misguided ways, Firmianus provided him with a reading list of anti-Quaker literature, to which Dubitantius replied, 'I am fully satisfied concerning the folly and madness of this Phanaticism, and from whence it sprang.'[7] It is an effective method of persuasive writing.

A key strategy of Quaker opponents was 'to prove their Quakers guilty from their own words'.[8] In his condemnation of Quakerism, Good does not effectively provide solid arguments but rather a simple dialogue, touching on the common criticisms, but he failed to support his arguments with scriptural evidence. His ultimately insubstantial arguments could be construed as an indication that he did not believe that the Quaker beliefs called for any serious thought or discussion with further corroboration.

Bourne took full advantage of this opportunity to defend Quakerism.

In his rebuttal, Bourne at once referred to Thomas Good as 'Friend'. He countered that Good's 'dialogue is rather a forgery, which thou and it are stuft with lyes'.[9] He stated that Good falsely accused and 'grossly' slandered the Quakers and that he 'doth much deserve to be blamed for using his Pen thus against the Innocent'.[10] Using legal terminology, such as forgery and slander, suggests a more sophisticated approach to framing their arguments against their transgressors that was not seen before in Bourne's work. He took Good's accusations seriously and crafted a careful response. Bourne's first issue with Good was the suggestion that 'to become a Quaker was a ready way to become a Papist'. He argued that if they were to be tried against each other, Anglicans versus Quakers, the Anglicans would be found to be more like Catholics than the Quakers.[11] Bourne then continued to address each issue Good raised, providing the scriptural evidence that Good's arguments lacked. Bourne addressed this, writing:

> Indeed thou givest no Reason at all; but 'tis only thy so saying, without giving or showing any Reason for it … if thou sayest, thou believest, it is sufficient for other to believe so too … they that be wise will require some further Testimony for thy so saying then thy bare Words … and so thou hast manifested thy own Folly and Envy in this Matter.[12]

His responses were measured and certainly lacked the zeal and fervour of the earlier Quaker writings of the 1650s, and even for Bourne, there was a noticeable change in tone from his early work. It could be argued that his language was perceptively different because this was written as a defensive piece, and it was important to give a measured, calm response to counter Good's accusations. Nevertheless, Bourne's experience as a writer is clear, as is his skill in responding to the claims that he felt were libellous. He was confident that the actions of the Quakers, certainly in 1675, were aligned with their words and most importantly, the word of God. They were still distressed at the state of society, those provoking 'the Holy God against their own souls' and 'evil manners'.[13] Good criticised the Quakers' outward appearance, commenting, 'we know a merry heart maketh a cheerful countenance, whereas a sad sour face … is a very probable sign of a disquieted, discontented, guilty, troubled, if not a malicious mind.'[14] Bourne responded that they 'cannot appear as one with People in their folly, being jolly and merry with them, out of the Fear of the Lord, which is because [they] know such Things are contrary to Godliness'.[15]

FIRMIANUS and DUBITANTIUS was published in 1674 and Good expressed concern that Quakers were not loyal subjects to the king. This was an ongoing suspicion from the moment the monarchy was restored. In the early 1660s, Fox was accused of 'imbruing the nation in blood' and holding meetings in order to plot insurrections against the king, while in 1661 several Quakers were released from Worcester Castle gaol under the condition that they appeared at the next assizes and did not disturb the king's peace.[16] In 1665, during a visitation of the plague and shortly after the Second Anglo-Dutch War commenced, the Quakers were perceived to be Dutch sympathisers who would aid the enemy if there was a land attack.[17] Loyalty was always a point of contention for Quaker opponents. The Test Act of 1673, which was primarily directed towards Catholics, required all officeholders to swear an oath of allegiance to the king and the established church, as well as signing a declaration denying the Catholic sacrament of transubstantiation.[18] As the Quakers would not swear any oath, their opponents doubted their loyalty to the king. As Dubitantius, Good wrote:

> Dubitantius: I see you are now in jest; you know that time was when they did take up arms in an hostile manner against the *King* and his Loyal subjects, and if they had a fair opportunity they would do the like again, and appear as cruel and bloody as ever did *Anabaptist* fifth Monarchy-man or *Jesuite*.
>
> Dubitantius: You are pleased to make your self mercy with these mens bare-fac'd hypocrisy, what a jugles this light within them? more unconstant then that of the moon, a meere phansy, a Diabolical suggestion; the Devil suits his tentations according as opportunities present themselves, when there is good probability of prevailing by rebellion and treason, then the light (or rather darkness within them) suggests unto them, 'tis lawful to take up arms, to plunder and murder their fellow subjects, yea the King himself, but when there is no probability to prosper by such villainous enterprises, then that light within them persuades them to be as quiet as Lambs, as innocent as so many pretty Pigeons.[19]

These accusations put the Quakers firmly on the defensive. It was their burden to prove their loyalty. Bourne admitted that yes, most of the Quakers had fought in the civil wars against the king but added that some also fought against Parliament.[20] While it can be argued that he did know Quakers who were Royalists, there is no extant evidence to support this. Most of them were ardently opposed to the king during the civil wars. This is an important distinction because Good implied that the Quakers were likely to take up arms against the monarchy again. His wariness of the Quakers was not entirely unjustified. Even the Quaker Peace Testimony of 1660 raised suspicions of their loyalty as their pacifism was declared when the state lacked a standing army and relied on its people for defence from foreign attack.[21] Bourne addressed this by stating that they had 'cast off [their] carnal weapons of war, with a Resolution never to return to them again. ... our peaceable deportment in our conversations to this time have given a faithful testimony to the reality of such our Resolution.'[22] He tried to reassure his readers that the Quakers were not the enemy and ended his response to Good with 'From a Lover of Immortal Souls, and the whole Creation of God'.[23] Again, here Bourne emphasised that he loved all of God's kingdom. He did not differentiate between the Quakers and those who still needed to be morally reformed.

The Quakers used writing to expose the spiritual and moral failings of seventeenth-century society. They used their platform to forewarn of a bleak future and they had the freedom to express these ideas in print, to share their message and to convey their fears for such a reprehensible society. Although they often felt obligated to defend themselves and their beliefs, they often used their publications to skilfully demonstrate their biblical knowledge. They had to show their opponents that they were just as, if not more, familiar with Christ's message and scripture. Their work was not overtly antagonistic to the government; they saved their judgement for the clergy, their persecutors and, more generally, the communities they lived in. When prompted by attacks in print they felt were misleading or libellous, Quakers wrote careful and meticulous responses. They also adapted their writing in times of political change and their own increased centralisation. As such, they were boldly confronting their world.

As the movement grew, the focus was less on convincement and admonition, and more on preservation. The evidence illustrates that Bourne adapted more easily to the change than Watkins. Perhaps because of age, perhaps because Bourne was more willing to fall into line with the wishes of the Quaker leadership, including George Fox and Margaret Fell. Despite the steady prosecution and harsh punishments meted out, the Quakers still flourished and rather than passively suffer, they shaped and refined their attitude towards the law and their persecutors, developing 'sophisticated, systematic, and relentless tactics ... [to] discourage and defeat their enemies'.[24] Edward Bourne and Morgan Watkins knew that Quakers were reviled, but they took great comfort from the belief that they were walking the same path as Christ. This comparison eased their physical and economic hardships, even if they remained disappointed with a wider society that refused to take their warnings seriously. They wanted to usher in a reformed society but, in doing so, they would disrupt societal and cultural norms that could jeopardise their religious communities. The Quakers in Herefordshire and Worcestershire were undeniably part of their respective religious communities, but they were willing to participate and integrate if it did not compromise their Quaker social principles. Indeed, those who did not abide by their code of conduct were swiftly confronted. Despite their occasional altercations with the authorities, they were increasingly aware of maintaining respectability in the wider communities. They remained steadfast social commentators, even though their hopes of a purified society proved untenable.

Chapter 12

Zealous: Humphrey Smith[1]

He lay very quiet and still, and not any unsavoury word proceeded out of his Mouth all the time of his Sickness, but he behaved himself like a Lamb, and he was very sensible unto the last Moment; he was faithful unto the Lord in his day, and a Crown Everlasting is upon his head, which shall rest upon him when all his Oppressors shall gnash their Tongues for pain and vexation of Heart yea, and the full Cup of the Lords Indignation is preparing for them who delight in Cruelty.[2]

As illustrated above in Nicholas Complin's testimony, Humphrey Smith of Little Cowarne, Herefordshire, died the ideal Quaker death in 1663, at peace and in silence. Complin also issued a stern, defiant warning to all those responsible for Smith's imprisonment and subsequent death.

Humphrey Smith's story is a snapshot of the early Quaker experience. His life was brief, but he wrote prolifically, not only about his travels and imprisonments as a Quaker but he also reminisced about his childhood and upbringing. At the very end of his life, when he could no longer write, others, like Nicholas Complin, wrote the end of his story on his behalf. Humphrey Smith was always in control of his narrative.

Smith was born in Stoke Bliss, a small parish that straddled the borders of Herefordshire and Worcestershire,[3] where he was baptised on 21 February 1624.[4] He described himself as spiritual child.[5] When reminiscing about his childhood, he wrote that he would:

> often pray to God (believing there was a God, though I knew him not) even earnestly did I pray with tears, and my heart was opened with his love, to whom also I should make my complaint in secret sometimes upon my knees, when I could get into such a place, that none could see me, nor at all come to know it.[6]

His recollections immediately inform the reader that he was an educated and literate child. Based on his account, he was a learner and deep thinker from when he was very young. Indeed, Smith was literate at an early age as his parents could afford to meet the costs of basic education. The education of boys in the early modern period was deemed important because male intelligence was seen as superior and the key to their future role as patriarchs.[7] It was thereby the responsibility of Smith's father to ensure he was suitably prepared for his future, but he could not foresee the future that lay ahead for his son. Smith wrote that as a child he would often wander off into the woods to think alone, sometimes for three or four hours.[8] This 'mournful state' resulted in criticism from his father and ridicule from his mother, as she 'laid her hands on him and said that his studying would make him a fool'.[9] He described himself as being 'usually disturbed and grieved', while his parents' response, although harsh, may have been coming from a place of sheer frustration rather than cruelty.[10] Nevertheless, further condemning his parents' attitude, he added that his father made him 'cry bitterly' at least six days a week.[11]

The Smith family were living in a world that was changing very quickly. Religious divisions were the most fundamental threat to the family and children who chose a different religious path could no longer see their parents as God's representatives in the most important areas of life.[12] It is not surprising to find that Smith was later deeply critical of his parents, Humphrey and Elinor Smith, especially his father, who was 'more eager than most men in labouring and caring for earthly things', but the public criticism of his upbringing is exceptional. Smith acquiesced to his parents' wishes but, as a result, later wrote that he grew up 'to nurse the evil earthly thing begotten in him'.[13] His outward acquiescence and deference to his parents would have been expected, as this was the foundation of the early modern parent-child relationship.[14] Parents were expected to nurture, provide for and educate their children, and children were obligated to obey, honour and meet the demands of their parents.[15] Conflict among family members was perceived to affect a family's honour because it pointed to disorder within the household.[16] In this case, Smith's parents may have viewed Humphrey's unbecoming behaviour as potentially demonstrating their failure as parents in properly performing their social roles.[17] Smith added that he was 'forced out' of God's love by his parents and was subsequently provoked to 'wrath, grief, and discontent', while his quiet nature was replaced with anger directed against his parents.[18] This resentful behaviour was not out of the ordinary during this time when the 'ideological underpinnings of repression' were beginning to break down.[19] In his recollections, Smith appeared to be challenging both the core values of his parents and their apparent lack of religious identity. In his writing, Smith was forced to confront that he needed something more than what his family and the prevailing religions of the day could offer. In his assessment, he placed the blame squarely on the shoulders of his parents. Based on his own childhood experiences, Smith later warned parents not to be 'the cause of the hardening of their children's hearts'.[20] He added:

> I do write to be an Example unto you, and a Warning, that you may not bring your Children into the like Alienation, Torment, and Condemnation as I was, and the more especially, because that few afterwards do return to God with all their Hearts, and enter in at the straight Gate.[21]

The Smiths were a yeoman family and likely opposed his pious solitude because they expected Humphrey to conform and become a farmer. This was because children were naturally expected to play their part in the household economy.[22] It was the commonly accepted view that hard work was rewarding and a person was only content if they were engaged with their labours.[23] This idea of solitude and introverted worship thereby conflicted with his parents' economic aspirations and they may have felt a duty of care to ensure that Humphrey developed into a hard-working adult. The benefit gained by parents from breaking a child's will at an early stage was that later he or she would accept with passive resignation their decisions in the two most important choices of his or her life, that of occupation and of a marriage partner.[24]

Initially, Smith complied and began to follow the traditional path laid out for him. In 1640, aged 16, he inherited a farm in Little Cowarne, Herefordshire, located between Stoke Bliss and Hereford.[25] Smith's farm was relatively prosperous, and in the Herefordshire Militia Assessment of 1663, his home was recorded as having four hearths; this made it one of the more sizable properties owned by early Quakers in the area and provides further evidence that he was raised in a prosperous family and, in turn, became a successful farmer himself.[26] In addition to his desire for 'earthly things', he also noted that he lived 'in all manner of sin and iniquity, except actual adultery, fornication and murder'.[27] Smith felt it was important to specify those exceptions.

This decision to forsake the Lord and his 'spiritual calling' subsequently had a significant impact on his life. The impact is evident when he reminisced about his upbringing, especially his spiritual regression in 1658:

> For when I was but young and void of the knowledge of God, or his Way of Holiness my mind ran much in the Earth with a covetous care, how to gain the Riches thereof. ... When I was in the height of the World's Way and Worship, and expecting riches to increase, even then in an unexpected time, did the dread of the Lord fall upon me, and his wonderful mighty power wrought exceedingly in me, to break me off from all my Wayes, and separate me from all of the Worship of the World.[28]

In another tract published in 1658, Smith further expressed his former affection of the 'world's way'. The tract was entitled *To the Musicioners, The Harpers, the Minstrels, the Singers, the Dancers, the Persecutors – From One who Loved Dancing and Music as His Life*.[29] In the vast catalogue of Smith's autobiographical writing, this titular sentence is the *only* reference he makes to any happiness from his former life.

Smith was living in arduous times, and the remainder of his personal tracts reveal youthful desperation and remorseful, almost miserable, regret for his misspent youth.

Herefordshire was a critical battleground for the Royalists and Parliamentarians. The events leading up to the civil wars, including Charles I's personal rule and the imposition of the prayer book by Archbishop William Laud, may have exposed Smith to political and religious dissent as a child. Smith's prolific writing output nevertheless does not reveal his influences outside of the Bible, and yet as a young man during the conflict, he would have been exposed to the voluminous amount of literature distributed at the time. This political propaganda encouraged dissent, and while it is unclear if Smith was directly influenced, he was both literate and of an impressionable age.

After the wars, perhaps influenced and inspired by preachers on the battlefield, Smith became an unpaid public preacher. His refusal to be paid for services is corroborated by his declaration in 1658 that the spirit 'encouraged him to do good and not accept payment' and that he 'refused their unrighteous gain and denied all their gifts and rewards'.[30] He also stated that he had 'never profited by any of them but lived in wickedness' as long as he followed them.[31] In his 1658 publication *Man Driven Out of the Earth and Darkness*, Smith did not hold from his condemnation that 'hireling priests were worse than publicans or harlots'.[32] His vehement opposition to a paid ministry may have been influenced by Hugh Peter(s), the most influential radical independent army preacher of the civil war period. In a sermon to Parliament in 1646, Peter declared: 'If you say that Money answer all things, yet you must heare the Lord say, the gold is mine, your silver is mine: It is not the drug, nor the bread that doth the work, but the spirit of them both.'[33]

Fellow Herefordshire Quaker preacher Morgan Watkins later echoed Smith's sentiments in 1664 when he wrote *Lamentation Over England*. In this, he cited the 'wickedness' of the Church and state authorities in England. Watkins observed that these 'Rulers, Priests and People' had 'erred, and strayed from the way of God; and follow too much the devices and desires of their own hearts; offending against his holy Laws ... to ensnare the Innocent'.[34] While appraising his own career, Smith wrote that he 'walked in darkness and wallowed in unrighteousness, and afterwards stood up as a tall cedar in the height of profession, preaching great and high things daily unto others, whereby then I was admired by many hundreds'.[35] He added that he 'was a zealous preacher', but he failed to bring 'souls home to God', and much to his disappointment, the people 'remained in their sins'.[36] He felt that clergymen were paid to help the people but did not know how to do so.[37] In contrast, men like Smith were known as 'mechanick preachers' and, as Christopher Hill comments, they would labour six days a week and would cost their congregations nothing.[38]

Smith preached across Herefordshire but soon grew less confident in his abilities and became increasingly despondent. In Stoke Bliss, he asserted that 'my mouth was stopped from the present, but if ever the Lord should open my mouth again, I shall preach indeed'.[39] He understood that people might have thought that he was a good and honest man, but he stressed that he felt his behaviour was 'contrary to the righteousness of God' and that he was a 'servant of corruption'.⁴⁰ Despite the admiration his congregation lavished on him, he went through this personal crisis of worthlessness. It is important to note that Seekers often had this deep anxiety that they were not worthy. In his 1652 tract entitled *Apocrypha*, William Erbery proclaimed:

> For my part, I am wholly silent, for though I speak sometimes unto men in the flesh, yet my Spirit is silent unto God; thus I am wholly silent, waiting as one of the dry bones in the dust, when the Lord will raise me with all his people out of our Graves, by revealing his glory in us.⁴¹

While this should not be construed as evidence that Smith engaged with Seekers in any manner, he may have been indirectly influenced by the Seekers and their writing before devoting his life to the ideas of George Fox and James Nayler.

Smith can be identified as a Quaker by early 1654 so he was likely one of the first convinced in the area.⁴² There is no extant documentation to show when or where he was convinced; however, it is highly probable that Richard Farnworth convinced him. Farnworth was one of the first missionary Quakers to visit the region, and Smith joined him, collaborating on a ninety-page tract titled *Antichrist's Man of War* (1655), which was a lengthy response to a sixty-five-page book written by Edmund Skipp entitled *The Worlds Wonder, or the Quakers Blazing Starr* (1654).⁴³ Skipp was the vicar of Bodenham, Herefordshire, from 1647 to 1657, and Smith had known him well when he was a public preacher.⁴⁴ In *The Worlds Wonder*, the frontispiece stated that the Quakers were 'deluded by Satan, both in their judgements and walkings: Together with a probable conjecture of the end of the World, and the estate of things in the interval'.⁴⁵ Skipp also referred to Quakerism as 'monster amongst men', 'poor beguiled wretches' and containing 'malevolent and contagious influences'.⁴⁶ In *Antichrist's Man of War*, Smith stated that Skipp 'wandered from the truth' and, like Farnworth, crafted a point-by-point response to Skipp's accusations and claims.⁴⁷ His first published piece exemplified what would be Smith's literary style – brimming with scriptural references and apocalyptical with a confrontational tone. To Skipp, he wrote, 'Oh take heed least it had been better for thee, than a Millstone had been hanged about thy neck, and thou cast into the Sea.'⁴⁸

Smith has been referred to as Farnworth's 'literary apprentice'.[49] Farnworth certainly influenced Smith, and this is reflected in the rich scriptural nature of his writing and preaching throughout the remainder of his life. Like Smith, Farnworth was described as a man of great conviction who insisted that he follow the course that he believed God had laid out for him.[50] Despite his initial lack of confidence as a public preacher in Herefordshire, Smith would prove to be a quite gifted minister and over the course of seven years convinced many to join the Quakers.[51] It can be argued that this success was partly due to the early literary influence of Farnworth. It is also likely that Smith's convincement, while undocumented, transformed him from suffering with crippling self-doubt to becoming a confident preacher. This change may have been driven by Farnworth's influence or Smith's sense of religious duty. Regardless of the true inspiration for his transformation, Smith gave the impression, through his writing, that it was the result of divine intervention.[52]

The earliest converts were zealous and compelled to spread their message, but in doing so, they risked their economic well-being, and the potential displacement of the family from their neighbourhood. Smith endured a £150 loss by leaving his farm in Little Cowarne, while his writing strongly suggests that he saw himself as a prophet. This reasoning would lead to the conclusion that he did not wilfully leave his family and farm, but he made the difficult choice to do so.

Smith relinquished his role as a provider and his role within his family. He condemned his parents for allowing him to conform to traditional behaviour as an adolescent and again, by leaving his own family he did not conform to the social norms of the period. Smith equated himself with biblical characters who all left their homes to preach the word of God.[53] When he was contemplating leaving his wife, Mary, and two children behind, he was overwrought with internal conflict. He discussed his missionary calling with Mary, who naturally pleaded with him to stay with them; he acquiesced but then fell into what could undoubtedly be described as a deep depression.[54] One night, as his family was going to sleep, he recalled that he 'thought they were people he should not be with'. He articulated his thoughts the following day, when he told his wife, 'Surely I should not be here,' and after an unknown period informed her and their family:

> With heaviness and tears ... I was not able to endure it any longer, and that I had abode with them in the way of the World for so long as possible I could, and that I must give up my life to serve the lord, desiring them (with tears) to be content, and in what I could, I should be careful for their good as ever I was.[55]

He added that he trusted in divine providence and that God would take care of his wife and children in his absence, and that if he only convinced one person it would all be worthwhile.[56] This statement alone is evidence of his zealous and single-minded commitment to Quakerism. An antiquarian biographer romanticised Smith's neglect of his family duties and wrote that 'he had forsaken his wife, children and lands, but he was to receive a hundredfold more'.[57] Antiquarian biographies of Smith demonstrate the need for modern historians to look closer at the impact a Quaker missionary's departure had on his or her immediate family. Smith was motivated by a higher power and because of this divine calling, he was able to justify essentially abandoning his family in rural Herefordshire. His family ties were not completely severed when he left them as the evidence suggests that this concern was not completely out of his mind. At the end of *Man Driven Out of Earth and Darkness*, he concluded:

> Let none think that I did wilfully neglect my outward employment, neither let any one think that I left my family as not regarding them, nor that I stay much out of that Country for any By-end; for the words are true, A prophet is not without Honour, save in his own country, and in his own house, and those that did seek to stop my mouth, did not well.[58]

His writing suggests that he was fully aware that he was being judged by his neighbours for what he had done, and added, 'what a Cross it was for me to leave what I did, let that of God judge.'[59] After he abandoned his family, Smith dared to later write, without a trace of irony, that men's wives also 'shall be left as widdows, their children as fatherless' if they did not turn to Quakerism – as he had done to his own family when he himself became convinced.[60]

Smith provided a full account of his struggle to leave his family and of how he put all his faith in God to care for them. *Man Driven Out of Earth and Darkness* is easily Smith's most personal piece of writing, and it was written for wider dissemination. His single-minded devotion was presented on a proverbial platter for his enemies and former neighbours to challenge, particularly as the critical role of an early modern parent was to provide economic security for his/her children.[61] As such, Smith was blatantly disregarding normative social behaviour as he accepted that duty to God might outweigh all other social obligations.[62] While his family may have accepted his fervent belief and even accepted his decision to leave, they would have faced judgement from their neighbours, a lack of support networks, and potential ostracism, in addition to the fundamental matter of how to avoid economic ruin and starvation in rural Herefordshire.

Smith left his family to a precarious future. He chose to be a 'prophet' over his obligations as a husband and father. The family he left behind had no choice in the matter. Thereby, his family's welfare was of limited consequence in comparison to the tasks at hand. There is a consensus amongst historians that the survival of the early movement was critically dependent on its itinerant ministry and the early Quakers believed that they were living on the precipice of the apocalypse, and that it was 'incumbent upon them to spread this teaching'.[63]

Smith began his life as an itinerant Quaker preacher by visiting Oxford in 1654 and the following year he found receptive audiences in Gloucestershire, Hampshire and Worcestershire.[64]

The first prominent court hearing involving the Quakers in Herefordshire and Worcestershire was the case of Smith and Thomas Cartwright of Bengeworth, located south of Evesham town centre, in Worcestershire. On Sunday, 19 August 1655, George Hopkins, the vicar of Evesham All Saints, preached a sermon in Bengeworth against Quakerism, equating it with witchcraft and, unsurprisingly, a local Quaker meeting in Cartwright's home was interrupted by Hopkin's congregation.[65] However, the meeting continued and the crowds shortly scattered, but later that evening, Cartwright and Smith were requested to swear the oath of abjuration (the oath renouncing papal supremacy), which they naturally refused, because Quakers would not swear at all, and were arrested.[66] Smith was further threatened with the Vagrancy Act – a measure often used against itinerant preachers, especially the Quakers. Smith and Cartwright were thereafter taken to the house of a prominent magistrate, Samuel Gardiner, where they were examined and were imprisoned the next day. Smith was not deterred, as he said, 'Repent and serve the Living God' out of the prison windows and, in response, Justice Robert Martin was alleged to have encouraged the people assembled to 'whoop' and begin an 'uproar' – some throwing stones and dirt at the windows, eventually breaking one of them. Martin allegedly tried to pull Smith out from the broken window, likely to allow the crowds to physically assault him.[67]

Throughout the following week, other Quakers were rounded up, including the former mayor of Evesham, magistrate and soldier Captain Edward Pitway.[68] Apart from Smith and Cartwright, fourteen other Quakers were brought before the authorities.[69] During his imprisonment, Smith still preached to anyone who would listen, and found a captive audience outside the 'gaol hole'. Despite this imprisonment, he continued his missionary work. In his tract *The Sufferings, Tryals and Purgings of the Saints at Evesham*, Smith accused the authorities of setting a trap for him and other Quakers.[70] Magistrates encouraged further maltreatment of these Quakers, while Robert Martin attempted to halt Smith's preaching and:

> bid the watchmen, if the people would not be gone from the gaol-hole, he then knock them down, and bid the men throw shuffles ful of dirt upon them in the dungeon, and set eight men with weapons ... to keep away all friends for coming to or speaking with them they had imprisoned.[71]

Smith, Cartwright and the other imprisoned Quakers were dismissed from the Autumn Quarter Sessions and returned to the gaol for not removing their hats. At the hearing, the judge advised, 'you might have had your liberty if you had not came in here in this contemptable way, with your hat on, therefore you shall turn back again to the Prison until you do come with your hat off.'[72] There are numerous suggestions that if the prisoners would merely remove their hats, they would be released. Subsequently, Smith and Thomas Woodrove wrote *The Cruelty of the Magistrates of Evesham, Worcestershire*. This tract detailed their experiences and the hostile response they received when they refused to remove their hats. Robert Atkins, the presiding judge, responded:

> You have come into the Court with your hats on, to fine you, and send you to Prison until you learn better manners, therefore I shall fine you every one and send you to Prison, where you shall lye from one Sessions til another, untill you come with your hats off.[73]

Smith added, 'let it first be made manifest whom we have offended, or what we have transgressed, or what errors I hold, if any can be proved, that the people may be convinced with us of any evil we may be accused of.' While being hauled away by the gaoler, he said, 'they have shamed all profession and all National Government.'[74]

Shortly after their initial imprisonment, a tract detailing the events taking place, partially authored by Smith, was published by the Quakers in 1655, entitled *A Representation of the Government of the Borough of Evesham*. This paper, although addressed to Oliver Cromwell, was certainly intended for a wider audience, beyond the borders of Worcestershire, as it provided a detailed account of their abuse and abusers in Evesham:

> [Robert Martin] caused stones to be thrown at our friends, and wished they would drown themselves; besides our friend [Humphrey Smith] in the common goale had stones thrown at him, spit at him, threw man's Dung in at him, some more filthy abuses he had which is a shame to name; one idle Drunken man came in with a Pike in his hand swearing and railing with so much violence, as though he would presently have murdered him, mentioning knocking him on the head in the night, & the Justice were acquainted with him, and no Officer would meddle with him; neither did they at all, for he said the best in the Town sent him.[75]

Cromwell responded to the publication after five months and delegated the investigation to James Berry, major general of Herefordshire, Shropshire and Wales, who issued a warrant for their release from gaol on 1 September 1656.[76] When Smith left Evesham in 1656, he wrote that he 'left behind him a people well established in the faith and hope of the gospel, and zealous for the honour and glory of Christ'. He possibly had this experience in his mind when he wrote *To the Flock of God Whom He Hath Gathered in Gloucestershire, Herefordshire, Worcestershire, etc.* while incarcerated in Winchester gaol in 1658. In the opening, he commented:

> The salutation of me, the Prisoner of Jesus Christ, with my own hand, unto you, my dear Ones ... among whom I have passed through good Report and evil Report.[77]

His early experiences in gaol did not deter him from his mission. Smith travelled extensively throughout southern England. Shortly after his release from Evesham in 1656, he was imprisoned in Exeter gaol, along with nineteen other Quakers; at the Assizes, the men, including Smith, were indicted for contempt, and fined twenty marks because they refused to remove their hats, like that which had occurred the previous year in Evesham.[78]

To the authorities, removing one's hat was a reasonable and straightforward request as it was a mark of deference. George Fox recorded in his journal: 'Oh the blows, punchings, beatings, and imprisonments that we underwent for not putting off our hats to men … for that soon tried all men's patience and sobriety.'[79] In 1661, Smith wrote: 'it was but only to please the Wills of men of corrupt minds, and until honest sober men were sent for out of their honest Employments, before Rulers, and into Courts, only to ensnare them about their Hats.'[80] Denying social superiors 'hat honour' was provocative and certainly challenged social protocols of the time.[81] Quakers sought to redefine the ideal of neighbourliness by challenging the status quo of societal niceties.[82]

As with most of their actions, scripture could be used to illuminate and justify their position. They suggested that the Bible did not require the removal of hats before superiors and referenced the Book of Daniel, where Shadrach, Meshach and Abednego were thrown into the furnace, in the presence of King Nebuchadnezzar, with their hats on.[83] By not removing his hat, it was an easy way to antagonise authorities and create unrest. However, with his refusal to comply with hat honour, Smith appeared to welcome abuse, imprisonment, and financial loss to drive forward his message and his path to martyrdom. Smith's message was also aided by subtle political undertones. In Evesham, he wrote that most of the Quakers that had been imprisoned, including Thomas Cartwright, were former soldiers who fought at Worcester 'for outward liberty, and now they are fined, or imprisoned, or both, without any Law transgressed, and are deprived of outward liberty'.[84]

In 1655, William Pitt of Worcester added that Smith was a 'friend of Parliament's Army, from the first firing of them, and afterwards ventured his naturall life, and suffered much loss by the king's army, and now we have not the least benefit of the liberty nor law of the Nation'.[85] While Smith did not expand on the specific losses he experienced, the billeting of Charles I's army, and plundering and deprivation of Herefordshire is well documented.

In *A Representation of the Government of the Borough of Evesham in the County of Worcester* it was noted that one of the justices in Evesham was a former Royalist who took arms against the present government, the implication being that their persecutors were harbouring malicious feelings against them for their involvement in the civil wars, as well for their religious beliefs.[86] Smith was imploring his readers to understand that Quakers were on the side of the government and their persecutors were the true enemies of the state.

Following the Nayler affair in October 1656, the authorities were quick to attempt to extinguish the activities of the troublesome Quakers. Smith made himself a nuisance to law enforcement for the rest of his life. On 25 October 1657, he travelled to Uphay in Axminster, Devon, for a meeting and was arrested for violating the Vagrancy Act of 1656.[87] The public demanded action against the 'idle' Quakers.[88] The Vagrancy Act was directed against 'all wandering persons' and Christopher Hill notes that the Quakers complained that the Act was so outrageous, it would have implicated Christ and the Apostles.[89] As punishment, Smith and his companion, Samuel Curtis, were sent to Bear Hall in Axminster, where they were stripped naked and whipped for their vagrancy.[90] Their books and papers were also burned at the time of their arrest.[91] Again, the authorities were publicly humiliating these disrupters and, by burning their literature, they attempted to ensure that no one else was influenced by their religious beliefs. The fear of these Quakers spread, and this is highlighted by Smith's reception in Sherborne, Dorsetshire, where he was met by a 'rude multitude' throwing stones, dirt and excrement at them all.[92]

In February 1658, Smith, William Bayley and Captain Anthony Melledge travelled to Ringwood, Hampshire, where Smith was asked to visit Mary Hinton, a sick woman.[93] Hinton was described as mentally ill and, following Smith's visit, she recovered. Her sudden recovery was enough to raise the suspicions of her employer, Stephen Jaye. Smith was subsequently accused of cursing Hinton rather than healing her – he denied both cursing and healing. Accusations like this illustrated the concerns that the Quakers were capable of supernatural powers 'to wish individuals ill'.[94] Smith and his companions were nevertheless not imprisoned, but this demonstrates the risk the Quakers faced in merely talking to outsiders and the intense distrust of their activities and potential influence.

Smith's persecution and abuse continued, yet his zeal remained undiminished. In addition to his gradual acceptance of persecution was an almost willingness to contravene the law, and he wrote that he left his livelihood while he expected to be 'exposed to want, hardships, revilings, imprisonments, whipping, stoning and all manner of cruel torture'.[95] While imprisoned in Dorchester in 1656, he penned a short accompaniment to Captain Melledge's tract entitled *A Dreadful Cry Against the Oppressors*, which concluded with the following paragraph:

> Written by the hand of him that hath learned to pray for his Enemies, and desires the good of all your souls, being a Friend to the peace of the people, and all that rule for God who hath made me willing to suffer for his Names sake in outward bonds, by the dark world unto whom I am known by the name of Humphrey Smith.[96]

Smith was standing on shifting sands, but refused to sink, even though the conditions in most mid-seventeenth-century prisons were appalling, and Quakers were often abused by over-zealous gaolers or fellow inmates.[97] He was no exception. Quakers were often able to write about the grim prison conditions while powerfully conveying the Quaker message. Throughout his travels, he endured constant persecution and abuse. Quaker opponents were trying to undermine them, psychologically and physically. It is possible that persecuted Quakers, like Smith, were accustomed to severe hardship and accepted that they needed to suffer yet again for God. During his imprisonment in Evesham, Smith wrote that there were:

> assaults made against us, both of the Heathens and the Rulers, who sought to vex us despitefully as they did. ... some threw stones in the prison the weight of five pound, and threw dirt and water on my lodging, and spit on me ... and pist at me several times, and once they pist on my food. ... but Friends feared none of these things.[98]

This published 'fearlessness' in the face of adversity was a testament to his strong convictions. Smith's unconditional devotion, during such a dark time in his life, would have served as a powerful testimony as Quakers who responded calmly to hostility and brutality were viewed as courageous and heroic by their peers. It can also be argued that Smith was almost sadistically loyal to his beliefs. During this period, apocalypticism was often used as an incentive to persecution, as every person sought to save others from 'falling into the abyss of damnation', no matter the cost.[99] Smith commented that the:

> most happy shall those be, who are found worthy to suffer, and endure all manner of trials, cruelties, and hardships for him, and his Name's sake ... and finish their course in righteousness, and lay down their lives for his sake, to live with Him for evermore![100]

Writing provided Smith, and other Quaker writers, with an opportunity to reach a larger audience. It also served as an outlet for self-reflection. In the earliest years of the movement, he wrote three single-authored pamphlets and contributed to another three by 1656, making him the joint tenth most prolific Quaker writer during the mid-1650s.[101] In comparison, most Quaker authors wrote fewer than three works,[102] and Smith was the most productive writer in 1658 during his imprisonment in Winchester gaol.[103] Like his contemporaries, Smith often referenced the Bible throughout his written work. In Evesham, Robert Atkin, clearly exasperated, observed: 'Smith, you are the Ring-Leader of this Sect, and of this people; I know you have Scripture enough, and you can tell of Paul's Condition, and many such things, but you lead people contrary to the wayes of God.'[104]

In his collected works, Smith referenced over 600 verses of the Bible. John 8:12 was the most cited verse in his work, referenced on six occasions. This verse very concisely summarises the message of the early Quakers: 'Then spake Jesus again unto them, saying, I am the light of the world: he that followeth me shall not walk in darkness, but shall have the light of life.' He frequently referenced the Books of John, Isaiah, and Hebrews. Each Book's purpose reflects a part of the spiritual journey. The Book of John aims to serve as proof that Jesus was in fact the son of God and as summarised in John 3:16, those 'who believe in him shall not perish but have eternal life'. The Book of Isaiah is about judgement, asking pagan nations to repent their sins, and provides a message of hope and forgiveness – God will provide salvation to those who are open to trusting the Lord. The Book of Hebrews was written primarily as a letter to those struggling with their new faith. In Hebrews, Christianity was viewed as vastly superior to Judaism, so Smith may have favoured Hebrews because he similarly believed that Quakerism was vastly superior to Anglicanism, Catholicism and other religious beliefs. In Hebrews, Christ criticised the idea that contact with God requires an intermediary – the same message that the early Quakers were trying to convey. Smith may have also identified with Christ's words on suffering in Hebrews 2:10: 'For it became him, for whom are all things, and by whom are all things in bringing many sons unto glory, to make the captain of their salvation perfect through sufferings.' This idea of perfection through suffering must have resonated with Smith as this was the foundation of his life since his convincement.

A result of his prolific writing was the convincement of new members. In Bridport, Dorset, Smith was credited for 'strengthening and confirming the newly convinced' in early 1657.[105] By all accounts, Smith was a powerful minister and he believed in his abilities as he declared:

> Hear I say, and let my words have entrance in you, and let the sound of my Voice take place in your Hearts, let the opening of my Lips give Astonishment to the Wicked, and the enlargement of my Hart the Confounding of the Heathen.[106]

While it cannot be determined how many Quakers were convinced by Smith, his reputation as a persuasive preacher was well established. It was noted that people were coming to his meetings to hear Smith preach and 'were mightily affected with him'.[107] His written work, the two passages below, written in 1658 and 1663, demonstrate the gulf that existed amongst those who were convinced and those who did not. As with all religious groups, there were severe penalties for the non-believers. Smith's passionate words would have inspired the newly convinced and served as a stern warning to the unconvinced. The first excerpt was written while imprisoned in Winchester in 1658 and the second was written five years later, in 1663.

> And the true desire of my present enlarged Heart for your Eternal Happiness, is, That as the Lord of Heaven and Earth hath counted you worthy of his Call, in the power of his Grace, which bringeth Salvation unto all, you may not judge your selves unworthy of the Kingdom of God, but may cleave unto his Truth in the inward parts, leaving all that which hath hindred you.[108]

> The Standard of the Lord is lifted up against you. ... he will plague you with the Beast and the Whore together for evermore, and your Seed shall be cut off the Earth, and your Children from among the Living; your Memorial shall Rot for evermore, and your Name blotted out from under Heaven; and all that hear of you shall Hiss at you, and an astonishment and a hissing shall you be unto all People.[109]

Smith created powerful imagery through his words and the bleak depiction of the unconvinced or those who actively opposed the Quakers is found throughout his writing. He was not subtle with his message and there is an urgency to his prose that suggests he felt a day of reckoning was imminent. Thematically, Smith frequently used apocalyptic biblical references and phrases, including, 'I will fill the Heathen with Horror, and all mine Enemies with the Blackness of Darkness.'[110] The passage below from *An Alarum Sounding Forth* best illustrates his graphic, apocalyptic style:

> In that Day shall the Songs of your Temples be turned into howling forever, the place of your Worship laid desolate, and the Dung of your solemn Feasts spread upon your Faces; your Rottenness shall appear, and you[r] Unfound parts be made manifest; the Skirts of the Whore shall be discovered, and all your Nakedness, that long in secret have committed Fornication with her, shall now appear to your everlasting shame. ... Torment shall take hold upon you, and Anguish shall seize upon your inward parts, a Fire shall be kindled in your Bowels forever, which shall burn, and non[e] shall quench it. ... The Wicked shall be turned into Hell, and all that forget God.[111]

Smith embraced this vision of a bleak, uncertain future, much like many of his contemporaries at this time, including Morgan Watkins. In 1658, in *The Just Complaint of the Afflicted ... To Be Delivered to the Judge of the Sessions at Winchester*, Smith warned, 'A day of Trouble is coming upon you, a day of Darkness, and not Light; yea, the Lord God is coming near to Judgement.'[112] In 1660, he wrote about a vision he had of a fire destroying London, six years before the 'Great Fire' devastated the city:

> As for the city herself, and her suburbs, and all that belonged to her [I beheld] a fire was kindled therein, but she knew not how, even in

her goodly palaces, and the kindling of it was in the foundation of her buildings. There was none could quench it, neither was there any able, and the burning thereof was exceedingly great and burned inward in an hidden manner, which cannot be expressed. ... O' City of London, thy sin hath been exceeding grievous, and thy iniquities beyond measure.[113]

However, the language used by Smith is non-specific and metaphorical, while the vision itself would have been viewed as a testimony to the vileness and immorality of London. Rebecca Rideal concludes that centuries of religious conditioning led the Christian world 'to see disasters and major events as signs of God's providence'.[114] It can be argued that Smith's 'vision' was that of a London cleansed of its sins and rising like a phoenix from the ashes. However, Quaker opponents could have used the publication of this vision to incarcerate them for incitement to arson. The Quakers were certainly arrested for much lesser offences.[115] It would only take one overenthusiastic zealot to read Smith's tract and its message of fire and brimstone, and the need to purge 'the city' to act upon this statement and turn it into reality.

Apocalyptic visions notwithstanding, a key to Smith's success as a Quaker preacher was his autobiographical writing. They were graphic insights into his beliefs as well as how he viewed seventeenth-century modes of behaviour and his place in this wider community. He wrote 'I have not learned nor received from men (the Lord God knoweth I lie not) but through the operation of the mighty power of God, whose indignation I have born, in whose judgements I rejoyce for ever.'[116] This personal approach to writing would have resonated with his readers, as his reflections on his life before convincement, combined with the use of apocalyptic passages from the Bible, would have served as a compelling cautionary tale. This apocalyptic style seamlessly merged with the autobiographical elements to produce work that was dynamic and engaging. Christopher Hill observes that these spiritual autobiographies confirmed the 'footlooseness' of the Quakers and demonstrated the ease with which they uprooted their lives and managed to live while travelling throughout the country.[117]

Smith was en route to visit his son on 14 October 1661 when he was imprisoned in Winchester following his arrest at a meeting in Alton, Hampshire. The presiding judge, Sir Thomas Terrill, gave Smith several opportunities to leave Winchester gaol, which Smith himself referred to as 'a filthy prison, and place unfit for men'.[118] Terrill gave him the option to pay bail and be released, while a year later, he offered the Quaker his freedom if he would hold no more meetings.[119] Smith found these terms to be disagreeable and consequently remained in prison. Again, this demonstrates Smith's stubborn and resolute determination. His interest was in controlling his narrative, and he seemed determined to die a martyr for the 'Lambs War' rather than return home to his family or continue preaching throughout England. Smith's final letter to his son, Humphrey Junior, demonstrates the implications for the displaced family of Quaker adherents.[120] It is critical to analyse this letter with discernment as the content further highlights the authority of his familial responsibilities and requests, despite his long absence. In this letter, he begins:

> My Son, The alone & only Son of me after the flesh (for I never had any other). I was called of the Lord from thee when thou wast young, & from all things else that were ever so dear unto me, to publish the Gospel of God, and to call Sinners to Repentance; in the which the Lord hath blessed me.
>
> And if it should be the will of God that I now finish my Testimony in this prison; yet have I so ordered & [taken] care for thee (my child) (and that according to the good will of God), that thou mayst spend thy Days in his Feare & walke uprightly in his Sight; & learne to labour honestly so with thy Hands, as may be of good Report among men & comfortable to thy selfe.[121]

Smith had perhaps undermined his family's future by abandoning them in 1654, culminating in his own untimely and entirely preventable death. Quakers, like Smith, were zealots – they saw only one path and not the world that they had created around them. Admittedly, they believed that their sacrifice would purify the world but at a tremendous personal cost to themselves, their wives, their families, their neighbours and their communities. Smith was willing to sacrifice himself for his beliefs but potentially unwilling to play his role as a husband, provider and father. In the opening lines of this letter, Smith openly admits that he was an absent father and acknowledges that, despite his absence, he has tried to care for him. He implores his son to carry on his legacy as a God-fearing, honest man. He further remarks:

> And now altho' as I said before, thou art my only Son, yet if thou refusest the Instructions of thy Father, & shalt reject the Counsel of God, and then not be obedient nor faithfull to thy Master, nor walk in God's holy Feare, nor keep in the Way of Truth, then let the Law of Men take hold of thy Body, let the Judgement of Friends pass upon thee, let the law of God seize upon thy Conscience & let Trouble & Feare & Poverty & Wretchedness & Shame overtake thee, inasmuch as thou dishonour thy Father & the Lord and his precious Truth.[122]

This warning is quite similar to the economic ultimatums imposed by fathers to their daughters in wills of the sixteenth century, but Smith uses this tactic to encourage his son to follow God's 'counsel' or face the most severe economic hardship and shame.

In many ways, this letter serves as his last will and testament, while the arrangements Smith made for an apprenticeship for his son are quite specific:

> And as for the Time thou art to be with thy Master from thy first going to him; I did intend & shall appoint some Friend to see the same performed; that thy Master, and the Schoolmaster, be paid and satisfied for one whole Yeares [Diet] & Teaching as likewise what I am to give with thee as an Apprentice & ye like; that thou being young & little, it might be easy to thee.
>
> And thenceforward thou art to be bound by indenture as an apprentice for eight yeares. And I do hereby appoint & desire George Weatherly and Robert Ludgater to see to the Drawing of the Indentures, and to be as Friends on thy Part.[123]

It was not mentioned in this final letter that Lucy Wyatt, a Worcestershire Quaker, would be left to care for Smith's son and that the child would later become an apprentice to Henry Abbot in Essex.[124] Wyatt was well known to Smith, and it is likely that Smith was responsible for her convincement in the 1650s. It is unknown why he placed his son in her care, but perhaps he felt secure in the knowledge that she would abide by his teachings and ensure that Humphrey Junior would be raised in the tenets of the Quaker community. An apprenticeship for a boy of Humphrey's age was not universal practice, but usually dependent on socio-economic factors.[125] In this case, it appears almost certain that the apprenticeship was made possible by his father's religious connections. Smith was fortunate that he had the opportunity to rely on the community of Quakers to outsource his role as a parent. In a traditional master-apprentice relationship, the master had the absolute power of a father and, in this case, Henry Abbot is likely to have provided Humphrey Junior with a stable fatherly presence for the first time in his life.[126]

At the close of this letter, Smith warns his son against visiting him in Winchester gaol and, in an austere way, which may have been typical of this father-son relationship, he uses this letter as a final goodbye to his son. With this letter, he was preparing his son for his absence without accepting the fact that he should be the person taking responsibility directly and guiding his son into adulthood. He ends the letter with:

> And as for coming to see me, think not on that: for many Friends have come severall Scores of Miles, to whom I have been scarce able to speake two Words, though the Lord hath given me so much Strength at present to write this unto thee. The which, if the Lord gather me to the eternal Rest of my Fathers, then mayst thou call this as my last Farewell. And the blessing of God be with thee for ever.[127]

Smith did not see his son again. This letter was written on 23 April 1663, and Smith died nearly two weeks later. On 6 May, he was buried in a Quaker burial ground in Bramshott, Hampshire.[128] Before his death, he wrote *The Cause of the Long Afflicted and Sore Oppressed Sent Forth in Brief from Winchester Prison Being a Copy of the Mittimus whereby Humphrey Smith was again Committed (into the place of his former long suffering, in the same streight unsavory Prison)*. By the time of its publication in early 1663, he had been imprisoned for fifteen months and was allegedly 'never called at Size or Sessions, nor suffered to come to any of the Rulers of the County to lay before them the true state of his Case'.[129] He continued to compare himself to the Apostle Paul and the authorities to killers of Christ. The tract ends with the following bleak biblical verses, predicting his own death and again comparing himself to Christ: 'the time cometh, that whosoever killeth you will think that he doth God Service',[130] and 'if the world hate you, ye know that it hated me before it hated you'.[131]

The earliest Quakers would have agreed that Smith lived a commendable life, but to outsiders, he was a religious zealot who abandoned his family for his faith; deserted a profitable farm to become an itinerant preacher; intentionally caused disruption with his preaching and his published work; and he was, for all intents and purposes, a lawbreaking vagrant. To Quakers, his dedication was inspirational, and his devotion was admirable. He was a martyr for their cause. His life was posthumously honoured in 1683, twenty years after his death, when his son compiled much of his father's written work into a large volume. The collected volume of Smith's work contains 48 tracts and spans 346 pages. As he died within the first wave of Quaker activity, this collection of tracts provides a very focused study of the earliest years of the Quakers. This volume also includes eyewitness accounts of his final days and testimonies written after his untimely death by the early leadership, including George Whitehead and George Fox. In 1683, Fox remembered, 'yet through the eternal power of the Lord, he [Smith] was upholden through his sufferings, and travelled through many hardships for the Lord Jesus Christ's sake, and did convert and turn many to the Lord Jesus Christ.'[132] It was later written that, during his final illness, Smith spoke 'many precious words to friends about Him, signifying that he was given up to the will of God, either in life or death'.[133] He died as he lived: persecuted yet devout, zealous and never wavering from his beliefs.

The sole eyewitness account of Smith's death comes from Nicholas Complin. He wrote and published his testimony in 1663 – unlike the others, which were written years later – thereby providing a more reliable account of Smith's final days. He commented that Smith 'lay very quiet and still, and not any unsavoury word proceeded out of his Mouth all the time of his Sickness, but he behaved himself like a Lamb, and he was very sensible unto the last Moment'.[134] This quiet departure is often recorded in Quaker testimonies. There was a dignity in this kind of death, particularly dying of a physically debilitating illness in a rancid prison. Complin concluded his nine-page memorial with a warning to those responsible for Smith's incarceration and subsequent death. He refers to them as bloodthirsty 'unsatiable, Vigorous, Tyrannical, Idolatrous Men' who should be cast into 'the dreadful Flames of the Burnings of his Vengeance'.[135] He added that

God would 'not spare the best of those that have had a hand in these things (and shall persist therein) but will destroy them utterly, and Curse them from his Presence for evermore; and in this, I shall be clear of all your Blood when it comes upon you'.[136] Complin's account was written as a provocative piece of Quaker literature. This provocation is made clear by the ferocious statements about their gaolers and others who had persecuted them. The intended audience for this would have naturally been the Quakers, but his distraught and often inflammatory testimony also would have stirred the interest of a general readership as well. To Complin, and to the Quakers, it was a story of Smith's undeserved incarceration while showing admiration for dignity and grace in which Smith spent his final days. Most importantly, Complin's account provides an insight into his own thoughts about their persecutors, mortality, and the righteousness of their beliefs, which also reflects the views that Quakers held more generally.

According to the accounts, Smith died the ideal Quaker death, in peace and silence. This, admittedly, was counter to his actions of an itinerant Quaker preacher. The Quaker ideal was to die in a state of holy quietude and composure. Indeed, the recorded deathbed sayings of many of the Quakers all have the same theme: inward peace, quietly and calmly expressed.[137] David Cressy argues that the natural fear of dying was challenged by the idea that 'none should fear death if buoyed by Christian Faith' and added that any fearful sentiments of those final moments were drowned out by 'promises of death as liberation'.[138]

Smith died a noble death in, by all accounts, grim circumstances. However, he did not die of natural causes. He did not die a painless death. He died of gaol fever, or what is commonly known as typhus. Gaol fever was very common in prisons, and it often occurred when prisoners were crowded together into dark, filthy, unventilated rooms.[139] It is therefore not surprising that Smith contracted this kind of illness in prison. Approximately ten days after contracting the illness, the infected could experience an intense fever, a watery acrid stool discharge, uncontrollable bowel movements or severe constipation, spotted skin or lesions, and emit putrid odours.[140] The symptoms of gaol fever suggests that Smith physically suffered and died a deeply uncomfortable and perhaps agonising death. The eyewitness accounts paint a very different picture, so what would be the motivation behind this?

It is easy to argue that the eyewitness accounts of a peaceful death served as propaganda for the movement.

To a lay reader, Smith's suffering was akin to that of Job in the Bible, and, like Job, Smith was faithful to the very end. He preferred to perish in prison than bend to Judge Terrill's disagreeable terms for release. The purpose of the Book of Job is to demonstrate why and how the righteous will prevail, despite intense suffering. It also seeks to define the meaning of truly unshakeable faith. As with Job, Smith's suffering and persecution reveal a deeper relationship with God. The words below, attributed to Job, could have easily been written by Smith himself:

> Till I die, I will not remove mine integrity from me. My righteousness I hold fast, and will not let it go: my heart shall not reproach me so long as I live. Let mine enemy be as the wicked, and he that riseth up against me as the unrighteous. For what is the hope of the hypocrite, though he hath gained when God taketh away his soul.[141]

These testimonies may have been published to exemplify an ideal Quaker death, but it is also important to examine other possibilities for Smith's deathbed depiction.

In his study of mental disorders in early modern England, Michael MacDonald argues that 'religious issues moved men to extremes of passion'.[142] In 1658, while in Hampshire gaol, Smith fell gravely ill, and he later wrote that he believed that he died in prison and came back from the dead.[143] Did Smith suffer from mental health issues or perhaps feel a sense of calm in his final moments because he did not think he was going to die? Sadly, it is difficult, if not impossible, to make a satisfying link to suggest that he had a mental illness. However, in times of severe distress, the brain can change. This is known as neuroplasticity. Neuroplasticity can exhibit itself as disassociation, where a person can completely detach from a threatening or stressful situation.[144] It is possible that, after frequent incarcerations in dreadful conditions, Smith's brain was forced to adapt to his chronically stressed situation.

As a comparison, Mary Penington's first husband, William Springett, died similarly to Smith.[145] Penington's eyewitness account of his death shares some similarities to Smith's accounts in that both died relatively peacefully, with lucidity and raised spirits, despite their physical suffering.[146] Without further evidence, it is most likely that the Quakers simply wanted him to be remembered in a way that was befitting of a man whose life was consumed by the desire to change hearts and minds, one who provided a path to salvation for those seeking a connection to God, who wrote voluminously and lived as they felt a God-fearing man should live. Apart from Nicholas Complin, all the testimonies were written in 1682 and 1683, just before the publication of the volume of Smith's written work. These testimonies comprise the introduction of the collection and would have given the reader an appreciation of the life and ultimate sacrifice of the author. They provide context to the events that Smith writes about and the issues he felt were most important.

In his testimony of Smith, written in 1683, George Fox referred to Smith as 'a worthy Souldier and Follower of the Lamb'.[147] Fox continued, 'yet through the eternal power of the Lord, he was upholden through his sufferings, and travelled through many hardships for the Lord Jesus Christ's sake, and did convert and turn many to the Lord Jesus Christ.'[148] George Whitehead's testimony declared that Smith was 'a man fearing God and hating Inequity, fervent and zealous against Deceit and Hypocrisie, and endued with a heavenly Gift and Gospel testimony, which he faithfully bore in his day'.[149] Nicholas Gates testified that Smith was 'very powerful to the convincing of many and turning them to the Light of Christ in themselves', and that he 'never murmured at the Exercises that he met withal, through Wicked and Unreasonable men'.[150] James Potter, another inmate at Winchester gaol, observed that Smith was 'diligent and laborious in his day and time, desiring to spend and be spent for the Gospels sake'.[151] Again, these testimonies are highlighting the essential qualities of an effective Quaker minister – the ability to convert souls and a good work ethic, alongside the ability to withstand the verbal and physical abuse from their challengers.

Smith's son, Humphrey, wrote a testimony honouring his father. He addressed the absence of his father in the first line: 'concerning my dear father, who to his unspeakable gain, but to my great sorrow and loss, the Lord took from me to himself, whilst I was young'.[152] This absence could simply be referring to Smith's death in Winchester gaol, or it could also be referencing his departure from the family home in the early 1650s. He added:

the great Opposition of Malicious, Cruel, and Ungodly men, by whom he suffered, more especially in Cromwell's time, Imprisonment, Dungeon, Whipping and much Affliction and Hardships; but being zealous for the glory of God, and the good of Souls, he valiantly endured it all.[153]

Humphrey Junior closes his testimony with the words 'we may follow the Lord fully and faithfully, and he may raise up in us the Same Love, Zeal, Diligence, and Vallour, as he did our Parents, is the earnest Desire of Humphrey Smith'.[154] The language used by Humphrey Junior shows that he did follow the advice of his father and matured into a God-fearing adult. This may demonstrate the conditioning he experienced under the care of Lucy Wyatt and Henry Abbot and suggests that he had accepted the narrative of his father's life as truth. In the twenty years since his death, the heroic version of Smith, the Quaker martyr, may have replaced the reality of Smith, the zealous deserter of his family.

These testimonies all share a common theme. Humphrey Smith was genuinely devout and passionate about his cause and was treated cruelly by men described as 'wicked and evil'. The verse chosen for the first page of the *Collection* is an appropriate summation of his life:

I have fought a good Fight. I have finished my Course. I have kept the Faith; henceforth there is laid up for me a Crown of Righteousness, which the Lord the Righteous Judge shall give me at that day, and not only to me but to them also that love his appearing (2 Timothy 4: 7–8).[155]

As the idea of a commendable life was extensively examined, this notion of a noble death must be considered, both among the Quakers and in the wider community.

Smith's death and last moments are depicted as a reflection of the values of the Quakers, but was this manner of death commonplace in mid-seventeenth-century England? David Stannard notes that death and expiration were 'matters of critical importance to the Puritans ... they constantly urged themselves to direct their lives toward that moment when their earthly pilgrimage would end'.[156] While Smith's worthiness can be debated, the way in which his death was depicted was universally ideal. Smith died peacefully, submitting himself to God's will, and was highly respected and admired by his peer group. In addition to celebrating Smith's life and work, the testimonies in this *Collection* may have provided part of the template used in later testimony writing and this acceptance of an ideal death may have convinced fellow preachers to maintain their divinely appointed path. Testimonies had developed into standard British Quaker practice and Smith was not the only one remembered in this manner. By the time of this publication in 1683, many of the leading Quakers had passed and were memorialised, including Edward Burrough, John Camm and Richard Hubberthorne.[157] In Edward Burrough's testimony, George Fox wrote that Burrough 'never turned his back on the Truth … a valiant warrior, more than a conqueror; who has got the Crown though death: who is dead but yet liveth amongst us, and amongst us is alive'.[158] They used memorial testimony writing to remind themselves and others of the importance of faithfulness in life and in death.[159]

Smith's prolific writing from 1655 to 1663 highlights his contributions to the early movement. His undiminished zeal burned brightly until the very end. While his zealous beliefs and negligent actions undermined the traditional values of the seventeenth century, Smith lived a commendable life in the eyes of the earliest Quakers. In 1658, during his first imprisonment at Winchester gaol, he wrote a passage that could be interpreted as his epitaph.

> By me who refused the Glory, Treasure, and Preferment of the world and did choose rather to suffer Affliction with the People of God. I have been often brought before Rulers, haled and beat out of the Synagogues, numbered among Transgressors, tryed at Assizes as an offender, yet there denyed the Liberty of a Murderer, being six time imprisoned, twice stript naked and whipt with rods, and since put into Bridewell; once put into and kept long in a Dungeon for Praying; often abused in Prison; sometimes near Death; in tryals often, in Perils often, in Loss of goods, in daily Reproaches, and in that which hath been greater than all these things; and yet have I been preserved unto this day by the Power of him who is the Light.[160]

Throughout Smith's life, he managed to control his narrative and, even in death, the image portrayed was one that would have satisfied him. Although his contribution to the early Quaker community is often overlooked, he was a prominent writer and preacher of the early movement and should be remembered as such. However, it is also imperative to view Smith as an individual driven to extreme lengths to pursue his religious identity, who deserted his family, suffered greatly at the hands of authorities, and died a premature death to satisfy his Quaker beliefs, like many of his contemporaries.[161]

Chapter 13

Legacy

The wars had a profound impact on society. In the aftermath of this internecine conflict, civilians were recoiling from violent experiences and clearly uncertain about the future. Moreover, as the residents of the counties were rebuilding their lives, homes and communities, they were also rebuilding their faith. During the wider political and religious upheaval and uncertainty of the late 1640s and early 1650s, there was an acceptance of new ideas. There was a receptive audience waiting, looking for confirmation that God, in the midst of chaos and destruction, was still there. Quaker missionaries and writers tapped into such anxieties and felt assured that their message of finding a personal connection with God reached receptive ears.

Quakers in Herefordshire and Worcestershire were regularly arrested for antagonising local officials, holding unlawful meetings, or refusing to swear oaths. The Quakers pushed back and asserted that their punishments did not match their alleged offences. To the authorities, they were purposefully breaking the law, so they reacted with robust measures required to keep the public peace.

Another critical factor for increased periods of persecution was the mindset of the local authorities. When the government found itself in an insecure position, both during the Interregnum and immediately after the restoration of the monarchy, the activities of the Quakers created instability and generated anxiety in the local community. Their actions risked the survival of the movement. However, persecution was not only dictated by national events. The investigation has shown that the influence of local opponents was widely felt. There was a local animosity to strangers and itinerant preachers, and for those authorities who could remember the civil wars, this mistrust in strangers with radical ideas was well placed.

Quakers increasingly had to fight back against what they felt was wrongful prosecution, thus creating a cycle of persecution. This cycle continued even when local authorities tried to show leniency in exchange for an agreement that the Quakers would not continue breaking the law. They did not believe they were in violation of God's law so they would not submit or admit fault. Consequently, the injustice the Quakers witnessed only served to embolden them.

Persecution shaped the Quakers' collective religious identity. Moreover, combined with their ability to disseminate their written work, it created a powerful motivational tool for the Quakers. Crafting their own narratives, they emerged as the heroic protagonists of the story, doing their best to redeem those they saw as misled. Quakers were emboldened by what they viewed as injustice and undue suffering caused by the local authorities. They were convinced that they were on a righteous path, like that of Christ and the Apostles. Their writing pleaded for urgency, and perhaps it was this heavy-handed approach that limited their impact. Quakers were driving their own narrative of martyrology. They needed to believe that they were being unfairly castigated for their overall narrative of suffering to work.

From their dynamic start, their intention can be clearly seen, and the zeal of these early Quakers is evident. The publications of their opponents demonstrate how they were viewed as serious threats to social order. As the final quarter of the century drew to a close, the Quakers were less focussed on convincement and admonishment, and more on preservation.

The Quakers needed to engage and interact with the wider world. This meant engaging with their neighbours, shaping their outward image to one of respectability, and focusing on the behaviour of their members rather than condemning the world around them. They needed to present a less threatening image to mainstream society. Arguably, the most important development in early Quakerism was the establishment of the Second Day Meetings. These meetings, which commenced in 1673, satisfied the growing need for more organisational structure. Critically, these meetings played a key role in reviewing and coordinating the publication of Quaker literature. Members would send their drafts to the Second Day Meeting for editorial review and approval. As Quakers relied heavily on their published materials to disseminate their message, this meeting ensured that their collective messaging was consistent and distanced from the early Quakers' radical past.

Their victories are evident in their lasting success and a legacy of peace and acceptance. Modern Quakerism could not be more distant to its antisocial past. Quakers succeeded where every other religious movement of the mid-seventeenth century failed. Their success should be attributed to the organisation of the early leadership, at a national and local level – they took control of the radical elements before they could illegitimise and destroy the entire movement. The zealous were sidelined and, in many cases, dead (from gaol fever etc.) by the start of the 1670s.

Quakerism was propelled by a legacy of discontent and a desire to find a direct connection to God. This began long before the first preachers began travelling and spreading the earliest Quaker message in the early 1650s. The traumatic experience of the civil wars reignited this yearning for faith and order. Yet, the history of early Quakerism is not just about the collective or the national leadership, it is about the regional figures who established these local religious communities and those who were willing to spread this message, no matter the sacrifice required. We have seen how individuals engaged with the structure of early Quakerism in these border counties and beyond. The individual experiences mattered and shaped early Quakerism.

Epilogue

On Colonial Shores

October 1659 – Boston, Massachusetts

'Mary Dyer, you shall go to the Place from whence you came and from thence to the Place of Execution and be hanged there until you are dead.'

She replied 'Yea, joyfully I shall go.'

A few days later, Quakers William Robinson, Marmaduke Stephenson and Mary Dyer walked hand in hand to the scaffold. The Quakers had been banished from Massachusetts Bay, but these Quakers repeatedly returned to hold meetings – even the threat of death would not deter them.

Robinson and Stephenson were executed. The noose was placed around Mary's neck, a kerchief covering her face. She was prepared to die for her faith.

She was not expecting a reprieve in these final moments, but her son successfully petitioned the court with not a moment to spare. She was released and warned to stay out of Boston.[1]

30 May 1660 – Boston, Massachusetts

Governor Endicott recognised the name before him from the previous year. She had indeed returned and was charged with the same crime.

'You must return to the prison, and there remain till to-morrow at nine o'clock; then thence you must go to the gallows, and there be hanged till you are dead.'

Mary replied, 'This is no more than what thou saidst before.'

'But now, it is to be executed.'

The following morning, she was led to the scaffold. She used her final moments to defiantly proclaim to her executors:

> I came to keep blood-guiltiness from you, desiring you to repeal the unrighteous and unjust law of banishment upon pain of death, made against the innocent servants of the Lord, therefore my blood will be required at your hands who wilfully do it; but for those that do it in the simplicity of their hearts, I do desire the Lord to forgive them. I came to do the will of my Father, and in obedience to his will I stand even to the death.[2]

There would be no last-minute reprieve.

Another Quaker had successfully achieved martyrdom.

Notes

Introduction
1. Andrew Fincham, 'Faith in Numbers—Re-quantifying the English Quaker Population during the Long Eighteenth Century', *Religions* 10, 83 (2019), 2.

Chapter 1: Prelude: The Road to War
1. Sir Barnabas Scudamore, *A Letter Sent to the Right Honourable the Lord Digby from Sir Barnabas Scudamore Governor of Hereford, Concerning the late Siedge of the Citty of Hereford* (Oxford: Leonard Litchfield, 1645), p. 3.
2. For details see Peter R. Pick, 'Interjections of Silence: The Poetics and Politics of Radical Protestant Writing, 1642–1660', University of Birmingham, Ph.D. thesis, 2000.
3. W.J. Sheils, 'Catholicism in England from the Reformation to the Relief Acts', in Sheridan Gilley and W.J. Sheils (eds.), *A History of Religion in Britain: Practice and Belief from Pre-Roman Times to the Present* (Oxford: Blackwell, 1994), p. 245.
4. Michael Questier, 'Catholic Loyalism in Early Stuart England', *English Historical Review*, 123, 504 (2008), 1143.
5. LPL, MSS., 943, Papers of William Laud and Others: Articles for the Visitation of Gloucester Cathedral 1635, pp. 447–50.
6. Michael Braddick, *God's Fury, England's Fire: A New History of the English Civil Wars* (London: Penguin, 2009), p. 72
7. Calvin Lane, *The Laudians and the Elizabethan Church: History, Conformity, and Religious Identity in Post-Reformation England* (London: Routledge, 2016), p. 1. The phrase 'beauty of holiness' comes from Psalms 29:2 – 'Give unto the Lord the glory due his name; worship the Lord in the beauty of holiness' and Psalms 96:9 'O worship the Lord in the beauty of holiness: fear before him, all the earth'.
8. Anon., *Articles to Be Inquired in the Metropolitical Visitation*, p. 2.
9. Ian Atherton, 'Viscount Scudamore's "Laudianism": The Religious Practices of the First Viscount Scudamore', *Historical Journal*, 34, 3 (1991), 585; George William Outram Addleshaw and Frederick Etchells, *The Architectural Setting of Anglican Worship* (London: Faber, 1948), p. 129.
10. HL, PO, JO, 10, 140, Main Papers: Archbishop Laud's Visitation (Worcester), 1635.
11. Jacqueline Eales, *Puritans and Roundheads* (Glasgow: Hardinge Simpole, 2002), p. 12.
12. Eales, *Puritans and Roundheads*, pp. 104, 110.
13. Norah Carlin, *The Causes of the English Civil War* (Oxford: Wiley-Blackwell, 1998), p. 67.
14. Jared van Duinen, '"An Engine Which the World Sees Nothing of": Revealing Dissent Under Charles I's "Personal Rule"', *Parergon*, 28, 1 (2011), 177–8.
15. See Henrick Langelüdecke, '"I Finde All Men & My Officers All Soe Unwilling": The Collection of Ship Money, 1635–1640', *Journal of British Studies*, 46, 3 (2007), 509–42.

16. Langelüdecke, 'I Finde All Men & My Officers All Soe Unwilling', 509.
17. Carlin, *Causes of the English Civil War*, p. 183.
18. Langelüdecke, 'I Finde All Men & My Officers All Soe Unwilling', 509.
19. Carlin, *Causes of the English Civil War*, p. 101.
20. Eales, *Puritans and Roundheads*, p. 87.
21. Langelüdecke, 'I Finde All Men & My Officers All Soe Unwilling', 533–41.
22. Sarah Waureghen, 'Covenanter Propaganda and Conceptualizations of the Public During the Bishops Wars, 1638–1640', *Historical Journal*, 52, 1 (2009), 65.
23. Waureghen, 'Covenanter Propaganda and Conceptualizations of the Public During the Bishops Wars', 66–7.
24. Kevin Sharpe, *The Personal Rule of Charles I* (New Haven: Yale University Press, 1992), p. 815.
25. Mark Charles Fissel, *The Bishops' Wars: Charles I's Campaigns Against Scotland, 1638–1640* (Cambridge: Cambridge University Press, 1994), p. 1.
26. Eales, *Puritans and Roundheads*, p. 114.
27. Anne Whiteman, 'The Protestation Returns of 1641–1642: Part I, The General Organisation', *Local Population Studies*, 55 (1995), 14.
28. Braddick, *God's Fury England's Fire*, p. 201.
29. John Whiteway, 'An Account of the Siege of Brampton Bryan Castle', *Archaeologia Cambrensis*, 10, 39 (1864), 233.
30. Gardiner (ed.), *Constitutional Documents of the Puritan Revolution*, p. 156.
31. Cressy, 'The Protestation Protested', 251–79.
32. Gardiner (ed.), *Constitutional Documents of the Puritan Revolution*, p. 156.
33. Cressy, 'The Protestation Protested', 251.
34. Braddick, *God's Fury England's Fire*, p. 144.
35. Eales, *Puritans and Roundheads*, p. 115.
36. *Mercurius Britanicus, Communicating the Affaires of Great Britaine for the Better Information of the People Issue*, 42, 1–8 July 1644, p. 334.
37. Fletcher, *Outbreak of the English Civil War*, pp. 83–4.
38. Cressy, 'The Protestation Protested', 278.
39. Whiteman, 'The Protestation Returns: Part I', 15.
40. Whiteman, 'The Protestation Returns: Part I', 14.
41. Whiteman, 'Protestation Returns: Part I', 17.
42. Whiteman, 'Protestation Returns: Part I', 20–1.
43. John Walter, *Covenanting Citizens: The Protestation Oath and Popular Political Culture in the English Revolution* (Oxford: Oxford University Press, 2016), p. 105.
44. Cressy, 'The Protestation Protested', 278.
45. Cressy, 'The Protestation Protested', 251–2.
46. Sir Thomas Aston, *A Collection of Sundry Petitions Presented to the Kings Most Excellent Majesty as Also, to the Two Most Honourable Houses, Now Assembled in Parliament, and Others Already Signed, By Most of the Gentry, Ministers and Freeholders of Several Counties* (Walter Davis: London, 1681), pp. 15–16.
47. Fletcher, *Outbreak of the English Civil War*, pp. 305–306.
48. Aston, *A Collection of Sundry Petitions*, frontispiece.
49. Aston, *A Collection of Sundry Petitions*, p. 16.
50. John Willis Bund, *Diary of Henry Townshend of Elmley Lovett, 1640–1663, Volume 2*, London: Mitchell Hughes and Clarke, 1920), II, p. 538.

51. Atherton, 'Viscount Scudamore's "Laudianism"', 589.
52. Bund, *Diary of Henry Townshend of Elmley Lovett, 1640–1663, Volume 2*, p. 539.
53. John Willis Bund, *The Civil War in Worcestershire, 1642–1646 and the Scotch Invasion of 1651* (Birmingham: Midland Educational Company, 1905), p. 123.
54. WRO, 1, 1, 79, 6, Quarter Sessions Rolls, 19 April 1642.
55. Sarah L. Bastow, '"Worth Nothing, But Very Wilful": Catholic Recusant Women of Yorkshire, 1536–1642', *Recusant History*, 25, 4 (2001), 599, 601.
56. Carlin, *Causes of the English Civil War*, p. 38.

Chapter 2: Misery, Total Ruin, Poor, Almost Wasted Kingdom

1. Bond (ed.), *Chamber Order Book of Worcester*, p. 354.
2. Bond (ed.), *Chamber Order Book of Worcester*, p. 355.
3. WRO, 1, 1, 79, 10, Quarter Sessions 1642 [fragment]. One of the contributors is Thomas Cartwright. The document does not identify where Cartwright lives in the county, so it is impossible to conclude that this is Thomas Cartwright, early Quaker of Bengeworth.
4. John Wroughton, *An Unhappy Civil War: The Experiences of Ordinary People in Gloucestershire, Somerset and Wiltshire, 1642–1646* (Bath: Lansdowne Press, 1999), p. 66.
5. Fletcher, *Outbreak of the English Civil War*, p. 356.
6. Judith M. Spicksley, *The Business and Household Accounts of Joyce Jeffreys, Spinster of Hereford, 1638–1648* (Oxford: Oxford University Press, 2012).
7. John Webb, 'Some Passages in the Life and Character of a Lady Resident in Herefordshire and Worcestershire during the Civil War', *Archaeologia: or Miscellaneous Tracts Relating to Antiquity*, 37 (1857), 206.
8. 'Charles I – volume 492: October 1642', in *Calendar of State Papers Domestic: Charles I, 1641–3*, ed. William Douglas Hamilton (London, 1887), pp. 398–400. *British History Online* http://www.british- history.ac.uk/cal-state-papers/domestic/chas1/1641-3/ pp. 398–403 [accessed 21 February 2021].
9. Thomas Kittermaster, *A Wonderfull Deliverance or Gods Abundant Mercy in Preserving from the Cavaliers the Towne of Draiton in the County of Hereford* (London: Printed by T.F. for I.H., 20 October 1642), frontispiece.
10. Kittermaster, *Wonderfull Deliverance*, p. 2.
11. Eales, *Puritans and Roundheads*, p. 125.
12. Kittermaster, *Wonderfull Deliverance*, p. 4.
13. John Nicholls (ed.), 'Letters of Lady Brilliana Harley', *Gentleman's Magazine and Historical Review* (July 1856 – May 1868), 474–5.
14. Whiteway, 'Account of the Siege', 236.
15. Whiteway, 'Account of the Siege', 236–7.
16. Braddick, *God's Fury England's Fire*, p. 393.
17. Wroughton, *An Unhappy Civil War*, p. 1.
18. William Bowen, *A Perfect and True Relation of the Great and Bloudy Skirmish Fought Before the City of Worcester* (London: Jo. Thomas, 1642), p. 7.
19. Mark Stoyle, *Soldiers and Strangers: An Ethnic History of the English Civil War* (New Haven: Yale University Press, 2008), p. 29.
20. Bund (ed.), *Diary of Henry Townshend*, p. 87.
21. Wroughton, *An Unhappy Civil War*, p. 151.

22. William Sheils, 'English Catholics at War and Peace', in Christopher Durston and Judith Maltby (eds.), *Religion in Revolutionary England* (Manchester: Manchester University Press, 2007), p. 140.
23. 'Charles I – vol. 459: July 1–13, 1640', in William Douglas Hamilton (ed.), *Calendar of State Papers Domestic: Charles I, 1640* (London, HMSO, 1880), pp. 434–74. British History Online http://www.british-history.ac.uk/cal-state-papers/domestic/chas1/1640/pp434-474 [accessed 25 May 2021]; Eales, *Puritans and* Roundheads, p. 97.
24. NA, SP, 16, 492, 321, 87, Nehemiah Wharton to George Willingham, 7 October 1642; Charles Carlton, *Going to the Wars: The Experiences of the British Civil Wars, 1638–1651* (London: Routledge, 1992), p. 82.
25. '5 December 1642 [Earl of Stamford's Letter, about securing the Papists]', *Journal of the House of Lords: Volume 5, 1642–1643* (London: HMSO, 1767–1830), 475. British History Online http://www.british-history.ac.uk/lords-jrnl/vol5/pp475-476 [accessed 11 May 2015].
26. Henry Ellis, 'Letters from a Subaltern Officer of the Earl of Essex's Army, Written in the Summer and Autumn of 1642', *Archaeologia*, 35, 2 (1854), 328, 330.
27. Eales, *Puritans and Roundheads*, p. 168.
28. Wroughton, *An Unhappy Civil War*, p. 33.
29. Eales, *Puritans and Roundheads*, pp. 156, 160.
30. Wroughton, *An Unhappy Civil War*, pp. 36, 45.
31. Wroughton, *An Unhappy Civil War*, p. 44.
32. WRO, 1, 1, 79, 4, Quarter Sessions Rolls: Presentment by the Great Inquest 11 April 1643.
33. Anon., *Foure Ordinances of the Lords and Commons Assembled in Parliament* (London, s.n., 1644), p. 2.
34. Scudamore, *A Letter Sent to the Right Honourable the Lord Digby*, p. 8.
35. HRO, AD30, 216, Personal Records/Transcripts Volume 1588–1823.
36. William Sheils, 'English Catholics at War and Peace', in Durston and Maltby (eds.), *Religion in Revolutionary England*, p. 139.
37. Wroughton, *An Unhappy Civil War*, pp. 22–33.
38. David Underdown, 'The Chalk and the Cheese: Contrasts among the English Clubmen', *Past & Present*, 85 (1979), 27.
39. Braddick, *God's Fury England's Fire*, p. 418.
40. Andy Wood, *Riot, Rebellion and Popular Politics in Early Modern England* (London: Palgrave, 2001), p. 145.
41. Braddick, *God's Fury England's Fire*, p. 421.
42. Bund, *Diary of Henry Townshend of Elmley Lovett, 1640–1663, Volume 2*, p. 227; Carlton, *Going to the Wars*, p. 294.
43. Carlton, *Going to the Wars*, p. 295.
44. Braddick, *God's Fury England's Fire*, p. 421.
45. Braddick, *God's Fury England's Fire*, p. 417.
46. Wood, *Riot, Rebellion and Popular Politics in Early Modern England*, p. 150.
47. Wroughton, *An Unhappy Civil War*, pp. 109, 126.
48. HRO, BG11, 17, 5, 46. Petition of Jane Merrick, who was injured while working to move earth for the defences of Hereford when it was besieged by the Scots.
49. Alexander Leslie Earl of Leven, *A Declaration of His Excellency the Earl of Leven Concerning the Rising of the Scotish Army from the Seige [sic] of the City of Hereford* (London: s.n., 1645), pp. 1–2.

50. Keith Lindley and David Scott (eds.), *The Journal of Thomas Juxon, 1644–1647* (London: Cambridge University Press, 1999), p. 83.
51. Stoyle, *Soldiers and Strangers*, pp. 146–7.
52. Stoyle, *Soldiers and Strangers*, p. 208. See also John and T.W. Webb (eds.), *Memorials of the Civil War ... as it Affected Herefordshire* (London: Longmans, 1879), p. 393.
53. Fletcher, *Outbreak of the English Civil War*, p. 376.
54. Wroughton, *An Unhappy Civil War*, pp. 68, 104, 122.
55. Thomas Morgan and John Birch, *Severall Letters from Colonel Morgan Governour of Gloucester and Colonel Birch* (London: John Wright, 24 December 1645), p. 4.
56. Morgan and Birch, *Severall Letters from Colonel Morgan*, p. 3.
57. Anon., *Mercurius Belgicus: or, A briefe Chronologie of the Battails, Sieges, Conflicts, and Other Most Remarkable Passages from the Beginning of This Rebellion, to the 25 of March 1646* (s.l.: s.n., 1646), pp. 55–6.
58. Anon., *Mercurius Belgicus ... 25 March 1646*, frontispiece.
59. Eales, *Puritans and Roundheads*, p. 177.
60. Carlton, *Going to the Wars*, p. 87.
61. Scudamore, *Letter Sent to the Right Honourable the Lord Digby*, p. 5.
62. Thomas Morgan and John Birch, *Two Letters Sent to the Honorable W. Lenthall Esq Speaker to the Honorable House of Commons: Concerning the Taking of Hereford on the 18. of this Instant Decem. 1645* (London: Edward Husband, 22 December 1645), pp. 3–4.
63. Anon., *Mercurius Belgicus ... 25 March 1646*, p. 58.
64. Anon., *A Petition of the Justices of the Peace ... at the Quarter Sessions holden at Hereford for the Same County Presented to the Right Honorable House of Commons Assembled in Parliament, 25 January 1648* (London: Giles Calvert, 1648/9).
65. Anon., *Petition of the Justices of the Peace*, p. 8.
66. WRO, 899, 749, 8782, 42, H14, 7. Counterpart lease for forty-one years from John Tyas. This lease describes property that was 'burnt or pulled down in the late wars'; WRO, 899, 749, 8782, 16, C30, 6. Mortgage by Demise from John Blurton of Worcester City. This mortgage describes a premises 'destroyed in the late warrs' on Foregate Street; WRO, 716, 02, 2071, V, A note of damage done at the Cathedral during the Civil War.
67. WRO, 899, 749, 8782, 42, H14, 5. Lease and counterpart lease for forty-one years from Sir Daniel Tyas, Knight; WRO, 899, 749, 8782, 16, C30, 6.
68. Anon., *An Exact and Perfect Relation of Every Particular of the Fight at Worcester* (London: Francis Leach, 1651), p. 1.
69. Sir Robert Stapylton, *A More Full Relation of the Great Victory Obtained by Our Forces near Worcester* (London: s.n., 1651), pp. 2–3.
70. Oliver Cromwell, *A Letter from the Lord General Cromwel, Dated September the Fourth, 1651 ... Touching the Taking of the City of Worcester and the Total Routing of the Enemies Army* (London: John Field, 1651), p. 7.
71. John Nickolls (ed.), *Original Letters and Papers of State, Addressed to Oliver Cromwell; Concerning the Affairs of Great Britain* (London: William Bowyer, 1743), p. 92.
72. Anon., *Exact and Perfect Relation*, p. 2.

Chapter 3: The Sparks of Radical Faith

1. Kate Peters, *Print Culture and the Early Quakers* (Cambridge: Cambridge University Press, 2005), p. 1.

2. Eales, *Puritans and Roundheads*, p. 7.
3. Christopher Hill, *The World Turned Upside Down: Radical Ideas During the English Revolution* (London: Penguin, 1991), p. 85.
4. Anon., *Tub-Preachers Overturn'd or Independency to be Abandon'd and Abhor'd as Destructive to the Majestracy and Ministery, of the Church and Common-Wealth of England* (London: *s.n.*, 1647).
5. Anon., *Tub-Preachers Overturn'd*, frontispiece.
6. Cressy, 'Revolutionary England', 71.
7. Braddick, *God's Fury England's Fire*, p. 436.
8. Arthur Leslie Morton, *The World of the Ranters: Religious Radicalism in the English Revolution* (London: Lawrence and Wishart, 1970), p. 14.
9. Carlin, *Causes of the English Civil War*, p. 48.
10. Bradstock, *Radical Religion in Cromwell's England*, p. 22; Michael Watts, *The Dissenters: From the Reformation to the French Revolution* (Oxford: Oxford University Press, 1985), p. 205.
11. Atherton, 'Viscount Scudamore's "Laudianism"', pp. 567–96.
12. Claire Cross, 'The Church in England 1646–1660', in G.E. Alymer (ed.), *The Interregnum: The Quest for Settlement, 1646–60* (London: Palgrave Macmillan, 1974), p. 112.
13. Cross, 'The Church in England, 1646–1660', p. 112.
14. Morton, *World of the Ranters*, p. 14.
15. Morton, *World of the Ranters*, p. 70.
16. Bernard Capp, 'The Fifth Monarchists and Popular Millenarianism', in J.F. Macgregor and Barry Reay (eds.), *Radical Religion in the English Revolution* (New York: Oxford University Press, 1984), p. 170.
17. Capp, 'The Fifth Monarchists and Popular Millenarianism', p. 170.
18. Bradstock, *Radical Religion in Cromwell's England*, p. 129.
19. Bradstock, *Radical Religion in Cromwell's England*, p. 130.
20. Bernard Capp, 'Extreme Millenarianism', in Peter Toon (ed.), *Puritans, the Millennium and the Future of Israel: Puritan Eschatology, 1600 to 1660* (London: James Clark & Co., 1970), p. 68.
21. Lilburne became a convert to Quakerism before his death in 1657.
22. M. Everett Green (ed.), *Calendar of State Papers, Domestic Series, [Commonwealth] 1649–1660, Preserved in the State Paper Department of Her Majesty's Public Record Office. Vol. 3: Jan–Oct 1651* (London: Longman & Co., [April 21] 1651), p. 514 http://go.galegroup.com/mss/i.do?&id=GALE%7CMC4326301667&v=2.1&u=tlem ea_spoa&it=r&p=SPOL&s w=w&viewtype=Calendar [accessed 17 December 2013].
23. Green (ed.), *Calendar of State Papers, Vol. 3*, p. 514; Nickolls (ed.), *Original Letters and Papers of State*, p. 92.
24. Nickolls (ed.), *Original Letters and Papers of State*, p. 92.

Chapter 4: A Plague of Northern Locusts
1. Michael Watts, *The Dissenters: From the Reformation to the French Revolution* (Oxford: Oxford University Press, 1985), p. 285.
2. Christopher Hill, *The World Turned Upside Down: Radical Ideas During the English Revolution* (London: Penguin, 1991), p. 95.

3. Leo Damrosch, *The Sorrows of the Quaker Jesus: James Nayler and the Puritan Crackdown on the Free Spirit* (Cambridge: Harvard University Press, 1996), p. 27.
4. Watts, *The Dissenters*, p. 193.
5. Watts, *The Dissenters*, p. 188.
6. John Spurr, 'From Puritanism to Dissent', in Christopher Durston and Jacqueline Eales (eds.), *The Culture of English Puritanism, 1560–1700* (London: Palgrave, 1996), p. 240.
7. Adrian Davies, *The Quakers in English Society, 1655–1725* (Oxford: Oxford University Press, 2000), p. 155.
8. H. Larry Ingle, *First Among Friends: George Fox and the Creation of Quakerism* (Oxford: Oxford University Press, 1994), p. 57.
9. Rosemary Moore, *The Light in Their Consciences: Early Quakers in Britain, 1646–1666* (rev. edn., University Park: Penn State Press, 2020), pp. 54, 71. Also, see Hugh Barbour and Arthur Roberts (eds.), *Early Quaker Writings* (Grand Rapids, MI: Eerdmans, 1973), p. 22; Kate Peters, *Print Culture and the Early Quakers* (Cambridge: Cambridge University Press, 2005), p. 2; Watts, *The Dissenters*, p. 196.
10. Nigel Smith (ed.), *George Fox: The Journal* (London: Penguin, 1998), pp. 10–11.
11. Rosemary Moore, 'The Early Development of Quakerism', in Richard C. Allen and Rosemary Moore, *The Quakers, 1656–1723: The Evolution of an Alternative Community* (University Park: Pennsylvania State University Press, 2018), pp. 11–12; Moore, *Light in Their Consciences*, pp. 82–3.
12. LSF, Swarthmore MSS., VII, 128, George Fox, A paper to be re[a]d among fr[i]ends at wo[rce]ster, undated.
13. Smith (ed.), *Journal*, pp. xxxix–xl.
14. Moore, *Light in Their Consciences*, p. 14.
15. William C. Braithwaite, *The Beginnings of Quakerism* (London: Macmillan, 1923), p. 141.
16. LSF, Swarthmore MSS., VI, 36, George Fox Epistle to the Flock of God, 1654.
17. Moore, *Light in Their Consciences*, p. 23.
18. Moore, *Light in Their Consciences*, p. 25.
19. LSF, Swarthmore MSS., I, 253, George Taylor and Thomas Willam to Margaret Fell, Kendal, 1655.
20. LSF, Swarthmore MSS., I, 250, George Taylor to Margaret Fell, Kendal, 1655.
21. Moore, *Light in Their Consciences*, p. 141.
22. Norman Penney (ed.), *The First Publishers of Truth: Being Early Records of The Introduction of Quakerism into The Counties of England and Wales* (London: Headley Brothers, 1907), p. 276.
23. Moore, *Light in Their Consciences*, pp. 74–6.
24. Alexandra Walsham, *Charitable Hatred: Tolerance and Intolerance in England, 1500–1700* (Manchester: Manchester University Press, 2009), p. 142; Barry Reay, 'Popular Hostility Towards Quakers in Mid-Seventeenth-Century England', *Social History*, 5, 3 (1980), 392; Martin Wyatt, *Quakers in Plymouth: A Friends' Meeting in Context, 1654 to the 1960s* (York: Quacks Books, 2017), p. 4.
25. Kay Taylor, 'Chalk, Cheese, and Cloth: The Settling of Quaker Communities in Seventeenth-Century Wiltshire', *Quaker Studies*, 10, 2 (2006), 169.
26. Richard Farnworth, *A Discovery of Truth and Falsehood* (London: Giles Calvert, 1653), frontispiece.

27. Richard Farnworth, *Light Risen out of Darkness* (London: Giles Calvert, 1654), frontispiece.
28. Andrew Bradstock, *Radical Religion in Cromwell's England* (London: I.B. Tauris, 2011), p. xvi.
29. Bradstock, *Radical Religion in Cromwell's England*, p. 103.
30. See Richard Farnworth, *A Discovery of Truth and Falsehood*, frontispiece; *A Brief Discovery of the Kingdome of Antichrist and the Downfall of it Hasteth Greatly. With a Difference Betwixt the Ordinances of Christ and of Antichrist* (London: s.n., 1653), frontispiece; *England's Warning Peece Gone Forth* (London: Tho. Wayte, 1653), frontispiece; *Light Risen out of Darkness*, frontispiece; *A Woman Forbidden to Speak in the Church the Grounds Examined, the Mystery Opened, the Truth Cleared, and the Ignorance Both of Priests and People Discovered* (London: Giles Calvert, 1654); frontispiece; and *Call Out of False Worships* (London: s.n., 1653), frontispiece.
31. Richard C. Allen, *Quaker Communities in Early Modern Wales: From Resistance to Respectability* (Cardiff: University of Wales, 2007), p. 4
32. Richard Bauman, 'Aspects of 17th Century Quaker Rhetoric', *Quarterly Journal of Speech*, 56 (1970), 69.
33. Swarthmore MSS., II, 55, Richard Farnworth to George Fox, Bromyard, Herefordshire, 26 April 1654.
34. Swarthmore MSS., III, 57, Richard Farnsworth to George Fox, Tewkesbury, Gloucestershire, 7 May 1654.
35. LSF, Swarthmore MSS., II, 55.
36. Penney (ed.), *First Publishers of Truth*, pp. 274–5.
37. LSF, Swarthmore MSS., III, 57.
38. LSF, Swarthmore MSS, II, 55.
39. Penney (ed.), *First Publishers of Truth*, p. xiii.
40. Moore, *Light in Their Consciences*, p. 14; Smith (ed.), *Journal*, pp. 140, 205.
41. Thomas Airey (also spelled Ayrey). See LSF, MSS. Box., P2, 15. 'The Journal of John Audland, 1654', in 'Letters of John Audland, 1653', pp. 32–4.
42. Richard T. Vann, *The Social Development of English Quakerism, 1655–1755* (Cambridge, Mass: Harvard University Press, 1969), p. 9.
43. Smith (ed.), *Journal*, p. 224.
44. £100 in 1655 is equal to approximately £22,570 in 2024. Bank of England Inflation Calculator. https://www.bankofengland.co.uk/monetary-policy/inflation/inflation-calculator [accessed 1 October 2024].
45. Smith (ed.), *Journal*, p. 224.
46. Penney (ed.), *First Publishers of Truth*, p. 124.
47. LSF, Portfolio MSS., 17, 3, James Merrick of Ross, a faithful servant and minister of Christ, and a sufferer for his name and of a good report among all men that feare God who finished his testimony in London.
48. Penney (ed.), *First Publishers of Truth*, p. 124.
49. Penney (ed.), *First Publishers of Truth*, p. 117.
50. Ingle, *First Among Friends*, p. 61.
51. LSF, Swarthmore MSS., II, 55.
52. LSF, Swarthmore MSS., II, 48, Richard Farnworth to Margaret Fell, Badsley, Warwickshire, 16 May 1654.

53. Richard Bailey, *New Light on George Fox and Early Quakerism* (San Francisco: Edwin Mellen Press, 1992), p. 126.
54. LSF, Swarthmore MSS., I, 231, Daniel Baker to George Fox, Worcester, 17 February 1664.
55. LSF, Swarthmore MSS., I, 238, Daniel Baker to George Fox, Worcester, 11 March 1664.
56. Moore, *Light in Their Consciences*, p. 79.
57. Ingle, *First Among Friends*, p. 89.
58. Daniel Baker, *Yet One Warning More, To Thee O England* (London: Robert Wilson, 1660), p. 8.
59. LSF, Swarthmore MSS., I, 231.

Chapter 5: An Organised Grassroots Effort

1. Joseph Besse, *A Collection of the Sufferings of the People Called Quakers Vol. I* (2 vols. London: L. Hinde, 1753), p. 145.
2. Joseph Besse, *A Collection of the Sufferings of the People Called Quakers Vol. II* (2 vols. London: L. Hinde, 1753), p. 766.
3. LSF, Portfolio MSS., 1, 45. Edward Bourne to King Charles II, Hereford Prison, 4 July 1664.
4. Samuel Pepys, *The Diary of Samuel Pepys: A Selection* (London: Penguin, 2003), p. 519.
5. Morgan Watkins, 'Letter from Morgan Watkins to Mary Penington, 18 August 1665', in Abram Rawlinson Barclay (ed.), *Letters & c. of Early Friends: Illustrative of the History of the Society from Nearly its Origin to About the Period of George Fox's Decease* (London: Harvey and Darton, 1841), p. 149.
6. Penney (ed.), *First Publishers of Truth*, pp. 114, 115, 124.
7. Penney (ed.), *First Publishers of Truth*, pp. 113, 121.
8. Penney (ed.), *First Publishers of Truth*, pp. 276–7.
9. Besse, *Sufferings*, II, pp. 62–3.
10. Besse, *Sufferings*, II, p. 71.
11. Moore, *Light in Their Consciences*, p. 229.
12. Moore, *Light in Their Consciences*, pp. 131, 229.
13. WRO, BA, 1303.
14. Davies, *Quakers in English Society*, p. 203.
15. Ilana Krausman Ben-Amos, 'Gifts and Favors: Informal Support in Early Modern England', *Journal of Modern History*, 72, 2 (June 2000), 337.
16. WRO, BA, 1303, 29 May 1665; WRO, BA, 1303, November 1665; WRO, BA, 1303, 21 November 1667; WRO, BA, 1303, 26 February 1668.
17. WRO, BA, 1303, 27 December 1670.
18. WRO, BA, 1303, 5 January 1675.
19. Laura Brace, *The Idea of Property in Seventeenth-Century England* (Manchester: Manchester University Press, 1998), p. 145.
20. WRO, BA, 1303, 4 March 1676, 23 May 1677.
21. NA, PROB. 11, 357, The Will of James Merrick, 1678.
22. WRO, BA, 1303, 13 July 1686.
23. WRO, BA, 1303, 28 December 1686.
24. WRO, BA, 1303, 29 March 1687.

25. For details see Nabil Matar, 'The Barbary Corsairs, King Charles I and the Civil War', *Seventeenth Century* 16, 2 (2001), 239.
26. Beatrice Saxon Snell (ed.), *The Minute Book of the Monthly Meeting of the Society of Friends for the Upperside of Buckinghamshire, 1669–1690* (High Wycombe: Hague & Gill, 1937), p. 75; Stephen C. Morland (ed.), *Somersetshire Quarterly Meeting, 1668–1699* (Surrey: Gresham Press, 1978), pp. 15–16, 105.
27. NA, PROB, 11, 357.
28. NA, PROB, 11, 357.
29. Isabel Southall, *Memorials of The Prichards of Almeley* (Birmingham: Privately Printed, 1893), p. 14.
30. NA, RG, 6, 1375. Monthly Minutes of Evesham and Alcester, 1648–1778; T.J.S. Bayliss, *Evesham Inns and Signs* (Evesham: Vale of Evesham Historical Society, 2008), p. 149.
31. George May, *A Descriptive History of the Town of Evesham, from the Foundation of Its Saxon Monastery, With Notices Respecting the Ancient Deanery of Its Vale* (London: Whittaker & Co., 1845), pp. 202–203.
32. Penney (ed.), *First Publishers of Truth*, p. 122.
33. In 1701, Bourne left land adjacent to his home on Sansome Walk, near Foregate Street, in Worcester for the construction of a meeting house, see John Noake, *Worcester Sects; Or, A History of the Roman Catholics and Dissenters of Worcester* (London: Longman, 1861), p. 256.
34. WRO, BA, 1303, 26 December 1682.
35. Penney (ed.), *First Publishers of Truth*, p. 113.
36. WRO, BA, 1303, 30 September 1684.
37. There are no extant minutes for the Leominster Monthly Meeting from until 1769.
38. George Fox, *A Collection of Many Select and Christian Epistles, Letters and Testimonies Written on Sundry Occasions, by That Ancient, Eminent, Faithful Friend and Minister of Christ Jesus, George Fox; The Second Volume* (London: T. Sowle, 1698), p. 291.
39. Gwynne Stock, 'Quaker Burial: Doctrine and Practice', in Margaret Cox (ed.), *Grave Concerns: Death and Burial in England, 1700–1850* (York: Council for British Archaeology, 1998), p. 129.
40. HRO, AS4, Register of Births, Marriages and Burials of Friends at Ross, Hereford, Leominster, and Bromyard, 1646–1845.
41. Besse, *Sufferings*, I, p. 255.
42. David Cressy, *Birth, Marriage & Death: Ritual, Religion, and the Life-Cycle in Tudor and Stuart England* (Oxford: Oxford University Press, 1999), pp. 417–18.
43. HRO, BD100, 37, Bargain and Sale Bargain and Sale (1) Henry Bedford sen. of Leominster, glover (2) Peter Young of Luston, farmer, Morgan Watkins of Hatfield, Thomas Holte of Stoke Prior [no occupation listed], Thomas Bach of Eyton, yeoman, Hugh Powle senior of Hide, Leominster, yeoman, and Charles Barnett of Leominster, baker, 1660.
44. NA, PROB. 11, 357.
45. WRO, BA, 1303, 7 January 1673.
46. Similarly, the Bristol Men's Meeting in February 1671 advised against the placement of gravestones at the Redcliffe burial ground. See Russell S. Mortimer (ed.), *Minute Book of the Men's Meeting of the Society of Friends in Bristol, 1667–1686* (Gateshead: Northumberland Press Ltd., 1971), pp. 40–1.
47. WRO, 892.2, 1303, 9, 19 December 1675.

48. WRO, 892.2, 1303, 9, 21 October 1679.
49. WRO, 892.2, 1303, 9, 17 September 1680.
50. WRO, 892.2, 1303, 9, 21 November 1680.
51. WRO, 892.2, 1303, 9, 19 December 1680.
52. Cressy, *Birth, Marriage & Death*, p. 332.
53. Moore, *Light in Their Consciences*, p. 138.
54. Russell S, Mortimer, 'Quakerism in Seventeenth Century Bristol', University of Bristol, MA thesis, 1946, p. 190.
55. Richard C. Allen, 'Living as a Quaker During the Second Period', in Richard C. Allen and Rosemary Moore, *The Quakers, 1656–1723: The Evolution of an Alternative Community* (University Park: Pennsylvania State University Press, 2018), p. 79.
56. Jack Wood, *Some Rural Quakers* (York: William Sessions Limited, 1991), p. 63.
57. WRO, 1303, 2, 20. Marriage certificate of Jonah Cater and Sarah Browne, 3 May 1686.
58. WRO, 892.2, 1303, 9, 20 March 1680.
59. WRO, 892.2, 1303, 9, 17 September 1681.
60. As was typical in the meeting records, actionable requests were not mentioned again in the meeting minutes.
61. NA, PROB, 11, 357; NA, RG, 6, 1343, General Register Office: Society of Friends' Registers, Notes and Certificates of Births, Marriages and Burials.
62. WRO, 892.2, 1303, 9, 23 June 1686.
63. Southall, *Memorials of The Prichards*, p. 19.
64. WRO, 892.2, 1303, 9, 18 December 1677.
65. Erin Bell, 'The Early Quakers, the Peace Testimony and Masculinity in England, 1660–1720', *Gender & History*, 23, 2 (2011), 287. Also, see Elizabeth A. Foyster, 'Male Honour, Social Control and Wife Beating in Late Stuart England', *Transactions of the Royal Historical Society 6th Series*, 6 (1996), 215–24; Anne Laurence, *Women in England, 1500–1760: A Social History* (London: Weidenfeld and Nicolson, 1996), p. 236.
66. Rosemary Moore, 'The Early Development of Quakerism', in Allen and Moore, *The Quakers, 1656–1723*, p. 17.
67. Moore, *Light in Their Consciences*, p. 139.
68. WRO, BA, 1303, 21 November 1667.
69. Mortimer, 'Quakerism in Seventeenth Century Bristol', p. 181.
70. Mortimer, 'Quakerism in Seventeenth Century Bristol', p. 165.
71. WRO, 892.2, 1303, 9, 17 October 1675, 18 September 1693.
72. WRO, 892.2, 1303, 9, 20 May 1688.
73. Mortimer, 'Quakerism in Seventeenth Century Bristol', p. 170.
74. Rhys Jenkins, 'Industries of Hereford in Bygone Times', *Transactions of the Newcomen Society*, 17 (1936), 6.
75. Edward Anthony Wrigley and Roger S. Schofield, *The Population History of England, 1541–1871* (Cambridge: Cambridge University Press, 1989), pp. 303–304.
76. Davies, *Quakers in English Society*, p. 207.
77. NA, PROB. 11, 359, The Will of Roger Prichard, Almeley, 1 March 1678.
78. NA, PROB, 11, 35, The Will of David Jones, Ross, 20 April 1676.
79. Davies, *Quakers in English Society*, p. 194.
80. NA, PROB, 11, 351.
81. Davies, *Quakers in English Society*, p. 195.

82. NA, PROB, 11, 357.
83. Davies, *Quakers in English Society*, p. 200.
84. NA, PROB, 11, 357.
85. WRO, BA, 1303, 4 July 1676.
86. WRO, 892.2, 1303, 9, 16 April 1678.
87. Mortimer, 'Quakerism in Seventeenth Century Bristol', p. 163.
88. Mary Forster, *These Several Papers Was Sent to the Parliament the Twentieth Day of the Fifth Moneth, 1659. Being Above Seven Thousand of the Names of the Hand-maids and Daughters of the Lord* ... (London: Mary Westwood, 1659), frontispiece; Mary Garman, *Hidden in Plain Sight: Quaker Women's Writings, 1650–1700* (Wallingford, PA: Pendle Hill Publications, 1996), p. 58.
89. Stephen Kent, '"Hand-Maids and Daughters of the Lord": Quaker Women, Quaker Families, and Somerset's Anti-Tithe Petition in 1659', *Quaker History*, 97, 1 (2008), 48.
90. Kent, 'Hand-Maids and Daughters of the Lord', 48.
91. Joseph Walton, *Incidents Illustrating the Doctrines and History of the Society of Friends* (Philadelphia: William H. Pile's Sons, 1897), pp. 380–1.
92. Thomas Wagstaff, *Piety Promoted in Brief Memorials and Dying Expressions of Some of the People Called Quakers* (9th part, 2nd edn., London: James Phillips & Son, 1798), p. 12.
93. Patricia Griffith, 'Early Quakers in Cornwall 1656–1750', University of Exeter, Ph.D. thesis, 2004; GA, DSF, 29, transcript.
94. Taylor, 'Chalk, Cheese, and Cloth: The Settling of Quaker Communities in Seventeenth-Century Wiltshire', 165.
95. NA, PROB, 11, 359.
96. NA, PROB, 11, 357.
97. Christine Trevett (ed.), *Women's Speaking Justified and Other Seventeenth Century Quaker Writings About Women* (London: Quaker Home Service, 1989), pp. 1–2.
98. Catherine M. Wilcox, *Theology and Women's Ministry in Seventeenth Century English Quakerism* (Lampeter: Edwin Mellen Press, 1995), pp. 236–7.
99. Trevett (ed.), *Women's Speaking Justified*, p. 3.
100. Caroline L. Leachman, 'From an "Unruly Sect" to a Society of "Strict Unity": The Development of Quakerism in England *c.*1650–1689', University College London: Ph.D. thesis, 1997, p. 105; Phyllis Mack, *Visionary Women: Ecstatic Prophecy in Seventeenth-Century England* (Berkeley, CA: University of California Press, 1992), p. 293.
101. LSF, Swarthmore MSS., V, 63, George Fox to the Women's Meetings, 5 October 1676.
102. Rosemary Moore, 'Gospel Order: The Development of Quaker Organization', in Allen and Moore, *The Quakers, 1656–1723*, p. 64.
103. Wilcox, *Theology and Women's Ministry*, p. 251.
104. LSF, Swarthmore MSS., V, 63.
105. George Fox, *The Woman Learning in Silence; or the Mystery of the Womans Subjection to Her Husband, Gospel Truth Demonstrated in a Collection of Doctrinal Books* (London: T. Sowle, 1656), p. 78.
106. LSF, Swarthmore MSS., V. 63.
107. LFS, MSS., 344, 159-60, John Penington Manuscripts Vol. 4.
108. Wilcox, *Theology and Women's Ministry*, p. 138.

109. Wilcox, *Theology and Women's Ministry*, p. 145.
110. Michele Lise Tarter and Catie Gill, *New Critical Studies on Early Quaker Women, 1650–1800* (Oxford: Oxford University Press, 2018), p. 3.
111. Allen, *Quaker Communities in Early Modern Wales*, p. 170.
112. Trevett, *Women and Quakerism in the Seventeenth Century*, pp. 130–1.
113. Hilary Hinds, *God's Englishwomen: Seventeenth-Century Radical Sectarian Writing and Feminist Criticism* (Manchester: Manchester University Press, 1996), pp. 1–2.
114. WRO, BA, 1303, April 1674.
115. Moore, 'Gospel Order', in Allen and Moore, *The Quakers, 1656–1723*, pp. 65, 68–71.
116. WRO, BA, 1303, 24 October 1676.
117. WRO, BA, 1303, 5 June 1681.
118. Jenkins, 'Industries of Hereford in Bygone Times', 185.
119. HRO, AM, 29, 1, Hearth Tax for Michaelmas 1665 for Herefordshire; Comparison with Militia Assessments 1663, Transcript by J. Harnden, 1984.
120. Davies, *Quakers in English Society*, p. 150.
121. Vann, *Social Development of English Quakerism*, p. 13.
122. HRO, BC, 9, 26, The Will of Edward Prichard, Almeley, 20 September 1725.
123. Humphrey Smith, *Man Driven Out of the Earth and Darkness by the Light, Life, and Mighty Hand of God* (London: s.n., 19 August 1658), p. 6.
124. Richard T. Vann, 'Literacy in Seventeenth-Century England: Some Hearth Tax Evidence', *Journal of Interdisciplinary History*, 5, 2 (1974), 287.
125. HRO, BC9. 9, Lease (release missing) (1) Edward Prichard of Almeley, glover and Elizabeth his wife, one of the daughters of Elizabeth, wife of Henry Wright of Shrewsbury, chapman. (2) Henry Lichfield of Little Eaton co. Derby, gent. Henry Wright of Shrewsbury and John Millington of Shrewsbury, baker, 7 June 1690. HRO, BC9, 10, Lease (1) Mary Prichard of Almeley, widow (2) Edward Prichard of Almeley, glover, her son and heir app, 7 January 1685.
126. Margaret Spufford, *The World of Rural Dissenters, 1520–1775* (Cambridge: Cambridge University Press, 1995), p. 64.
127. Richard C. Allen, 'Living as a Quaker During the Second Period', in Allen and Moore, *The Quakers 1656–1723*, p. 87.
128. WRO, 892.2, 1303, 9, 20 December 1678.
129. WRO, BA, 1303, 7 March 1673, 2 September 1673, 24 October 1676, 30 December 1684, 7 April 1685.
130. WRO, BA, 1303, 2 September 1673.
131. WRO, BA, 1303, 24 October 1676.

Chapter 6: Early Quakers and Their Fierce Opponents

1. LSF, GBS, II, Worcestershire, p. 1.
2. Charles Cherry, 'Enthusiasm and Madness: Anti-Quakerism in the Seventeenth Century', *Quaker History*, 73, 2 (1984), 11.
3. Nigel Gilbert, *A History of Kidderminster* (Chichester: Phillimore, 2004), p. 46.
4. William M. Lamont, *Richard Baxter and the Millennium* (Guildford: Biddles, 1979), p. 176.
5. Edward Burrough, *Many Strong Reasons Confounded, Which Would Hinder Any Reasonable Man from Being a Quaker* (London: Thomas Simmons, 1657), p. 1. The three tracts were *The Worcestershire Petition Defended*, *Quakers Catechism*, and *One Sheet Against the Quakers*.

6. James Nayler, *An Answer to a Book Called the Quakers Catechism, Put Out by Richard Baxter. Wherein the Slanderer is Searched, His Questions Answered, and His Deceit Discovered His Own Bosom* (London, s.n., 1656), p. 17; Richard Hubberthorne, *The Light of Christ Within Proved to be Sufficient to Lead unto God, In Answer to a Book Put Forth by John Tombes and Richard Baxter* (London: Thomas Simmons, 1660); R[ichard] F[arnworth], *A True Testimony Against the Popes Wayes, &c. In a Return to That Agreement of 42 of Those That Call Themselves Ministers of Christ (But Are Proved to Be Wrongers of Men and of Christ) in the County of Worcester, and Some Adjacent Parts* (London: Giles Calvert, 1656).
7. LSF, GBS, II, Worcestershire, p. 1.
8. Richard Baxter, 'Answer to the Quakers Queries', in Richard Baxter, *The Quakers Catechism* (London: Thomas Underhill, 1655), p. 3.
9. Baxter, 'Answer to the Quakers Queries', p. 3.
10. Baxter, *The Quakers Catechism*. Richard Farnworth also interrupted Baxter's service in Kidderminster in 1655 but was forcibly removed from the church and avoided imprisonment. See LSF, GBS, II, Worcestershire, p. 1.
11. LSF, GBS, II, Worcestershire, p. 1.
12. Baxter, *The Quakers Catechism*, frontispiece.
13. Baxter, 'Answer to the Quakers Queries', pp. 122–3.
14. Baxter, 'Answer to the Quakers Queries', p. 129.
15. Baxter, 'Answer to the Quakers Queries', pp. 135, 136.
16. Baxter, 'Answer to the Quakers Queries', pp. 124–5.
17. Baxter, 'Answer to the Quakers Queries', p. 142.
18. Baxter, 'Answer to the Quakers Queries', p. 144.
19. Richard Baxter, 'An Answer to a Young Unsettled Friend', in Baxter, *The Quakers Catechism*, p. 117.
20. Baxter, 'Answer to a Young Unsettled Friend', p. 118.
21. Baxter, 'Answer to a Young Unsettled Friend', p. 115.
22. Baxter, 'Answer to a Young Unsettled Friend', pp. 115–16.
23. Cherry, 'Enthusiasm and Madness', 13.
24. Rosemary Moore, *The Light in Their Consciences: Early Quakers in Britain, 1646–1666* (rev. edn., University Park: Penn State Press, 2020), pp. 21, 118.
25. Richard Farnworth, *The Ranters Principles and Deceits Discovered and Declared Against, Denied and Disowned by Us Whom the World calls Quakers* (London: Giles Calvert, 1654), frontispiece.
26. Ariel Hessayon, 'Early Quakerism and its Origins', in John Coffey (ed.), *The Oxford History of Protestant Dissenting Traditions: Volume I: The Post-Reformation Era, c.1559–c.1689* (Oxford: Oxford University Press, 2020), p. 145.
27. Baxter, 'Answer to a Young Unsettled Friend', pp. 114–15.
28. Baxter, 'Answer to a Young Unsettled Friend', p. 114.
29. Esmond Samuel de Beer (ed.), *The Diary of John Evelyn, Volume III: Kalendarium, 1650–1672* (Oxford: Oxford University Press, 2000), p. 179.
30. John Deacon, *The Grand Imposter Examined: or the Life, Tryal, and Examination of James Nayler* (London: Henry Brome, 1657), pp.33–4.
31. Deacon, *The Grand Imposter Examined*, pp. 37–8.
32. Ralph Farmer, *Satan Enthroned in his Chair of Pestilence* (London: Edward Thomas, 1657), p. 41.

33. Henry More, *A Collection of Several Philosophical Writings of Dr Henry More ... as namely, His Antidote Against Atheism, Appendix to the Said Antidote, Enthusiasmus Triumphatus* (London: James Flesher, 1662).
34. Henry More, 'A Brief Discourse of The Nature, Causes, Kindes, and Cures of Enthusiasm' in Henry More, *A Collection of the Several Philosophical Writings of Dr Henry More*, p. 1.
35. Cherry, 'Enthusiasm and Madness', 4.
36. Richard Blome, *The Fanatick History or An Exact Relation and Account of The Old Anabaptists and New Quakers* (London: J. Sims, 1660), frontispiece.
37. Blome, *The Fanatick History*, pp. 145–6.
38. Humphrey Smith, *Something Further Laid Open of the Cruel Persecution of the People Called Quakers by the Magistrates and People of Evesham* (London: s.n., 1656), p. 6.
39. Smith, *Something Further Laid Open*, p. 6.
40. Richard Baxter, *One Sheet Against the Quakers* (London: Robert White, 1657), p. 11.
41. Edward Bourne, *The Truth of God Cleared, and Above the Deceite Advanced ...* (London: Thomas Simmons, 1657), p. 12.
42. Kay. S. Taylor, 'Society, Schism and Sufferings: The First 70 Years of Quakerism in Wiltshire', University of the West of England: Ph.D. thesis, 2006, p. 57; Christopher Hill, 'Quakers and the English Revolution', *Journal of the Friends Historical Society*, 56, 3 (1992), 165–79; and John Wroughton, *An Unhappy Civil War: The Experiences of Ordinary People in Gloucestershire, Somerset, and Wiltshire, 1642–1646* (Bath: Lansdowne Press, 1999), p. 17.
43. Bourne, *Truth of God Cleared*, p. 12.
44. Baxter, *One Sheet Against the Quakers*, p. 6.
45. Miller, 'A Suffering People': English Quakers and Their Neighbours, c.1650–c.1700', *Past & Present*, 188 (2005), 75.

Chapter 7: The Blasphemous Susanna Pierson

1. Henry Cadbury (ed.), *George Fox's Book of Miracles* (Cambridge: Cambridge University Press, 2012), p. 5.
2. Charles Cherry, 'Enthusiasm and Madness: Anti-Quakerism in the Seventeenth Century', *Quaker History*, 73, 2 (1984), 3. Rosemary Moore, *The Light in Their Consciences: Early Quakers in Britain, 1646–1666* (rev. edn., University Park: Pennsylvania State University Press, 2020), p. 133.
3. Cadbury (ed.), *Book of Miracles*, p. 147.
4. Cadbury (ed.), *Book of Miracles*, p. 57.
5. *Mercurius Politicus*, 26 February to 5 March 1657, pp. 7639–40; *Publick Intelligencer*, 2 March–9 March 1657, pp. 1234–5.
6. *Publick Intelligencer*, 2 March–9 March 1657, p. 1234.
7. The extant Quarter Session records and the Great Book of Sufferings up to 1657 show no reference to William Pool or George Knight. The 1642 Protestation return for the St Nicholas parish of Worcester was signed by a George Knight, likely to be Pool's employer. See PO, JO, 10, 1, 108, 39. Protestation Return – Worcester (City) St Nicholas, 1642.
8. Anon., *A Sad Caveat to All Quakers: Not to Boast Any More That They Have God Almighty by The Hand, When They Have the Devil By The Toe* (London: W. Gilbertson, 1657), pp. 8–9.
9. Anon., *A Sad Caveat to All Quakers*, p. 11.

10. Ralph Houlbrooke, *Death, Religion, and the Family in England, 1480–1750* (Oxford: Clarendon Press, 1998), p. 210.
11. Richard Baxter, *The Right Method for a Settled Peace of Conscience...* (London: Printed for T. Underhill, F. Tyton and W. Raybould, 1653), pp. 267, 369.
12. Will Coster, *Family and Kinship in England, 1450–1800* (London: Pearson, 2001), p. 85.
13. Houlbrooke, *Death, Religion, and the Family in England*, p. 336.
14. Anon., *A Sad Caveat to All Quakers*, p. 11.
15. *Publick Intelligencer*, 2 March–9 March 165, p. 1234.
16. Richard Bauman, *Let Your Words Be Few: Symbolism of Speaking and Silence Among Seventeenth-Century Quakers*, (4th edn., Tucson: Wheatmark, 2009), p. 84.
17. Anon., *A Sad Caveat to All Quakers*, pp. 15–16.
18. Baxter, *One Sheet Against the Quakers*, p. 12.
19. Anon., *The Grand Imposter Examined or The Life, Tryal, and Examination of James Nayler* (London: Henry Brome, 1656), p. 34.
20. Erin Bell, 'Eighteenth-Century Quakerism and the Rehabilitation of James Nayler, Seventeenth-Century Radical', *The Journal of Ecclesiastical History*, 59, 3 (2008), 426–46.
21. LSF, Swarthmore MSS., II, 195. George Fox to James Nayler, unknown location, 1656.
22. William Sewell, *The History of the Rise, Increase, and Progress of the Christian People Called Quakers* (Philadelphia: Uriah Hunt, 1832), pp. 125–6.
23. Nigel Smith (ed.), *George Fox: The Journal* (London: Penguin Books, 1998), p. 124.
24. Smith (ed.), *The Journal*, pp. 94–5.
25. Sewell, *The History of the Rise*, p. 128.
26. William Bray (ed.), *The Diary of John Evelyn, Volume I* (London: M. Walter Dunne, 1901), p. 311.
27. Thomas Underhill, *Hell Broke Loose or An History of the Quakers Both Old and New* (London: Thomas Underhill and Simon Miller, 1660), p. 34.
28. E. Hockliffe (ed.), The Diary of the Rev. Ralph Josselin 1616–1683 (London: Royal Historical Society, 1908), p. 115.
29. Christine Trevett, *Women and Quakerism in the 17th Century* (York: Sessions, 1991), pp. 16, 28.
30. Anon., *A Sad Caveat to All Quakers*, pp. 10–11; Catie Gill, *Women in the Seventeenth-Century Quaker Community: A Literary Study of Political Identities, 1650–1700* (London: Routledge, 2005), p. 31.
31. *Mercurius Politicus*, 26 February to 5 March 1657, pp. 7639–40; *Publick Intelligencer*, 2 March–9 March 1657, pp. 1234–5.
32. *Mercurius Politicus*, 26 February to 5 March 1657, p. 7639.
33. Baxter, *One Sheet Against Quakers*, p. 4.
34. Anon., *A Sad Caveat to All Quakers*, frontispiece.
35. Anon., *A Sad Caveat to All Quakers*, p. 16.
36. LSF, Swarthmore MSS., I, 217. Tho[mas] Willam to M[argaret] F[ell], 1654 [the date is listed incorrectly].
37. LSF, Swarthmore MSS., I, 217.
38. LSF, Swarthmore MSS., I, 217.
39. Anon., *The Quakers Quaking: or, The Most Just and Deserved Punishment Inflicted on the Person of James Naylor...* (London: W. Gilbertson, 1657), p. 2.
40. Anon., *Quakers Quaking*, p. 1.

41. Moore, *Light in Their Consciences* (rev. edn., University Park: Pennsylvania State University Press, 2020), p. 136.
42. Baxter, *One Sheet Against the Quakers*, p. 5.

Chapter 8: Persecution or Prosecution?
1. Joseph Besse, *A Collection of the Sufferings of the People Called Quakers Vol. I* (2 vols. London: L. Hinde, 1753), p. 254.
2. Besse, *Sufferings*, I, p. 255.
3. LSF, GBS, II, p. 653.
4. John Noake, *Worcester Sects; Or, A History of the Roman Catholics and Dissenters of Worcester* (London: Longman, 1861), p. 36.
5. William Simpson, *From One Who Was Moved of the Lord God to Go a Sign Among the Priests …* (London: Thomas Simmons, 1659), p.8.
6. Robert J. Acheson, *Radical Puritans in England, 1550–1660* (London: Longman, 1990), p. 71.
7. William Simpson, *Going Naked as a Signe* (London: Printed for M.W., 1659), frontispiece.
8. John Miller, '"A Suffering People": English Quakers and Their Neighbours, c.1650–c.1700', *Past & Present*, 188 (August 2005), 71.
9. Miller, 'A Suffering People', 71.
10. Rosemary Moore, *The Light in Their Consciences: Early Quakers in Britain, 1646–1666* (rev. edn., University Park: Pennsylvania State University Press, 2020), p. 184.
11. Richard Bauman, 'Aspects of 17th Century Quaker Rhetoric', *Quarterly Journal of Speech*, 56 (1970), 69.
12. LSF, GBS, II, pp. 644–71; Besse, *Collection of the Sufferings*, I, pp. 254–6.
13. LSF, GBS, II, pp. 660–7.
14. It is likely that Gervase was the husband of Susanna. Their names are often together in the records.
15. LSF, GBS, II, pp. 660–1.
16. LSF, GBS, II, p. 662.
17. LSF, GBS, II, p. 663.
18. LSF, GBS, II, p. 662.
19. LSF, GBS, II, p. 663.
20. LSF, GBS, II, p. 664.
21. Besse, *Sufferings*, I, p. 257.
22. LSF, GBS, II, pp. 658–9.
23. LSF, GBS, II, p. 659.
24. LSF, GBS, II, p. 669.
25. Moore, *Light in Their Consciences*, p. 162.
26. LSF, GBS, II, pp. 644–71.
27. Richard C. Allen, 'Restoration Quakerism', in Stephen W. Angell and Pink Dandelion (eds.), *The Oxford Handbook of Quaker Studies* (Oxford: Oxford University Press, 2013), p. 31.
28. Allen, 'Restoration Quakerism', p. 31.
29. This is common in most discussions of Quakerism. For an example, see Kay Taylor, 'Chalk, Cheese, and Cloth: The Settling of Quaker Communities in Seventeenth-Century Wiltshire', *Quaker Studies*, 10, 2 (2006), 171.
30. Allen, 'Restoration Quakerism', p. 31.

31. Adrian Davies, *The Quakers in English Society, 1655–1725* (Oxford: Clarendon Press, 2000), p. 169.
32. There were very minor increases in Herefordshire and Worcestershire during the Popish Plot, *c.*1679–81.
33. LSF, GBS, II, p. 669.
34. LSF, GBS, II, Worcestershire, 1670, p. 669; Joseph Besse, *A Collection of the Sufferings of the People Called Quakers Vol. II* (2 vols. London: L. Hinde, 1753), p. 69.
35. Besse, *Sufferings*, I, p. 257.
36. Besse, *Sufferings*, I, p. 259.
37. WRO, BA, 1303, Herefordshire Quarterly Meeting Minutes, 1665–1790, February 1677.
38. Besse, *Sufferings*, I, p. 259.
39. Miller, 'A Suffering People', 99.
40. Besse, *Sufferings*, I, p. 259.
41. Besse, *Sufferings*, I, p. 257.
42. Barry Reay, 'Popular Hostility Towards Quakers in Mid-Seventeenth-Century England', *Social History*, 5 (1980), 390.
43. Reay, 'Popular Hostility', 400–1; Stephen K. Roberts, 'The Quakers in Evesham 1655–1660: A Study in Religion, Politics and Culture', *Midland History*, 16 (1991), 81; Alan A. Anderson, 'A Study in the Sociology of the Religious Persecution: The First Quakers', *Journal of Religious History*, 9, 3 (1977), 249.
44. NA, E179, 119, 487 Herefordshire Hearth Tax Records, 1665; Cecil Anthony Francis Meekings, S. Porter and Ian Roy (eds.), *The Hearth Tax Collectors' Book for Worcester, 1678–1680* (Leeds: Worcestershire Historical Society, 1983), pp. 40–116.
45. Reay, 'Popular Hostility', 392.
46. Reay, 'Popular Hostility', 394.
47. Besse, *Sufferings*, I, pp. 254–61.
48. LSF, GBS, II, pp. 644–71.
49. Nigel Smith (ed.), *George Fox: The Journal* (London: Penguin Books, 1998), p. 425.
50. Smith (ed.), *Journal*, p. 426.
51. Besse, *Sufferings*, II, p. 71.
52. Besse, *Sufferings*, II, p. 72.
53. Besse, *Sufferings*, II, p. 73.
54. Besse, *Sufferings*, II, p. 73; WRO 110, 1, 119. 1673 Quarter Sessions Calendar of Prisoners. George Fox is listed but the document is unable to be examined at Worcestershire Record Office because it has been deemed too fragile to be issued.
55. Besse, *Sufferings*, II, p. 73.
56. Besse, *Sufferings*, II, p. 75.
57. Besse, *Sufferings*, II, pp. 75–6.
58. Moore, *Light in Their Consciences*, p. 159.
59. Roberts, 'The Quakers in Evesham', 72.
60. Miller, 'A Suffering People', 74.
61. Edward Bourne, *An Epistle to Friends* (London: J. Bringhurst, 1682), frontispiece.
62. Besse, *Sufferings*, I, p. 256.
63. Heming was either a widow or her husband was not a Quaker as there are no others with this surname in the GBS.
64. LSF, GBS, II, pp. 645, 655, 668.

Notes 175

65. Thomas Danson, *The Quakers Folly Made Manifest to All Men* (London: J.H. for John Allen, 1659), p. ii.
66. LSF, Swarthmore MSS., I, 240. D[aniel] Baker to G[eorge] F[ox], Worcester, c.1666.
67. Baxter, *One Sheet Against the Quakers*, p. 11.
68. Baxter, *One Sheet Against the Quakers*, p. 3.
69. Edward Burrough, 'Truth Defended or Certain Accusations Answered', in his *The Memorable Works of a Son of Thunder and Consolation Namely That True Prophet and Faithful Servant of God and Sufferer for the Testimony of Jesus, Edward Burroughs, Who Dyed a Prisoner for the Word of God in the City of London, the Fourteenth of the Twelfth Moneth, 1662* (s.l.: s.n., 1662), p. 134.
70. Baxter, 'Answer to the Quakers Queries', p. 2.

Chapter 9: The Evil Multitudes
1. Morgan Watkins, *Lamentation Over England* (London: s.n., 1664), frontispiece.
2. Watkins, *Lamentation Over England*, p. 2.
3. Watkins, *Lamentation Over England*, pp. 6, 14, 16.
4. John Miller, '"A Suffering People": English Quakers and Their Neighbours, c.1650–c.1700', *Past & Present*, 188 (2005), 95.
5. Adrian Davies, *The Quakers in English Society, 1655–1725* (Oxford: Clarendon Press, 2000), p. 201.
6. Watkins, *Lamentation Over England*, p. 42.
7. Geoffrey F. Nuttall, 'Overcoming the World: The Early Quaker Programme', *Studies in Church History*, 10 (1972), 146.
8. Watkins, *Lamentation Over England*, p. 6.
9. Humphrey Smith, *To the Musicioners, The Harpers, the Minstrels, the Singers, the Dancers, the Persecutors* (London, s.n., 1658), p. 3.
10. Morgan Watkins, *The Things That are Caesar's Rendered unto Caesar and the Things that are God's Rendered Unto God* (London: s.n., 1666), p. 18.
11. Tim Harris, 'Problematising Popular Culture', in Tim Harris (ed.), *Popular Culture in England, c.1500–1850* (London: Macmillan, 1995), p. 10.
12. Andrew Hadfield, Matthew Dimmock and Abigail Shinn, 'Thinking About Popular Culture in Early Modern England', in Andrew Hadfield, Matthew Dimmock and Abigail Shinn (eds.), *The Ashgate Research Companion to Popular Culture in Early Modern England* (London: Routledge, 2014), p. 16.
13. Keith Wrightson, *English Society, 1580–1680* (London: Hutchinson, 1982), p. 12.
14. Phil Withington, 'Citizens, Community, and Political Culture in Restoration England', in Alexandra Shepard and Phil Withington (eds.), *Communities in Early Modern England* (Manchester: Manchester University Press, 2000), p. 136.
15. Steve Hindle, 'A Sense of Place? Becoming and Belonging in the Rural Parish, 1550–1650', in Shepard and Withington (eds.), *Communities in Early Modern England*, p. 97.
16. Hindle, 'A Sense of Place?', p. 97.
17. Watkins, *The Things That are Caesar's*, p. 9.
18. David Underdown, *Revel, Riot and Rebellion: Popular Politics and Culture in England, 1603–1660* (Oxford: University Press, 1985), pp. 11, 14.
19. Wrightson, *English Society*, p. 62.

20. 'March 1654: An Ordinance for Prohibiting Cock-Matches', in C.H. Firth and R.S. Rait (eds.), *Acts and Ordinances of the Interregnum, 1642–1660* (London: His Majesty's Stationery Office, 1911), p. 861. British History Online, http://www.british-history.ac.uk/no-series/acts-ordinances-interregnum/p861 [accessed 10 January 2022]; 'July 1654: An Ordinance Prohibiting Horse-Races for Six Monenths', in Firth and Rait (eds.), *Acts and Ordinances of the Interregnum*, pp. 941–2. British History Online http://www.british-history.ac.uk/no-series/acts-ordinances-interregnum/ pp. 941–2 [accessed 10 January 2022]; John I. Day, 'Horse Racing and the Pari-mutuel', *Annals of the American Academy of Political and Social Science*, 269, 1, (1950), 56.
21. Oliver Cromwell, *A Proclamation of His Highness, Prohibiting Horse-Races in England and Wales for Eight Monenths* (London: Henry Hills and John Field, 1658).
22. Christopher Durston, 'Puritan Rule and the Failure of Cultural Revolution, 1645–1660', in Christopher Durston and Jacqueline Eales (eds.), *The Culture of English Puritanism, 1560–1700* (Palgrave Macmillan: Basingstoke, 1996), pp. 217–18.
23. Underdown, *Revel, Riot and Rebellion*, p. 46.
24. Barry Reay, 'Popular Culture in Early Modern England', in Barry Reay (ed.), *Popular Culture in Seventeenth-Century England* (Routledge: London, 1988), p. 21.
25. Peter Burke, 'Popular Culture in Seventeenth-Century London', *London Journal*, 3, 2 (1977), 145.
26. Mark Hailwood, *Alehouses and Good Fellowship in Early Modern England* (Woodbridge: Boydell Press, 2014), p. 225.
27. Wrightson, *English Society*, p. 129.
28. Alan Dyer, 'Small Market Towns, 1540–1700', in Peter Clark (ed.), *The Cambridge Urban History of Britain Volume II, 1540–1840* (Cambridge: Cambridge University Press, 2000), p. 425.
29. Underdown, *Revel, Riot and Rebellion*, p. 242.
30. Ben Watson, *Cider, Hard, and Sweet: History, Traditions, and Making your Own* (Woodstock, VT: Countryman Press, 2013), p. 20.
31. John Burnett, *Liquid Pleasures: A Social History of Drinks in Modern Britain* (London: Routledge, 1999), p. 157; Watson, *Cider, Hard, and Sweet*, p. 22.
32. Wrightson, *English Society*, p. 168.
33. Paul Griffiths, John Landers, Margaret Pelling, Robert Tyson, 'Population and Disease, Estrangement and Belonging, 1540–1700', in Peter Clark (ed.), *The Cambridge Urban History of Britain* (Cambridge: Cambridge University Press, 2000), p. 228.
34. Wrightson, *English Society*, p. 168.
35. Samuel Pepys, *The Diary of Samuel Pepys: A Selection* (London: Penguin, 2003), pp. 26, 69, 101, 104–105, 118, 132–3, 139, 152, 157, 216.
36. Susan Dwyer Amussen, 'The Gendering of Popular Culture in Early Modern England', in Harris (ed.), *Popular Culture in England*, p. 63.
37. Wrightson, *English Society*, p. 167; James Brown, 'Alehouse Licensing and State Formation in Early Modern England', in Jonathan Herring, Ciaran Regan, Darin Weinberg and Phil Withington (eds.), *Intoxication and Society: Problematic Pleasures of Drugs and Alcohol* (Basingstoke: Palgrave Macmillan, 2013), p. 110.
38. Durston, 'Puritan Rule and the Failure of Cultural Revolution', in Durston and Eales (eds.), *Culture of English Puritanism*, p. 230.
39. James A. Sharpe, *Crime in Early Modern England* (Longman: London, 1999), p. 8.
40. Jonathan Barry, 'Popular Culture in Seventeenth-Century Bristol', in Reay (ed.), *Popular Culture in Seventeenth-Century England*, pp. 74–5.

41. Christopher Durston, 'Puritan Rule and the Failure of Cultural Revolution, 1645–1660', in Durston and Eales (eds.), *The Culture of English Puritanism*, p. 218.
42. Nigel Smith (ed.), *George Fox: The Journal* (London: Penguin, 1998), p. 280.
43. Stephen Porter, Stephen K. Roberts, Ian Roy (eds.), *The Diary and Papers of Henry Townshend, 1640–1663* (Bristol: Worcestershire Historical Society, 2014), p. 282.
44. Watkins, *Lamentation Over England*, p. 14.
45. Martin Ingram, 'From Reformation to Toleration: Popular Cultures in England, 1540–1690', in Harris (ed.), *Popular Culture in England*, p. 102; Underdown, *Revel, Riot and Rebellion*, p. 255.
46. Underdown, *Revel, Riot and Rebellion*, p. 275.
47. Daniel Baker, *Yet One Warning More, To Thee O England* (London: Robert Wilson, 1660), p. 5.
48. Smith (ed.), *Journal*, p. 280.
49. WRO, 1, 1, 90; WRO, 1, 1, 93; WRO, 1, 1, 97; WRO, 1, 1, 101; WRO, 1, 1, 104. Quarter Sessions (Worcester) 1660, 1661, 1662, 1664 and 1675.
50. WRO, 1, 1, 97.
51. WRO, 1, 1, 101; WRO, 1, 1, 121.
52. Richard Farnworth, *A Character Whereby the Fast Christs, or Antichrists, Seducers, False Prophets, and House Creepers May Be Known* (London: Giles Calvert, 1654), p. 6.
53. Morgan Watkins, *Swearing Denyed in the New Covenant* (London: Robert Wilson, 1660), p. 4.
54. Jonathan Harlow, 'Preaching for Hire: Public Issues and Private Concerns in a Skirmish of the Lamb's War', *Quaker Studies*, 10, 1 (2005), 41; Alexandra Walsham, *Charitable Hatred: Tolerance and Intolerance in England, 1500–1700* (Manchester: Manchester University Press, 2006), p. 46.
55. Joseph L. Black (ed.), *The Martin Marprelate Tracts: A Modernized and Annotated Edition* (Cambridge: Cambridge University Press, 2011), p. xix.
56. Ingram, 'From Reformation to Toleration', p. 108.
57. Ingram, 'From Reformation to Toleration', p. 122.
58. Alexander Parker, *A Tryall of a Christian* (London: Thomas Simmons, 1658), p. 10.
59. Hugh Barbour and Arthur Roberts (eds.), *Early Quaker Writings* (Grand Rapids, MI: Eerdmans, 1973), p. 52.
60. Watkins, *Lamentation Over England*, p. 2.
61. Watkins, *Day Manifesting the Night*, p. 9.
62. Morgan Watkins, *The Day Manifesting the Night and the Deeds of Darkness Reproved by the Light* (London: Thomas Simmons, 1660), p. 4.
63. Watkins, *Lamentation Over England*, p. 2.
64. Watkins, *Lamentation Over England*, p. 19.
65. Watkins, *Lamentation Over England*, p. 7.
66. Watkins, *Lamentation Over England*, p. 7.
67. Watkins, *Lamentation Over England*, p. 11.
68. Pepys, *Diary of Samuel Pepys*, p. 257. Pepys frequently fell asleep during sermons, even on Christmas Day and Easter Sunday.
69. Watkins, *Lamentation Over England*, p. 22.
70. Watkins, *Lamentation Over England*, p. 11.
71. Richard Baxter, 'An Answer to a Young Unsettled Friend', in his *The Quakers Catechism* (London: Thomas Underhill, 1655), p. c3.

72. Watkins, *Lamentation Over England*, p. 10.
73. Watkins, *Lamentation Over England*, p. 13.
74. Richard Davies, *An Account of the Convincement, Exercises, Services, and Travels of ... Richard Davies* (London: James Phillips, 1794), pp. 4, 9–10, 13.
75. Morgan Watkins, *The Marks of the True Church* (London: s.n., 1675), p. 25.
76. Watkins, *Marks of the True Church*, p. 13.
77. Watkins, *Marks of the True Church*, p.1.
78. Rosemary Moore, *The Light in Their Consciences: Early Quakers in Britain, 1646–1666* (rev. edn., University Park, PA: Pennsylvania State University Press, 2020), p. 49.
79. Edward Bourne, *The Truth of God Cleared* (London: Thomas Simmons, 1657), p. 7.
80. Bourne, *Truth of God Cleared*, p. 6.
81. Bourne, *Truth of God Cleared*, p. 1.
82. Bourne, *Truth of God Cleared*, pp. 5–6.
83. Bourne, *Truth of God Cleared*, p. 10.
84. Durston, 'Puritan Rule and the Failure of Cultural Revolution', in Durston and Eales (eds.), *Culture of English Puritanism*, p. 232.
85. Moore, *Light in Their Consciences*, p. 172; Rosemary Moore, 'Seventeenth-Century Context and Quaker Beginnings', in Stephen W. Angell and Pink Dandelion (eds.), *The Oxford Handbook of Quaker Studies* (Oxford: Oxford University Press, 2013), p. 27.
86. Richard Hubberthorne, *An Answer to a Book Called a Just Defence and Vindication* (London: Robert Wilson, 1660), p. 14.
87. Edward Bourne, *A Warning from the Lord God Out of Sion, Who is Mighty and Terrible Sounded Forth Unto the Inhabitants of the City of Worcester* (London: Robert Wilson, 1660), p. 9.
88. Bourne, *Warning from the Lord God ... Worcester*, p. 10.
89. Bourne, *Warning from the Lord God ... Worcester*, p. 8.
90. Watkins, *Day Manifesting the Night*, p. 13.
91. Watkins, *Swearing Denyed*, p. 3.
92. Richard Bauman, *Let Your Words Be Few: Symbolism of Speaking and Silence Among Seventeenth-Century Quakers* (4th edn., Tucson: Wheatmark, 1983), p. 84.

Chapter 10: Writing Like the World is Ending
1. LSF, Swarthmore MSS., III, 4, 188, M[organ] Watkins to G[eorge] F[ox], Torbans (presumably Torbay, Devon), 1660. Watkins does not identify who asked him to draft *Swearing Denyed in the New Covenant*.
2. Morgan Watkins, *Swearing Denyed in the New Covenant* (London: Robert Wilson, 1660), frontispiece.
3. Morgan Watkins, *The Day Manifesting the Night and the Deeds of Darkness Reproved by the Light* (London: Thomas Simmons, 1660), frontispiece.
4. Watkins, *Day Manifesting the Night*, p. 3.
5. Watkins, *Day Manifesting the Night*, pp. 10–11.
6. Edward Bourne, *A Warning from the Lord God to the Inhabitants of the Town and County of Warwick* (s.l.: s.n., 1661), frontispiece.
7. Morgan Watkins, *Lamentation Over England* (London: s.n., 1664), frontispiece.
8. Watkins, *Lamentation Over England*, p. 46.
9. Watkins, *Lamentation Over England*, p. i.
10. Watkins, *Lamentation Over England*, p. 1.

11. Watkins, *Lamentation Over England*, p. 8.
12. Rosemary Moore, *The Light in Their Consciences: Early Quakers in Britain, 1646–1666* (rev. edn., University Park: Pennsylvania State University Press, 2020), pp. 158–61.
13. Joseph Besse, *A Collection of the Sufferings of Early Quakers Vol. II* (2 vols. London: Luke Hinde, 1753), p. 67.
14. Besse, *Sufferings*, II, p. 67.
15. Watkins, *Lamentation Over England*, pp. 27, 44.
16. Watkins, *Lamentation Over England*, pp. 40, 44.
17. Watkins, *Lamentation Over England*, p. 5.
18. Watkins, *Lamentation Over England*, pp. 4, 36.
19. Pepys, *Diary of Samuel Pepys*, p. 414.
20. Watkins, *Lamentation Over England*, pp. 14, 18.
21. Watkins, *Lamentation Over England*, p. 25.
22. Sylvia Stevens, 'Travelling Ministry', in Angell and Dandelion (eds.), *The Oxford Handbook of Quaker Studies*, p. 299. Stevens suggests that Fox's message that Christ had returned to be their inward teacher 'carried the implication that they were participating in an end-time and that it was incumbent upon them to spread this teaching'.
23. Nuttall, 'Overcoming the World', p. 151.
24. LSF, Swarthmore MSS., I, 4, 52, E[dward] Born [sic] to G[eorge] F[ox], Hereford, 1664.
25. Watkins, *Lamentation Over England*.
26. Watkins, *Lamentation Over England*, p. 10.
27. Revelations 8: 7–9.
28. Rebecca Rideal, *1666: Plague, War, and Hellfire* (London: John Murray, 2016), p. 223.
29. Anonymous, *Flagellum Dei, or, A Collection of the Several Fires, Plagues, and Pestilential Diseases That Have Happened in London Especially, and Other Parts of This Nation From the Norman Conquest to This Present* (London: s.n., 1668).
30. Thomas Vincent, *God's Terrible Voice in the City* (s.l.: s.n., 1667), p. 46.
31. Rosemary Moore, 'The Early Development of Quakerism', in Richard C. Allen and Rosemary Moore, *The Quakers, 1656–1723: The Evolution of an Alternative Community* (University Park, PA: Pennsylvania State University Press, 2018), p. 25.
32. Watkins, *Things That are Caesar's*, pp. 12–13.
33. Moore, *Light in Their Consciences*, p. 157. Also, see Douglas Gwyn, 'James Nayler and the Lamb's War', *Quaker Studies*, 12, 2 (2008), 174. Gwyn referred to this phenomenon as an 'apocalyptic revelation' that inspired a powerful aversion to the state church.
34. John Spurr, 'From Puritanism to Dissent, 1660–1700', in Christopher Durston and Jacqueline Eales (eds.), *The Culture of English Puritanism, 1560–1700* (Basingstoke: Palgrave Macmillan, 1996), p. 262.
35. LSF, Swarthmore MSS., III, 1,129, Morgan Watkins to M[argaret] F[ell], London, 1665.
36. Watkins, *Things That are Caesar's*, pp. 4–5.
37. Watkins, *Things That are Caesar's*, pp. 19, 30.
38. Watkins, *Things That are Caesar's*, p. 20.
39. Watkins, *Things That are Caesar's*, p. 8.
40. Watkins, *Things That are Caesar's*, p. 21.
41. Watkins, *Things That are Caesar's*, p. 25.
42. Pepys, *Diary of Samuel Pepys*, pp. 230, 243, 247, 350, 828, 846.

43. Edward Bourne, *Certain Queries Answered, Which Were Sent by a PAPIST for the People Called QUAKERS to Answer* (s.l.: s.n., 1667), frontispiece.
44. Neil H. Keeble and Geoffrey F. Nuttall (eds.), *Calendar of the Correspondence of Richard Baxter, Volume 1, 1638–1660* (Oxford: Clarendon Press, 1991), p. 170; William M. Lamont, *Richard Baxter and the Millennium* (London: Croom Helm, 1979), p. 175.
45. Walsham, *Charitable* Hatred, p. 206.
46. Bourne, *Certain Queries Answered*, pp. 1–2.
47. Bourne, *Certain Queries Answered*, p. 13.
48. Bourne, *Certain Queries Answered*, p. 16.
49. Bourne, *Certain Queries Answered*, pp. 19–20.
50. Jessie Childs, *God's Traitors: Terror and Faith in Elizabethan England* (London: Bodley Head, 2014), p. 13.
51. Bourne, *Certain Queries Answered*, p. 25.
52. Bourne, *Certain Queries Answered*, pp. 22–3.
53. Bourne, *Certain Queries Answered*, p. 25.
54. Richard G. Bailey, 'Francis Ellington's Use of Prophecy to Explain the Appearance, Deliverance, and Apocalyptic Role of Quakers in the Last Days', *Quaker Studies*, 3, 2 (1998), 114.
55. Bailey, 'Francis Ellington's Use of Prophecy', 117.
56. Edward Bourne, *A Looking-Glass Discovering to All People what Image They Bear* (s.l.: s.n., 1671).
57. Bourne, *A Looking-Glass*, p. 7.
58. Raymond Brown and Alan P. Sell, 'Quakers and Dissenters in Dispute', in Allen and Moore, *The Quakers, 1656–1723*, p. 146.
59. Pepys, *Diary of Samuel Pepys*, p. 942.
60. Bourne, *A Looking-Glass*, pp. 15–16.
61. Bourne, *A Looking-Glass*, p. 16.
62. Bourne, *A Looking-Glass*, p. 25.
63. John Spurr, *The Restoration Church in England, 1646–1689* (New Haven: Yale University Press, 1981), p. 61.
64. George Southcombe, 'The Quakers and Politics, 1660–1689', in Allen and Moore, *The Quakers, 1656–1723*, p. 175.
65. Madeleine Pennington, *Quakers, Christ, and the Enlightenment* (Oxford: Oxford University Press, 2021), p. 131.
66. Watkins, *Marks of the True Church*, p. 22.
67. Watkins, *Marks of the True Church*, p. 24.
68. Edward Bourne, *For the Inhabitants of Worcester to View and Consider Well of, Especially They of Nicholas Parish* (s.l.: s.n., 1682), frontispiece.
69. Bourne, *For the Inhabitants of Worcester*, pp. 3–4.
70. Richard C. Allen, 'Living as a Quaker During the Second Period', in Allen and Moore, *The Quakers, 1656–1723*, p. 83.
71. Thomas Robertson, Richard Blank, John Bowater, and William Ingram, *To the Bishops and Clergy of England and Wales, The State of the Cruel Persecution, Imprisonment (Many to Death) and Spoil of Goods Inflicted Upon the People called Quakers* (London: s.n., 1685), p. 3.
72. John Bowater, *Something Concerning the Proceedings of Thomas Willmate, Vicar of the Parish of Bromsgrove, in the County of Worcester, Against Me John Boweter, (Who Am a*

Prisoner for the Testimony of Christ Jesus) with a Salutation of Love to My Loving and Kind Neighbours (London: s.n., 1681), pp. 1–2.
73. Bourne, *For the Inhabitants of Worcester*, p. 5.
74. Edward Bourne, *An Epistle to Friends* (London: J. Bringhurst, 1682), frontispiece.
75. Ralph Stevens, *Protestant Pluralism: The Reception of the Toleration Act, 1689–1720* (Woodbridge: Boydell & Brewer, 2018), p. 53.
76. Peters, *Print Culture and the Early Quakers*, p. 176.
77. Ted L. Underwood, *Primitivism, Radicalism, and the Lamb's War: The Baptist-Quaker Conflict in Seventeenth-Century England* (Oxford: Oxford University Press, 1997), p. 123.
78. Moore, *Light in Their Consciences*, p. 206.

Chapter 11: The Good Argument Against Quakerism

1. Edward Bourne, *An Answer to Doctor Good (so called) His DIALOGUE against those call'd QUAKERS* (s.l.: s.n., 1675), frontispiece.
2. Thomas Good, *FIRMIANUS and DUBITANTIUS, OR Certain DIALOGUES Concerning Atheism, Infidelity, Popery, and other Heresies and Schisme's That Trouble the Peace of the Church, and Are Destructive of Primitive Piety* (Hereford: L. Litchfield, 1674).
3. Good, *Firmianus and Dubitantius*, p. iii.
4. Good, *Firmianus and Dubitantius*, p. 90.
5. Good, *Firmianus and Dubitantius*, pp. 88–9.
6. Good, *Firmianus and Dubitantius*, p. 92.
7. Good, *Firmianus and Dubitantius*, p. 92.
8. David Manning, 'Accusations of Blasphemy in English Anti-Quaker Polemic, c. 1660–1701', *Quaker Studies*, 14, 1 (2009), 36. Also, see Thomas Hicks, *The Quaker Condemned Out of His Own Mouth* (London: R.W. for Peter Parker, 1674).
9. Bourne, *Answer to Doctor Good*, p. 5.
10. Bourne, *Answer to Doctor Good*, pp. 4–5.
11. Bourne, *Answer to Doctor Good*, p. 3.
12. Bourne, *Answer to Doctor Good*, p. 15.
13. Bourne, *Answer to Doctor Good*, p. 11.
14. Good, *Firmianus and Dubitantius*, pp. 93–4.
15. Bourne, *Answer to Doctor Good*, p. 11.
16. Smith (ed.), *Journal*, pp. 289, 320. In 1656, Fox was accused of trying to restore the king; Porter, Roberts, Roy (eds.), *Diary and Papers of Henry Townshend*, p. 297.
17. Rebecca Rideal, *1666: Plague, War, and Hellfire* (London: John Murray, 2016), p. 68.
18. Erin Bell, 'Quakers and the Law', in Allen and Moore, *The Quakers, 1656–1723*, p. 270.
19. Good, *Firmianus and Dubitantius*, pp. 96–7.
20. Bourne, *Answer to Doctor Good*, p. 20.
21. Walsham, *Charitable Hatred*, p. 47.
22. Bourne, *Answer to Doctor Good*, p. 20.
23. Bourne, *Answer to Doctor Good*, p. 24.
24. Craig W. Horle, *The Quakers and the English Legal System, 1660–1688* (Philadelphia: University of Pennsylvania Press, 1988), p. 149.

Chapter 12: Zealous: Humphrey Smith

1. Erica Canela, 'The Commendable Life and Noble Death of Humphrey Smith', *Quaker Studies*, 25, 1 (2020), 3–26. This chapter is an unabridged version of this article.
2. Nicholas Complin, 'The Faithfulness of the Upright Made Manifest Being a Testimony Concerning the Life, Death, and Sufferings of ... Humphrey Smith', in Anon (ed.), *A Collection of the Several Writings and Faithful Testimonies of ... Humphrey Smith* (London: Andrew Sowle, 1683), pp. 6–7.
3. In 1897, Stoke Bliss was transferred to Worcestershire.
4. Stephen. K. Roberts, 'Smith, Humphrey (bap. 1624 – d.1663)', *Oxford Dictionary of National Biography* (Oxford: Oxford University Press, 2004). www.oxforddnb.com/view/article/25818 [accessed 16 May 2014].
5. For example, Richard Farnworth had a similar experience as a teenager and struggled with internal conflict regarding religion until he received 'divine guidance'. For further analysis of Farnworth's spiritual journey, see Michael Birkel and Stephen W. Angell, 'The Witness of Richard Farnworth: Prophet of Light, Apostle of Church Order', in Stephen W. Angell and Pink Dandelion (eds.), *Early Quakers and Their Theological Thought, 1647–1723* (Cambridge: Cambridge University Press, 2015), pp. 83–101.
6. Humphrey Smith, *To All Parents of Children Upon the Face of the Whole Earth* (London: Thomas Simmons, 1660), pp. 6–7.
7. Anthony Fletcher, *Growing up in England: The Experience of Childhood, 1600–1914* (New Haven: Yale University Press, 2008), p. 12.
8. Smith, *To All Parents of Children*, p. 17.
9. Smith, *To All Parents of Children*, pp. 5, 16.
10. Smith, *To All Parents of Children*, pp. 16–17.
11. Smith, *To All Parents of Children*, p. 7.
12. Ralph Houlbrooke, *The English Family, 1450–1700* (London: Longman, 1984), p. 168.
13. Smith, *To All Parents of Children*, p. 7.
14. Lawrence Stone, *The Family, Sex and Marriage in England, 1500–1800* (London: Penguin, 1979), p. 123.
15. Ilana Krausman Ben-Amos, 'Reciprocal Bonding: Parents and Their Offspring in Early Modern England', *Journal of Family History*, 25, 3 (2000), 292.
16. Courtney Thomas, 'The Honour & Credite of the Whole House', *Cultural and Social History*, 10, 3 (2013), 332.
17. Thomas, 'The Honour & Credite of the Whole House', 332.
18. Smith, *To All Parents of Children*, pp. 5–6.
19. Stone, *Family, Sex and Marriage*, p. 121.
20. Smith, *To All Parents of Children*, p. 8.
21. Smith, *To All Parents of Children*, p. 7.
22. Keith Wrightson, *Earthly Necessities: Economic Lives in Early Modern Britain, 1470–1750* (London: Penguin, 2002), p. 49.
23. Keith Thomas, *The Ends of Life: Roads to Fulfilment in Early Modern England* (Oxford: Oxford University Press, 2010), p. 96.
24. Stone, *Family, Sex and Marriage*, p. 127.
25. Roberts, 'Smith, Humphrey', p. 1.
26. HRO, AM 29, 1, Hearth Tax for Michaelmas 1665 for Herefordshire and Comparison with Militia Assessments 1663 (transcript by J. Harnden), p. 133.

27. Humphrey Smith, *Man Driven Out of the Earth and Darkness by the Light, Life, and Mighty Hand of God* (London: s.n., 1658), p. 4.
28. Smith, *Man Driven Out of the Earth and Darkness*, p. 6.
29. Humphrey Smith, *To the Musicioners, The Harpers, the Minstrels, the Singers, the Dancers, the Persecutors …* (London: s.n., 1658), frontispiece.
30. Smith, *Man Driven Out of the Earth and Darkness*, pp. 10, 12.
31. Smith, *Man Driven Out of the Earth and Darkness*, p. 6.
32. Smith, *Man Driven Out of the Earth and Darkness*, p. 12.
33. Hugh Peters, *Gods Doings and Mans Duty, Opened in a Sermon Preached Before Both Houses of Parliament … 1645* (London: Giles Calvert, 1646), p. 21.
34. Morgan Watkins, *Lamentation Over England* (London, 1664), frontispiece.
35. Smith, *Man Driven Out of the Earth and Darkness*, p. 3.
36. Smith, *Man Driven Out of the Earth and Darkness*, p. 11.
37. Humphrey Smith, *A Sad and Mournful Lamentation for the People of These Nations, but Especially for the Priests and Leaders …* (London: s.n., 1660), p. 2.
38. Christopher Hill, *The World Turned Upside Down: Radical Ideas During the English Revolution* (London: Penguin, 1991), p. 99.
39. Smith, *Man Driven Out of the Earth and Darkness*, p. 10.
40. Smith, *Man Driven Out of the Earth and Darkness*, pp. 11–12.
41. William Erbery, *Apocrypha* (London: s.n., 1652), p. 4.
42. Norman Penney (ed.), *First Publishers of Truth* (London: Headley Bros, 1907), p. 212.
43. Farnworth and Smith, *Antichrist's Man of War*; Edmund Skipp, *The Worlds Wonder or the Quakers Blazing Starr* (London: Henry Hills, 1654).
44. Nuttall, 'Another Baptist Vicar?', 331–4.
45. Skipp, *The Worlds Wonder*, frontispiece.
46. Skipp, *The Worlds Wonder*, pp. A4, 4.
47. Farnworth and Smith, *Antichrist's Man of War*, pp. 69–90.
48. Farnworth and Smith, *Antichrist's Man of War*, p. 85.
49. Kate Peters, *Print Culture and the Early Quakers* (Cambridge: Cambridge University Press, 2005), p. 50.
50. H. Larry Ingle, *First Among Friends: George Fox and the Creation of Quakerism* (Oxford: Oxford University Press, 1994), p. 85.
51. George Fox, 'George Fox's Testimony Concerning Humphrey Smith', in Anon (ed.), *A Collection*, p. i; Edward Waldren, 'Edward Waldren's Testimony Concerning Humphry Smith, in Anon. (ed.), *A Collection*, p. viii.
52. Smith, *Man Driven Out of the Earth and Darkness*, p. 1; Humphrey Smith, *To New-Englands Pretended Christians who Contrary to Christ, Have Destroyed the Lives of Men* (London: Robert Wilson, 1660), p. 1; Smith, *To All Parents of Children*, p. 21.
53. Smith, *Man Driven Out of the Earth and Darkness*, p. 5.
54. Smith, *Man Driven Out of the Earth and Darkness*, pp. 7–8.
55. Smith, *Man Driven Out of the Earth and Darkness*, pp. 9–10.
56. Smith, *Man Driven Out of the Earth and Darkness*, pp. 7, 9.
57. Alfred Brown, *Evesham Friends in the Olden Time* (London: West Newman & Co., 1885), p. 32.
58. Smith, *Man Driven Out of the Earth and Darkness*, p. 11.
59. Smith, *Man Driven Out of the Earth and Darkness*, p. 3.
60. Smith, *A Sad and Mournful Lamentation*, p. 7.

61. Ben-Amos, 'Reciprocal Bonding', 292.
62. Rosemary Moore, *The Light in Their Consciences: Early Quakers in Britain, 1646–1666* (rev. edn., University Park: Penn State Press, 2020), p. 122.
63. Sylvia Stevens, 'Travelling Ministry', in Stephen W. Angell and Pink Dandelion (eds.) *The Oxford Handbook of Quaker Studies* (Oxford: Oxford University Press, 2013), p. 299; Ingle, *First Among Friends*, pp. 118–19; Rosemary Moore, 'The Early Development of Quakerism', in Richard C. Allen and Rosemary Moore, *The Quakers, 1656–1723: The Evolution of an Alternative Community* (University Park, PA: Pennsylvania State University Press, 2018), p. 15.
64. Penney (ed.), *First Publishers of Truth*, pp. 105–106, 108, 112, 212.
65. Humphrey Smith, 'The Sufferings, Tryals and Purgings of the Saints at Evesham', in Anon (ed.), *A Collection of the Several Writings and Faithful Testimonies of ... Humphrey Smith* (London: Andrew Sowle, 1683), pp. 5–6.
66. Roberts, 'The Quakers in Evesham, 1655–1660', 66.
67. Anon., *A Representation of The Government of the Borough of Evesham*, frontispiece.
68. Smith and Woodrove, *Cruelty of the Magistrates of Evesham*, p. 9.
69. Humphrey Smith, *Something Further Laid Open of the Cruel Persecution of the People Called Quakers by the Magistrates and People of Evesham* (London: s.n., 1656), frontispiece.
70. Smith, 'The Sufferings, Tryals and Purgings of the Saints at Evesham', pp. 1–4.
71. Smith and Woodrove, *Cruelty of the Magistrates of Evesham*, p. 1.
72. Smith and Woodrove, *Cruelty of the Magistrates of Evesham*, p. 4.
73. Smith and Woodrove, *Cruelty of the Magistrates of Evesham*, p. 5.
74. Smith and Woodrove, *Cruelty of the Magistrates of Evesham*, p. 4.
75. Anon., *A Representation of The Government of the Borough of Evesham*, frontispiece.
76. Joseph Besse, *A Collection of the Sufferings of Early Quakers Vol. II* (2 vols. London: Luke Hinde, 1753), p. 56.
77. Humphrey Smith, 'To the Flock of God Whom He Hath Gathered in Gloucestershire, Herefordshire, Worcestershire, etc', in Anon (ed.), *A Collection*, p. 137.
78. Joseph Besse, *A Collection of the Sufferings of the People Called Quakers Vol. I* (2 vols. London: L. Hinde, 1753), p. 149. James Nayler was also imprisoned with Smith at this time.
79. Nigel Smith (ed.), *George Fox: The Journal* (London: Penguin, 1998), p. 36.
80. Humphrey Smith, *Sound Things Asserted* (s.l.: s.n., 1662), p. 4.
81. Kathleen H. Thomas, *The History and Significance of Quaker Symbols in Sect Formation* (Lampeter: Edwin Mellen Press, 2002), pp. 36–7.
82. Adrian Davies, *The Quakers in English Society, 1655–1725* (Oxford: Clarendon Press, 2000), p. 202.
83. Moore, *Light in Their Consciences*, p. 59.
84. Smith and Woodrove, *Cruelty of the Magistrates of Evesham*, p. 7.
85. Pitt cited in Humphrey Smith and Thomas Woodrove, *The Cruelty of the Magistrates of Evesham, Worcestershire ...* (London: Giles Calvert, 1655) p. 8.
86. Anon., *A Representation of The Government of the Borough of Evesham*, frontispiece.
87. Besse, *Sufferings*, I, p. 150.
88. David Underdown, *Revel, Riot, and Rebellion: Popular Politics and Culture in England, 1603–1660* (Oxford: Oxford University Press, 1985), p. 244.
89. Hill, *World Turned Upside Down*, pp. 49–50.
90. Penney (ed.), *First Publishers of Truth*, p. 86.

91. Besse, *Sufferings*, I, p. 150.
92. Penney (ed.), *First Publishers of Truth*, p. 86.
93. Johnson, 'The Case of the Distracted Maid', 33.
94. Johnson, 'The Case of the Distracted Maid', 47.
95. Smith, *Man Driven Out of the Earth and Darkness*, p. 5.
96. Melledge, *A True Relation of the Former Faithful and Long Service*, p. 8.
97. Richard C. Allen, 'Restoration Quakerism, 1660–1691', in Angell and Dandelion (eds.), *Oxford Handbook of Quaker Studies*, p. 33.
98. Smith, 'The Sufferings, Tryals and Purgings of the Saints at Evesham', p. 9.
99. Alexandra Walsham, *Charitable Hatred: Tolerance and Intolerance in England, 1500–1700* (Manchester: Manchester University Press, 2006), p. 46.
100. LSF, MSS., Vol. S, 213, p. 107.
101. M. Kate Peters, 'Quaker Pamphleteering and the Development of the Quaker Movement, 1652–1656', University of Cambridge, Ph.D. thesis, 1996, p. 27.
102. Betty Hagglund, 'Quakers and the Printing Press', in Dandelion and Angell (eds.), *Early Quakers and Their Theological Thought*, p. 36.
103. Moore, *Light in Their Consciences*, p. 164.
104. Smith and Woodrove, *Cruelty of the Magistrates of Evesham*, p. 4.
105. Norman Penney (ed.), *First Publishers of Truth*, p. 83.
106. Humphrey Smith, *The Sounding Voice of the Dread of Gods Mighty Power to All the Judges and Rulers of the Earth Who Rise Up Against the Lamb* (London: Thomas Simmons, 1658), p. 2.
107. Norman Penney (ed.), *First Publishers of Truth*, p. 106.
108. Humphrey Smith, *To the Young and Tender, and to the Late Convinced People of God … In and Near the County of Essex* (London: s.n., 1663), p. 2.
109. Humphrey Smith, *An Alarum Sounding Forth unto All the Inhabitants of the Earth …* (London: s.n., 1658), pp. 21–2.
110. Smith, *An Alarum Sounding Forth*, frontispiece.
111. Smith, *An Alarum Sounding Forth*, pp. 4–5.
112. Humphrey Smith, *The Just Complaint of the Afflicted … To Be Delivered to the Judge of the Sessions at Winchester* (s.l.: s.n., 24 October 1658), p. 1.
113. Humphrey Smith, *The Vision of Humphrey Smith Which He Saw Concerning London* (London: Thomas Simmons, 1660), p. 2.
114. Rebecca Rideal, *1666: Plague, War, and Hellfire* (London: John Murray, 2016), p. 1.
115. Moore, *Light in Their Consciences*, p. 71.
116. Humphrey Smith, *Hidden Things Made Manifest by the Light …* (London: Thomas Simmons, 1664), pp. 19–20.
117. Hill, *World Turned Upside Down*, p. 50. Other notable Quakers who left their families include Sarah Cheevers of Wiltshire. See Kay. S. Taylor, 'Society, Schism and Sufferings: The First 70 Years of Quakerism in Wiltshire', University of the West of England, Ph.D. thesis, 2006, p. 292.
118. Smith, *Just Complaint of the Afflicted*, p. 1.
119. Complin, 'The Faithfulness of the Upright Made Manifest', pp. b1–b2.
120. Humphrey Smith's son was not referred to as 'Junior' but for clarity, the suffix will be used here.
121. LSF, Portfolio MSS., 36, 101, Smith's Letter to His Son, 1663.
122. LSF, Portfolio MSS., 36, 101.

123. LSF, Portfolio MSS., 36, 101.
124. Thomas Wagstaff, *Piety Promoted in Brief Memorials and Dying Expressions of some of the People called Quakers* (9th part, 2nd edn., London: James Phillips & Son, 1798), p. 14.
125. Bernard Capp, *The Ties That Bind: Siblings, Family, and Society in Early Modern England* (Cambridge: Cambridge University Press, 2018), p. 13; Patrick Wallis, 'Apprenticeship and Training in Premodern England', *Journal of Economic History*, 68, 3 (2008), 835; Will Coster, *Family and Kinship in England, 1450–1800* (London: Pearson Education, 2001), p. 54.
126. Coster, *Family and Kinship in England*, p. 55.
127. LSF, Portfolio MSS., 36, 101.
128. HaRO, 24M54, 25, 3. General Meeting of Dorsetshire and Hampshire, Burials.
129. Humphrey Smith, *The Cause of the Long Afflicted and Sore Oppressed Sent Forth in Brief from Winchester Prison* (s.l.: s.n., 1663), p. 7.
130. John 16:2
131. John 15:18; Smith, *The Cause of the Long Afflicted*, p. 8.
132. George Fox, 'Testimony Concerning Humphrey Smith', p. i.
133. William Evans and Thomas Evans (eds.), *Piety Promoted* (Philadelphia: Friends Books Store, 1854), p. 55.
134. Complin, 'Faithfulness of the Upright Made Manifest', pp. xii–xiii.
135. Complin, 'Faithfulness of the Upright Made Manifest', p. xii.
136. Complin, 'Faithfulness of the Upright Made Manifest', p. xiii.
137. Houlbrooke, *Death, Religion, and the Family in England*, p. 179.
138. David Cressy, *Birth, Marriage and Death: Ritual, Religion, and the Life-Cycle in Tudor and Stuart England* (Oxford: Oxford University Press, 1999), pp. 381–2.
139. Kevin Siena, *Rotten Bodies: Class and Contagion in Eighteenth-Century Britain* (New Haven: Yale University Press, 2019), pp. 102, 104.
140. Siena, *Rotten Bodies*, pp. 109–11.
141. Job 27: 5–8.
142. Michael MacDonald, *Mystical Bedlam: Madness, Anxiety, and Healing in Seventeenth-Century England* (Cambridge: Cambridge University Press, 1981), p. 68.
143. Smith, *An Alarum Sounding Forth unto All the Inhabitants of the Earth*, p. 24.
144. Iris-Tatjana Kolassa and Thomas Elbert, 'Structural and Functional Neuroplasticity in Relation to Traumatic Stress', *Current Directions in Psychological Science*, 16, 6, (2007), 321–5.
145. Springett died from calenture fever. It is defined as a tropical fever, but presumably may have been typhus or typhoid.
146. Mary Penington, *Some Account of Circumstances ... of Mary Penington* (London: Harvey and Darton, 1821), pp. 77–89.
147. Fox, 'Testimony Concerning Humphrey Smith', p. ii.
148. Fox, 'Testimony Concerning Humphrey Smith', pp. i–ii.
149. George Whitehead, 'A Testimony Concerning the Servant of Christ, Humphrey Smith ...', in Anon (ed.), *A Collection*, p. iii.
150. Nicholas Gates, 'The Testimony of Nicholas Gates concerning Humphrey Smith', in Anon (ed.), *A Collection*, p. xv.
151. James Potter, 'James Potter's Testimony Concerning Humphrey Smith', in Anon (ed.), *A Collection*, p. xvi.

152. Humphrey Smith, 'Humphrey Smith's Testimony Concerning His Father', in Anon (ed.), *A Collection*, p. xxi.
153. Smith, 'Testimony Concerning His Father', p. xxi.
154. Smith, 'Testimony Concerning His Father', p. xxiii.
155. 2 Timothy 4: 7–8; Anon. (ed.), *A Collection*, frontispiece
156. David Stannard, *The Puritan Way of Death: A Study in Religion, Culture, and Social Change* (Oxford: Oxford University Press, 1977), p. 93.
157. Moore, *Light in Their Consciences*, pp. 208–10.
158. Elizabeth Vipont, *George Fox and the Valiant Sixty* (London: Hamish Hamilton, 1975), pp. 110–11.
159. Erica Canela and Robynne Rogers Healey, 'Our Dear Friend Has Departed This Life: Memorial Testimony Writing in the Long Eighteenth Century', in Robynne Rogers Healey (ed.), *Quakerism in the Atlantic World, 1690–1830* (University Park: The Pennsylvania State University Press, 2021), p. 39.
160. Humphrey Smith, *The True and Everlasting Rule of God Discovered* (London: Thomas Simmons, 1658), pp. 25–6.
161. There are similarities between Smith, his mentor Richard Farnworth, and also James Nayler. There is scope for future research exploring the journeys of all three men and particularly Nayler's influence on Farnworth and Farnworth's influence on Smith. All three were from similar socio-economic backgrounds, were prolific writers and died whilst on their travels. Nayler died in 1660 after a brutal assault while travelling to the north. Farnworth died at a similarly young age to Smith in 1666 of a summer fever. See Moore, *Light in Their Consciences*, pp. 45, 228; Douglas Gwyn, 'James Nayler and the Lamb's War', *Quaker Studies*, 12, 2, (2008), 171–88; Leo Damrosch, *The Sorrows of the Quaker Jesus: James Nayler and the Puritan Crackdown on the Free Spirit* (Cambridge, Massachusetts: Harvard University Press, 1996); Erin Bell, 'Eighteenth-Century Quakerism and the Rehabilitation of James Nayler, Seventeenth-Century Radical, *The Journal of Ecclesiastical History*, 59 (3) 2008, 426–46.

Epilogue: On Colonial Shores

1. Joseph Bolles and Ellis Hookes, *Spirit of the martyrs revived; An addition to the book, entituled, The spirit of the martyrs revived. It being a short acount of some remarkable persecutions in New-England; especially of four faithful martyrs of our Lord and Saviour Jesus Christ, who suffered death at Boston* (New London, Connecticut: n.p., 1758).
2. Horatio Rogers, *Mary Dyer of Rhode Island: The Quaker Martyr that was hanged on Boston Common, June 1, 1660* (Providence, Preston and Rounds, 1896), pp. 68–71.

Bibliography

Primary Sources

<u>Archives</u>
Glamorgan Archives, Cardiff (GA)
DSF, 29.   Birth marriage and burial records relating to the General Meeting of Herefordshire, Worcestershire, and Wales 1650–1838, transcript.

Gloucestershire Archives, Gloucester (GLA)
D1340, A.   Gloucestershire Quarterly Meetings 1668–1788.
G3, SO, 2.   Quarter Sessions Order Book 1633–1670/1.
G3, SO, 6.   Quarter Sessions Order Book 1654–1663.

House of Lords Record Office, London (HLA)
PO, JO, 10, 1, 108, 33.   Protestation Return – Worcester (City) All Saints, 1642.
PO, JO, 10, 1, 108, 34.   Protestation Return – Worcester (City) St Alban, 1642.
PO, JO, 10, 1, 108, 35.   Protestation Return – Worcester (City) St Andrew, 1642.
PO, JO, 10, 1, 108, 36.   Protestation Return – Worcester (City) St Clement, 1642.
PO, JO, 10, 1, 108, 37.   Protestation Return – Worcester (City) St Helen, 1642.
PO, JO, 10, 1, 108, 38.   Protestation Return – Worcester (City) St Martin, 1642.
PO, JO, 10, 1, 108, 39.   Protestation Return – Worcester (City) St Nicholas, 1642.
PO, JO, 10, 1, 108, 40.   Protestation Return – Worcester (City) St Peter, 1642.
PO, JO, 10, 1, 108, 41.   Protestation Return – Worcester (City) St Swithin, 1642.
PO, JO, 10, 140.   Main Papers: Archbishop Laud's Visitation (Worcester), 1635.

Hampshire Record Office, Hampshire (HaRO)
24M54, 25, 3.   General Meeting of Dorsetshire and Hampshire, Burials.

Herefordshire Record Office, Hereford (HRO)
A85, 1.   Herefordshire Quarterly Meeting, 1692–1796.
AD30, 216.   Personal Records/Transcripts Volume 1588–1823.
AH65.   Index to digest registers, 1650–1836.
AJ14, 5.   Story of the Quakers in Ross (typescript).
AJ17, 5.   E.S. Whiting, 'The Story of the Quakers in Ross, 1665–1960', typescript: 1966.
AM29, 1.   Hearth Tax Assessment for Michaelmas 1665 for Herefordshire and Comparison with the Herefordshire

	Militia Assessments of 1663, Transcribed by J. Harden in 1984.
AS4.	Register of Births, Marriages and Burials of Friends at Ross, Hereford, Leominster, and Bromyard 1646–1845.
B28, 1.	Marriage Settlement of Roger Prichard, Almeley, 1712.
BA31, 1–249.	Misc. Herefordshire (Ross-on-Wye, etc.) and Gloucestershire (Cirencester, etc.) deeds and papers and Merrick family papers.
BC9, 9.	Lease (release missing) (1) Edward Prichard of Almeley, glover and Elizabeth his wife, one of the daughters of Elizabeth, wife of Henry Wright of Shrewsbury, chapman. (2) Henry Lichfield of Little Eaton co. Derby, gent. Henry Wright of Shrewsbury and John Millington of Shrewsbury, baker, 7 June 1690.
BC9, 10.	Lease (1) Mary Prichard of Almeley, widow (2) Edward Prichard of Almeley, glover, her son and heir app, 7 January 1685.
BD100, 37–36.	Deeds to South Street Leominster for land to be used as a meeting house and burial ground.
BG11, 17, 5, 46.	Petition of Jane Merrick, who was injured while working to move earth for the defences of Hereford when it was besieged by the Scots.
BG11, 17, 5, 49.	Depositions of Daniel Holder, Master of the Company of Clothiers and Weavers, and Walter Merrick, Baker.
BG11, 11, 27.	Francis Finch to Roger Pritchard, Glover.
Microfilm X110.	Hereford, Worcestershire, and Wales, births 1635–1837.

Lambeth Palace Library, London (LPL)

MSS., 943.	Papers of William Laud and Others: Articles for the visitation of Gloucester cathedral 1635.

Library of the Society of Friends, London (LSF)

ARB, 81.	Edward Bourne's letter to George Fox from Warwick gaol, 1660.
ARB, 130.	Edward Bourne's letter to George Fox from Worcester 1690.
Charles Lloyd MSS. Extracts.	Letter by Morgan Watkins.
Gibson, 1.	Edward Bourne's letter to George Whitehead from Worcester, 1696.
MSS. Box., P2, 15.	The Journal of John Audland, 1654, in 'Letters of John Audland, 1653'.
MSS. Vol. 210.	Biographical Memoirs of Edward Bourne Vol. 2, 289.
MSS. Vol. 213.	Biographical memoirs by Thomas J. Backhouse and Thomas Mounsey, containing biographies of Friends, Vol. 5, S–Y.
MSS. 344, 159–60.	John Penington MSS, Vol. 4.
Penn MSS. 131.	Letter to George Fox from William Penn, 1674.

Portfolio MSS. 1, 45.	Edward Bourne's Letter to King Charles II, Hereford Prison, 4 July 1664.
Portfolio MSS. 1, 46.	Letter to the King, 1684 [Edward Bourne].
Portfolio MSS. 15, 143.	Edward Bourne's letter to George Fox from Worcester, 1685.
Portfolio MSS. 16, 51.	A Minister Deceased [Edward Bourne], 1708.
Portfolio MSS. 17, 3.	James Merrick of Ross, a faithful servant and minister of Christ, and a sufferer for his name and of a good report among all men that feare God who finished his testimony in London.
Portfolio MSS. 36, 101.	Humphrey Smith's letter to his son, 1663.
Spence MSS. III, 175.	Edward Bourne's letter to George Fox from Worcester, 1676.
Spriggs I MSS. 156, 25.	Edward Bourne's letter to George Fox from Worcester, 1676.
Swarthmore MSS., 7, 16.	G[eorge] F[ox] to Clemen[t] Rider in Wo[rce]ster, 1656.
Swarthmore MSS., I, 4, 52.	E[dward] Born[e] to GF from Hereford, 1664.
Swarthmore MSS., I, 217.	Tho. Willam to M[argaret] F[ell], 1654.
Swarthmore MSS., I, 231.	Daniel Baker to George Fox, Worcester, 17 February 1664.
Swarthmore MSS., I, 238.	Daniel Baker to George Fox, Worcester, 11 March 1664.
Swarthmore MSS., I, 240.	D[aniel] Baker to G[eorge] F[ox] presener [sic] at wo[rce]ster abought 1666.
Swarthmore MSS., II, 195.	George Fox to James Nayler, 1656.
Swarthmore MSS., II, 48.	Richard Farnworth to Margaret Fell, Badsley, Warwickshire, 16 May 1654.
Swarthmore MSS., II, 55.	Richard Farnworth to George Fox, Bromsgrove, 26 April 1654.
Swarthmore MSS., III, 57.	Richard Farnworth to George Fox, Tewkesbury, Gloucestershire, 7 May 1654.
Swarthmore MSS., III, 1, 129.	Morgan Watkins to Margaret Fell, 1665.
Swarthmore MSS., III, 4, 188.	M[organ] Watkins to G[eorge] F[ox] at Torbans (presumably Torbay, Devon), 1660.
Swarthmore MSS., III, 253–4.	George Taylor and Thomas Willam to Margaret Fell, 1655.
Swarthmore MSS., III, 304.	George Taylor and Thomas Willam to Friends, 1655.
Swarthmore MSS., V, 63.	George Fox to the Women's Meetings, 5 October 1676.
Swarthmore MSS., IV, 52.	Edward Bourne's letter to George Fox from Hereford, 1664.
Swarthmore MSS., VI, 36.	George Fox Epistle to the Flock of God, 1654.
Swarthmore MSS., VII, 128.	George Fox, A paper to be red among frends at woster, undated.
YM, MfS, GBS.	Great Book of Sufferings, II, 1650–1680.

Bibliography 191

National Archives, Kew (NA)
E179, 119, 487.	Herefordshire Hearth Tax Records, 1665.
PROB, 11, 351.	Will of David Jones, Ross, 23 April 1676.
PROB, 11, 357.	Will of James Merrick, Tanner of Ross, Herefordshire, 2 November 1675.
PROB, 11, 359.	Will of Roger Prichard, Almeley, 1 March 1678.
PROB, 11, 361.	Will of John Merricke, Tanner of Ross, Herefordshire.
RG, 6, 1375.	Monthly Minutes of Evesham and Alcester, 1648–1778 [including burial, marriage, and death records].
SP, 16, 492, 321, 87.	Nehemiah Wharton to George Willingham, 7 October 1642.
EM, 1281–1488.	Papers of Royalist Supporters.

Shropshire Archives, Shropshire (SALA)
XMO, 445, 268.	Paper copy of a private charter, 7 July 1419.

Woodbrooke Quaker Study Centre Library, Birmingham (WQSCL)
Bevan-Naish Collection, Vol. 1817.	The Letters of John Ellis 1708.
Bevan-Naish Collection, Vol. 2261.	Tracts 33. Before 1708.
Bevan-Naish Collection, Vol. 2205.	Tracts Vol. 5.

Worcester Record Office, Worcester (WRO)
1, 1, 79, 4.	Quarter Sessions Rolls: Presentment by the Great Inquest 11 April 1643.
1, 1, 79, 6.	Quarter Sessions 19 April 1642.
1, 1, 79, 10.	Quarter Sessions 1642 [fragment].
1, 1, 90.	Quarter Sessions Easter/Midsummer/Michaelmas, 1660, 1661 Epiphany.
1, 1, 93.	Quarter Sessions Easter/Midsummer/Michaelmas, 1661, 1662 Epiphany.
1, 1, 97.	Quarter Sessions Easter/Midsummer/Michaelmas, 1662, 1663 Epiphany.
1, 1, 101.	Quarter Sessions Easter/Midsummer/Michaelmas, 1664, 1665 Epiphany.
1, 1, 104.	Quarter Sessions Easter/Midsummer/Michaelmas, 1675, 1676 Epiphany.
110, 1, 119.	1673 Quarter Sessions Calendar of Prisoners.
899, 799, 8782, 42, H14, 5.	Lease and counterpart lease for forty-one years from Sir Daniel Tyas, Knight.
899, 749, 8782, 42, H14, 7.	Counterpart lease for forty-one years from John Tyas.
899, 749, 8782, 16, C30, 6.	Mortgage by demise from John Blurton of Worcester City.
716, 02, 2071, V.	A note of damage done at the Cathedral during the Civil War.
795.02, 2059.	Consistory and Probate Court Case Lists, 1668–1672, 1669–1671.
898.2, 1303, 9.	Ross Monthly Meeting Minutes, 1674–1778

898.2, 2208.	Howard E. Collier, 'The Worcester Meeting of the Religious Society of Friends, 1655–1949', Unpublished typescript 1949.
1303, 2, 20.	Marriage Certificate of Jonah Cater and Sarah Browne, 3 May 1686.
1303, 2, 20.	Marriage Certificate of Joseph Player and Mary Cater, 16 November 1686.
1303, 2, 20.	Marriage Certificate of Daniell Lodge and Jane James, 13 July 1687.
8001, 3, 3, 2.	Quarter Sessions Order Books from 1632–1655 and 1656–1673.
BA, 1303.	Herefordshire Quarterly Meeting Record of Business Minutes, 1665–1790

Printed Primary Sources

Anon. (ed.), *A Collection of the Several Writings and Faithful Testimonies of … Humphry Smith*, (London: Andrew Sowle, 1683).

Anon., *A Copy of a Letter, With Its Answer Concerning a Context at Worcester Between a Minister and a Quaker* (s.l.: s.n., 1656).

Anon., *A Petition of the Justices of the Peace … at the Quarter Sessions Holden at Hereford for the Same County Presented to the Right Honorable House of Commons Assembled in Parliament, 25 January 1648* (London: Giles Calvert, 1649).

Anon., *A Representation of The Government of the Borough of Evesham in the County of Worcester Directed unto the Protector of England, Scotland, and Ireland* (s.l.: s.n., 1655).

Anon., *A Sad Caveat to All Quakers: Not to Boast Any More That They Have God Almighty by The Hand, When They Have the Devil By The Toe* (London: W. Gilbertson, 1657).

Anon., *An Exact and Perfect Relation of Every Particular of the Fight at Worcester* (London: Francis Leach, 1651).

Anon. *Articles to Be Inquired in the Metropolitical Visitation … for the Diocese of Worcester in the Yeere of Our Lord God 1635* (London: Richard Badger, 1635).

Anon., *Flagellum Dei, or, A Collection of the Several Fires, Plagues, and Pestilential Diseases That Have Happened in London Especially, and Other Parts of This Nation from the Norman Conquest to This Present* (London: s.n., 1668).

Anon., *Foure Ordinances of the Lords and Commons Assembled in Parliament* (London: s.n., 1644).

Anon., *The Grand Imposter Examined or The Life, Tryal, and Examination of James Nayler* (London: Henry Brome, 1656).

Anon., *The Quakers Quaking: or, The Most Just and Deserved Punishment Inflicted on the Person of James Naylor …* (London: W. Gilbertson, 1657).

Anon., *Tub-Preachers Overturn'd or Independency to Be Abandon'd and Abhor'd as Destructive to the Majestracy and Ministery, of the Church and Common-Wealth of England* (London: s.n., 1647).

Aston, Sir Thomas, *A Collection of Sundry Petitions Presented to the Kings Most Excellent Majesty as Also, to the Two Most Honourable Houses, Now Assembled in Parliament, and Others Already Signed, By Most of the Gentry, Ministers and Freeholders of Several Counties* (London: Walter Davis, 1681).

Baker, Daniel, *Yet One Warning More, To Thee O England* (London: Robert Wilson, 1660).

Bale, John, *A Brefe Chronycle Concerning the Examination and Death of the Blessed Martir of Christ Sir John Oldecastell the Lord Cobham* (London: Anthony Scoloker and Wyllya[m] Sere, 1548).
Baxter, Richard, 'Answer to the Quakers Queries', in *The Quakers Catechism* (London: Thomas Underhill, 1655).
Baxter, Richard, *One Sheet Against Quakers* (London: Robert White, 1657).
Baxter, Richard, *Reliquiae Baxterianae: or, Mr. Richard Baxter's Narrative of the Most Memorable Passages of His Life and Times* (London: T. Parkhurst, J. Robinson, J. Lawrence and J. Dunton, 1696).
Baxter, Richard, *The Quakers Catechism* (London: Thomas Underhill, 1655).
Baxter, Richard, *The Right Method for a Settled Peace of Conscience* ... (London: Printed for T. Underhill, F. Tyton and W. Raybould, 1653).
Blome, Richard, *The Fanatick History or, An Exact Relation and Account of the Old Anabaptists and New Quakers: Being the Summe of All That Hath Been Yet Discovered About Their Most Blasphemous Opinions, Dangerous P[r]actises, and Malitious Endevours* ... (London: J. Sims, 1660).
Bolles, Joseph and Hookes, Ellis, *Spirit of the martyrs revived*; An addition to the book, entituled, *The spirit of the martyrs revived. It being a short account of some remarkable persecutions in New-England; especially of four faithful martyrs of our Lord and Saviour Jesus Christ, who suffered death at Boston* (New London, Connecticut: n.p., 1758).
Bourne, Edward, *A Looking-Glass Discovering to All People what Image They Bear* (s.l.: s.n., 1671).
Bourne, Edward, *A Warning from the Lord God to the Inhabitants of the Town and County of Warwick* (s.l.: s.n., 1661).
Bourne, Edward, *A Warning from the Lord God Out of Sion, Who is Mighty and Terrible Sounded Forth Unto the Inhabitants of the City of Worcester* (London: Robert Wilson, 1660).
Bourne, Edward, *An Answer to Doctor Good (so called) His DIALOGUE against those call'd QUAKERS* (s.l.: s.n., 1675).
Bourne, Edward, *An Epistle to Friends* (London: J. Bringhurst, 1682).
Bourne, Edward, *Certain Queries Answered, Which Were Sent by a PAPIST for the People Called QUAKERS to Answer*, (s.l.: s.n., 1667).
Bourne, Edward, *For the Inhabitants of Worcester to View and Consider Well of, Especially They of Nicholas Parish* (s.l.: s.n., 1682).
Bourne, Edward, *The Truth of God Cleared, and Above the Deceite Advanced* ... (London: Thomas Simmons, 1657).
Bowater, John, *Something Concerning the Proceedings of Thomas Willmate, Vicar of the Parish of Bromsgrove, in the County of Worcester, Against Me John Boweter, (Who Am a Prisoner for the Testimony of Christ Jesus) with a Salutation of Love to My Loving and Kind Neighbours* (London: s.n., 1681).
Bowen, William, *A Perfect and True Relation of the Great and Bloudy Skirmish Fought Before the City of Worcester* (London: Jo. Thomas, 1642).
Burrough, Edward, *Many Strong Reasons Confounded, Which Would Hinder Any Reasonable Man from Being a Quaker* (London: Thomas Simmons, 1657).
Burrough, Edward, 'Truth Defended or Certain Accusations Answered', in Anon. (ed.), *The Memorable Works of a Son of Thunder and Consolation Namely That True Prophet and Faithful Servant of God and Sufferer for the Testimony of Jesus, Edward Burroughs, Who Dyed a Prisoner for the Word of God in the City of London, the Fourteenth of the Twelfth Moneth, 1662* (s.l.: s.n., 1662).

Complin, Nicholas, 'The Faithfulness of the Upright Made Manifest Being a Testimony concerning the Life, Death, and Sufferings of a precious Servant of the Lord, called, Humphry Smith', in Anon. (ed.), *A Collection of the Several Writings and Faithful Testimonies of ... Humphry Smith* (London: Andrew Sowle, 1683).

Cromwell, Oliver, *A Letter from the Lord General Cromwel, Dated September the Fourth, 1651 ... Touching the Taking of the City of Worcester and The Total Routing of the Enemies Army* (London: John Field, 1651).

Cromwell, Oliver, *A Proclamation of His Highness, Prohibiting Horse-Races in England and Wales for Eight Moneths* (London: Henry Hills and John Field, 1658).

Danson, Thomas, *The Quakers Folly Made Manifest to All Men* (London: J.H. for John Allen, 1659).

Davies, Richard, *An Account of the Convincement, Exercises, Services, and Travels of ... Richard Davies* (London: James Phillips, 1794).

Deacon, John, *The Grand Imposter Examined: or the Life, Tryal, and Examination of James Nayler* (London: Henry Brome, 1657).

Edwards, Thomas, *The First and Second Part of Gangrena*, (3rd ed., London: T.R. and E.M., 1646).

Erbery, William, *Apocrypha* (London: s.n., 1652).

Farmer, Ralph, *Satan Enthroned in his Chair of Pestilence* (London: Edward Thomas, 1657).

F[arnworth], R[ichard], *A Brief Discovery of the Kingdome of Antichrist and the Downfall of it Hasteth Greatly. With a Difference Betwixt the Ordinances of Christ and of Antichrist* (London: s.n., 1653), frontispiece.

Farnworth, Richard, *A Character Whereby the Fast Christs, or Antichrists, Seducers, False Prophets, and House Creepers May Be Known* (London: Giles Calvert, 1654).

Farnworth, Richard, *A Discovery of Truth and Falsehood* (London: Giles Calvert, 1653).

F[arnworth], R[ichard], *A True Testimony Against The Popes Wayes, &c. In a Return to That Agreement of 42 of Those That Call Themselves Ministers of Christ (But Are Proved to Be Wrongers of Men and of Christ) in the County of Worcester, and Some Adjacent Parts* (London: Giles Calvert, 1656).

F[arnworth], R[ichard], *A Woman Forbidden to Speak in the Church the Grounds Examined, the Mystery Opened, the Truth Cleared, and the Ignorance Both of Priests and People Discovered* (London: Giles Calvert, 1654).

F[arnworth], R[ichard], *Call Out of False Worships* (London: s.n., 1653).

F[arnworth], R[ichard], *England's Warning Peece Gone Forth* (London: Tho. Wayte, 1653).

Farnworth, Richard, *Light Risen out of Darkness* (London: Giles Calvert, 1654).

Farnworth, Richard, *The Ranters Principles and Deceits Discovered and Declared Against, Denied and Disowned by Us Whom the World calls Quakers* (London: Giles Calvert, 1654)

Farnworth, Richard and Smith, Humphrey, *Antichrist's Man of War, Apprehended and Encountered Withal, by a Souldier of the Armie of the Lamb* (London: Giles Calvert, 1655).

Forster, Mary, *These Several Papers Was Sent to the Parliament the Twentieth Day of the Fifth Moneth, 1659. Being Above Seven Thousand of the Names of the Hand-maids and Daughters of the Lord ...* (London: Mary Westwood, 1659).

Fox, George, *A Collection of Many Select and Christian Epistles, Letters and Testimonies Written on Sundry Occasions, by That Ancient, Eminent, Faithful Friend and Minister of Christ Jesus, George Fox; The Second Volume* (London: T. Sowle, 1698).

Fox, George, 'George Fox's Testimony Concerning Humphrey Smith', in Anon. (ed.), *A Collection of the Several Writings and Faithful Testimonies of ... Humphry Smith* (London: Andrew Sowle, 1683).

Fox, George, *Gospel Truth Demonstrated in a Collection of Doctrinal Books* (London: T. Sowle, 1656).
Gates, Nicholas, 'The Testimony of Nicholas Gates concerning Humphrey Smith', in Anon (ed.), *A Collection of the Several Writings and Faithful Testimonies of ... Humphry Smith* (London: Andrew Sowle, 1683).
Good, Thomas, *FIRMIANUS and DUBITANTIUS, OR Certain DIALOGUES Concerning Atheism, Infidelity, Popery, and Other Heresies and Schisme's That Trouble the Peace of the Church, and Are Destructive of Primitive Piety* (Hereford: L. Litchfield, 1674).
Hicks, Thomas, *The Quaker Condemned Out of His Own Mouth* (London: R.W. for Peter Parker, 1674).
Hubberthorne, Richard, *An Answer to a Book Called A Just Defence and Vindication* (London: Robert Wilson, 1660).
Hubberthorne, Richard, *The Light of Christ Within Proved to be Sufficient to Lead unto God, In Answer to a Book Put Forth By John Tombes and Richard Baxter* (London: Thomas Simmons, 1660).
Kittermaster, Thomas, *A Wonderfull Deliverance or Gods Abundant Mercy in Preserving from the Cavaliers the Towne of Draiton in the County of Hereford* (London: Printed by T.F. for I.H., 20 October 1642).
Leven, Alexander Leslie Earl of, *A Declaration of His Excellency the Earl of Leven Concerning the Rising of the Scotish Army from the Seige [sic] of the City of Hereford* (London: M. B[ell], 1645).
Melledge, Anthony, *A True Relation of the Former Faithful and Long Service ... of Anthony Melledge* (s.l.: s.n., 1656).
Mercurius Belgicus: or, A briefe Chronologie of the Battails, Sieges, Conflicts, and Other Most Remarkable Passages from the Beginning of This Rebellion, to the 25 of March 1646.
Mercurius Britanicus, Communicating the Affaires of Great Britaine for the Better Information of the People, Issue 42. 1–8 July 1644.
Mercurius Politicus, 26 February to 5 March 1657.
More, Henry, *A Collection of Several Philosophical Writings of Dr Henry More ... as Namely, His Antidote Against Atheism, Appendix to the Said Antidote, Enthusiasmus Triumphatus* (London: James Flesher, 1662).
More, Henry, *Enthusiasmus Triumphatus, or, A Discourse of the Nature, Causes, Kindes, and Cures, of Enthusiasm* (London: J. Flesher, 1656).
Morgan, Thomas and Birch, John, *Severall Letters from Colonel Morgan Governour of Gloucester and Colonel Birch* (London: John Wright, 24 December 1645).
Morgan, Thomas and Birch, John, *Two Letters Sent to the Honorable W. Lenthall Esq Speaker to the Honorable House of Commons; Concerning the Taking of Hereford on the 18. of This Instant Decem. 1645* (London: Edward Husband, 22 December 1645).
Nayler, James, *An Answer to a Book Called the Quakers Catechism, Put Out by Richard Baxter. Wherein the Slanderer is Searched, His Questions Answered, and His Deceit Discovered His Own Bosom* (London: s.n., 1656).
Nickolls, John (ed.). *Original Letters and Papers of State, Addressed to Oliver Cromwell; Concerning the Affairs of Great Britain* (London: William Bowyer, 1743).
Parker, Alexander, *A Tryall of a Christian* (London: Thomas Simmons, 1658).
Penington, Mary, *Some Account of Circumstance ... of Mary Penington* (London: Harvey and Darton, 1821).
Peters, Hugh, *Gods Doings and Mans Duty, Opened in a Sermon Preached Before Both Houses of Parliament ... 1645* (London: Giles Calvert, 1646).

Pepys, Samuel, *Memoirs of Samuel Pepys, Esq. comprising His Diary and a Selection from His Private Correspondence* (London: Fredrick Warne and Co., 1879).

Potter, James, 'James Potter's Testimony Concerning Humphrey Smith', in Anon. (ed.), *A Collection of the Several Writings and Faithful Testimonies of ... Humphry Smith* (London: Andrew Sowle, 1683).

Publick Intelligencer, 2–9 March 1657.

Robertson, Thomas, Blank, Richard, Bowater, John and Ingram, William, *To the Bishops and Clergy of England and Wales, the State of the Cruel Persecution, Imprisonment (Many to Death) and Spoil of Goods Inflicted Upon the People Called Quakers* (London: s.n., 1685).

Rogers, Horatio, *Mary Dyer of Rhode Island: The Quaker Martyr that was hanged on Boston Common, June 1, 1660* (Providence, Preston and Rounds, 1896).

Scudamore, Sir Barnabas, *A Letter Sent to the Right Honourable the Lord Digby from Sir Barnabas Scudamore Governor of Hereford, Concerning the late Siedge of the Citty of Hereford* (Oxford: Leonard Litchfield, 1645).

Sewell, William, *The History of the Rise, Increase, and Progress of the Christian People Called Quakers* (Philadelphia: Uriah Hunt, 1832).

Simpson, William, *From One Who Was Moved of the Lord God to Go a Sign Among the Priests ...* (London: Thomas Simmons, 1659).

Simpson, William, *Going Naked as a Signe* (London: Printed for M.W., 1659).

Skipp, Edmund, *The Worlds Wonder, or the Quakers Blazing Starr* (London: Henry Hills, 1654).

Smith, Humphrey, *An Alarum Sounding Forth unto All the Inhabitants of the Earth ...* (London: s.n., 1658).

Smith, Humphrey, *A Sad and Mournful Lamentation for the People of These Nations, but Especially for the Priests and Leaders ...* (s.l.: M.W,1660).

Smith, Humphrey, *Concerning Tithes* (s.l.: s.n., 1659).

Smith, Humphrey, *Hidden Things Made Manifest by the Light ...* (London: s.n., 1664).

Smith, Humphrey, *Man Driven Out of the Earth and Darkness by the Light, Life, and Mighty Hand of God* (London: s.n., 1658).

Smith, Humphrey, *Something Further Laid Open of the Cruel Persecution of the People Called Quakers by the Magistrates and People of Evesham* (London: s.n., 1656).

Smith, Humphrey, *Sound Things Asserted* (s.l.: s.n., 1662).

Smith, Humphrey, *To the Young and Tender, and to the Late Convinced People of God ... In and Near the County of Essex* (London: s.n., 1663).

Smith, Humphrey, *The Cause of the Long Afflicted and Sore Oppressed Sent Forth in Brief from Winchester Prison* (s.l.: s.n., 1662).

Smith, Humphrey, *The Just Complaint of the Afflicted ... To Be Delivered to the Judge of the Sessions at Winchester* (s.l.: s.n., 24 October 1658).

Smith, Humphrey, *The Sounding Voice of the Dread of Gods Mighty Power to All the Judges and Rulers of the Earth Who Rise Up Against the Lamb* (London: T. Simmons,1658).

Smith, Humphrey 'The Sufferings, Tryals and Purgings of the Saints at Evesham', in Anon. (ed.), *A Collection of the Several Writings and Faithful Testimonies of ... Humphry Smith* (London: Andrew Sowle, 1683).

Smith, Humphrey, *The Vision of Humphrey Smith Which He Saw Concerning London* (London: Thomas Simmons, 1660).

Smith, Humphrey, *The True and Everlasting Rule of God Discovered* (London: Thomas Simmons, 1658).

Smith, Humphrey, *To All Parents of Children Upon the Face of the Whole Earth* (London: Thomas Simmons, 1660).
Smith, Humphrey, *To New-Englands Pretended Christians Who Contrary to Christ, Have Destroyed the Lives of Men* (London: Robert Wilson, 1660).
Smith, Humphrey, *To the Musicioners, The Harpers, the Minstrels, the Singers, the Dancers, the Persecutors* (London: s.n., 1658).
Smith, Humphrey and Woodrove, Thomas, *The Cruelty of the Magistrates of Evesham, Worcestershire ...* (London: Giles Calvert, 1655).
Smith, Humphrey III, 'Humphrey Smith's Testimony concerning his Father', in Anon. (ed.), *A Collection of the Several Writings and Faithful Testimonies of ... Humphry Smith* (London: Andrew Sowle, 1683).
Stapylton, Sir Robert, *A More Full Relation of the Great Victory Obtained By Our Forces Near Worcester* (London: s.n., 1651).
Underhill, Thomas, *Hell Broke Loose or An History of the Quakers Both Old and New* (London: Thomas Underhill and Simon Miller, 1660).
Vincent, Thomas, *God's Terrible Voice in the City* (s.l.: s.n., 1667).
Watkins, Morgan, *Swearing Denyed in the New Covenant* (London: Robert Wilson, 1660).
Watkins, Morgan, *Lamentation Over England* (London: s.n., 1664).
Watkins, Morgan, *The Day Manifesting the Night and the Deeds of Darkness Reproved by the Light* (London: Thomas Simmons, 1660).
Watkins, Morgan, *The Marks of the True Church* (London: s.n., 1675).
Watkins, Morgan, *The Things That are Caesar's Rendered unto Caesar and the Things That are God's Rendered Unto God* (s.l.: Printed for M.W., 1666).
Whitehead, George, 'A Testimony Concerning the Servant of Christ, Humphrey Smith ...' in Anon (ed.), *A Collection of the Several Writings and Faithful Testimonies of ... Humphry Smith* (London: Andrew Sowle, 1683).

Secondary Sources

Books
Abbott, Margery Post, *Historical Dictionary of the Friends (Quakers)* (Lanham, MD: Scarecrow, 2012).
Acheson, Robert J, *Radical Puritans in England, 1550–1660* (London: Longman, 1993).
Addleshaw, George William Outram and Etchells, Frederick, *The Architectural Setting of Anglican Worship* (London: Faber, 1948).
Allen, Richard C., *Quaker Communities in Early Modern Wales: From Resistance to Respectability* (Cardiff: University of Wales, 2007).
Angell, Stephen W. and Dandelion, Pink (eds.), *The Oxford Handbook of Quaker Studies* (Oxford: Oxford University Press, 2013).
Aston, Margaret, *Lollards and Reformers: Images and Literacy in Late Medieval Religion* (London: Hambledon Press, 1984).
Atkin, Malcolm, *The Civil War in Worcestershire* (Stroud: Sutton, 1995).
Atkin, Malcolm, *Worcestershire under Arms: An English County During the Civil Wars* (Barnsley: Leo Cooper/Pen & Sword Books, 2004).
Bailey, Richard, *New Light on George Fox and Early Quakerism* (San Francisco: Mellen, 1992).
Barbour, Hugh, *The Quakers in Puritan England* (New Haven: Yale University Press, 1964).

Barbour, Hugh and Roberts, Arthur (eds.), *Early Quaker Writings* (Grand Rapids, MI:Eerdmans, 1973).
Bauman, Richard, *Let Your Words Be Few: Symbolism of Speaking and Silence Among Seventeenth-Century Quakers* (4th edn., Tucson, AZ: Wheatmark, 2009).
Bayliss, T.J.S., *Evesham Inns and Signs* (Evesham: Vale of Evesham Historical Society, 2008).
Bellers, John, *John Bellers: 1654 to 1725; Quaker Visionary: His Life, Times, and Writings*, George Clarke (ed.) (York: Sessions Book Trust, 1987).
Bennett, Martyn, *The English Civil War, 1640–1649* (London: Longman, 1995).
Besse, Joseph, *A Collection of the Sufferings of the People Called Quakers* (2 vols. London: L. Hinde, 1753).
Black, Joseph L. (ed.), *The Martin Marprelate Tracts: A Modernized and Annotated Edition* (Cambridge: Cambridge University Press, 2011).
Bond, Shelagh (ed.), *The Chamber Order Book of Worcester, 1602–1650* (Leeds: WS Maney & Son, 1974).
Brace, Howard, *The First Minute Book of the Gainsborough Monthly Meeting of the Society of Friends, 1669–1719* (Hereford: Hereford Times, Ltd, 1948).
Brace, Laura, *The Ideas of Property in Seventeenth-Century England: Tithes and the Individual* (Manchester: Manchester University Press, 1998).
Braddick, Michael, *God's Fury, England's Fire: A New History of the English Civil Wars* (London: Penguin, 2009).
Bradstock, Andrew, *Radical Religion in Cromwell's England* (London: I.B. Tauris and Co., 2011).
Braithwaite, William C., *The Beginnings of Quakerism* (London: Macmillan, 1912).
Braithwaite, William C., *The Second Period of Quakerism* (London: Macmillan, 1919).
Bray, William (ed.), *The Diary of John Evelyn, Volume I* (London: M. Walter Dunne, 1901).
Briggs, Asa, *A Social History of England* (London: Penguin, 1999).
Briggs, John, Harrison, Christopher, McInnes, Angus and Vincent, David (eds.), *Crime and Punishment in England: An Introductory History* (London: University College London Press, 1996).
Brown, Alfred, *Evesham Friends in the Olden Time* (London: West, Newman & Co., 1885).
Bund, J. Willis, *Diary of Henry Townshend of Elmley Lovett, 1640–1663 Vol. 2* (London: Mitchell Hughes and Clarke, 1920).
Bund, J. Willis, *The Civil War in Worcestershire, 1642–1646 and the Scotch Invasion of 1651* (Birmingham: Midland Educational Company, 1905).
Burnett, John, *Liquid Pleasures: A Social History of Drinks in Modern Britain* (London: Routledge, 1999).
Cadbury, Henry (ed.), *George Fox's Book of Miracles* (Cambridge: Cambridge University Press, 2012).
Capp, Bernard, *England's Culture Wars: Puritan Reformation and its Enemies in the Interregnum, 1649–1660* (Oxford: Oxford University Press, 2012).
Capp, Bernard, *The Ties That Bind: Siblings, Family, and Society in Early Modern England* (Cambridge: Cambridge University Press, 2018).
Carlin, Norah, *The Causes of the English Civil War* (Oxford: Blackwell, 1999).
Carlton, Charles, *Going to the Wars: The Experiences of the British Civil Wars, 1638–1651* (London: Routledge, 1992).
Childs, Jessie, *God's Traitors: Terror and Faith in Elizabethan England* (London: Bodley Head, 2014).

Bibliography 199

Chu, Jonathan, *Neighbors, Friends, or Madmen: The Puritan Adjustments to Quakerism in Seventeenth-Century Massachusetts Bay* (Westport, CT: Greenwood Press, 1985).
Copeland, Rita, *Pedagogy, Intellectuals and Dissent in the Later Middle Ages: Lollardy and Ideas of Learning* (Cambridge: Cambridge University Press, 2001).
Coffey, John (ed.), *The Oxford History of Protestant Dissenting Traditions: Volume I: The Post-Reformation Era, c.1559–c.1689* (Oxford: Oxford University Press, 2020).
Corbin, Peter and Sedge, Douglas (eds.), *The Oldcastle Controversy: Sir John Oldcastle, Part I and The Famous Victories of Henry V* (Manchester: Manchester University Press, 1991).
Coster, Will, *Family and Kinship in England, 1450–1800* (New York: Longman, 2001).
Crawford, Patricia, *Women and Religion in England 1500–1720* (London: Routledge, 1996).
Cressy, David, *Birth, Marriage, and Death: Ritual, Religion, and the Life-Cycle in Tudor and Stuart England* (Oxford: Oxford University Press, 1999).
Cressy, David and Ferrell, Lori Anne, *Religion and Society in Early Modern England: A Sourcebook* (London: Routledge, 1996).
Cromwell, Oliver and Roots, Ivan Alan, *Speeches of Oliver Cromwell* (London: Dent, 1989).
Damrosch, Leo, *The Sorrows of the Quaker Jesus: James Nayler and the Puritan Crackdown on the Free Spirit* (Cambridge: Harvard University Press, 1996).
Daniell, Christopher, *Death and Burial in Medieval England, 1066–1550* (London: Taylor & Francis Group, 1996).
Davies, Adrian, *The Quakers in English Society, 1655–1725* (Oxford: Clarendon Press, 2000).
de Beer, Esmond Samuel (ed.), *The Diary of John Evelyn, Volume III: Kalendarium, 1650–1672* (Oxford: Oxford University Press, 2000).
Duffy, Eamon, *The Stripping of the Altars: Traditional Religion in England, c.1400–c.1580* (New Haven: Yale University Press, 1992).
Durston, Christopher and Maltby, Judith D., *Religion in Revolutionary England* (Manchester: Manchester University Press, 2006).
Eales, Jacqueline, *Puritans and Roundheads* (Glasgow: Hardinge Simpole, 2002).
Eales, Jacqueline, *Women in Early Modern England, 1500–1700* (London: UCL, 1998).
Emmott, Elizabeth, *The Story of Quakerism* (London: Headley Brothers, 1908).
Erickson, Amy Louise, *Women and Property in Early Modern England* (London: Routledge, 1995).
Evans, Jennifer and Read, Sara, *Maladies and Medicine: Exploring Health and Healing, 1540–1740* (Barnsley: Pen & Sword History, 2017).
Evans, William and Evans, Thomas (eds.), *Piety Promoted* (Philadelphia: Friends Books Store, 1854).
Faraday, Michael A., *Herefordshire Militia Assessments of 1663* (London: Royal Historical Society, 1972).
Fissel, Mark Charles, *The Bishops' Wars: Charles I's Campaigns against Scotland, 1638–1640* (Cambridge: Cambridge University Press, 1994).
Fletcher, Anthony, *The Outbreak of the English Civil War* (London: Edward Arnold, 1981).
Fletcher, Anthony and Stevenson, John (eds.), *Order & Disorder in Early Modern England* (Cambridge: Cambridge University Press, 1987).
Forrest, Ian and Whittick, Christopher (eds.), *The Visitation of Hereford Diocese in 1397* (Woodbridge: Boydell & Brewer, 2021).
French, Henry R., *The Middle Sort of People in Provincial England 1600–1750* (Oxford: Oxford University Press, 2007).

Gardiner, Samuel R. (ed.), *The Constitutional Documents of the Puritan Revolution 1625–1660* (3rd edn., Oxford: Oxford University Press, 1958).
Garman, Mary, *Hidden in Plain Sight: Quaker Women's Writings, 1650–1700* (Wallingford, PA: Pendle Hill Publications, 1996).
Gaskill, Malcolm, *Crime and Mentalities in Early Modern England* (Cambridge: Cambridge University Press, 2000).
Gaskill, Malcolm, *Witchfinders: A Seventeenth-Century English Tragedy* (London: John Murray, 2006).
Gilbert, Nigel, *A History of Kidderminster* (Chichester: Phillimore, 2004).
Gill, Catie, *Women in the Seventeenth-Century Quaker Community: A Literary Study of Political Identities, 1650–1700* (London: Routledge, 2005).
Gilley, Sheridan, *A History of Religion in Britain: Practice and Belief from Pre-Roman Times to the Present* (Oxford: Blackwell, 1994).
Grell, O.P., Israel, J.I. and Tyacke, N. (eds.), *From Persecution to Tolerance* (Oxford: Clarendon Press, 1991).
Gummere, Amelia Mott, *Witchcraft and Quakerism: A Study in Social History* (London: Headley Brothers, 1908).
Gwyn, Douglas, *The Covenant Crucified: Quakers and the Rise of Capitalism* (London: Quaker Books, 2006).
Hailwood, Mark, *Alehouses and Good Fellowship in Early Modern England* (Woodbridge: Boydell Press, 2014),
Harlow, Jonathan (ed.), *The Ledger of Thomas Speed, 1681–1690* (Bristol: 4word, 2011).
Hatton, Jean, *George Fox: The Founder of the Quakers* (Oxford: Monarch, 2007).
Hawkins, Brian, *Taming the Phoenix: Cirencester and the Quakers, 1642–1686* (York: William Sessions, 1998).
Heath-Agnew, E., *Roundhead to Royalist: A Biography of Colonel John Birch 1615–1691* (Hereford: Print Logic, 1977).
Hill, Christopher, *Puritanism and Revolution: Studies in Interpretation of the English Revolution of the 17th Century* (London: Secker & Warburg, 1995).
Hill, Christopher, *The Century of Revolution, 1603–1714* (London: Cardinal, 1975).
Hill, Christopher, *The World Turned Upside Down: Radical Ideas During the English Revolution* (London: Penguin, 1991).
Hinds, Hilary, *George Fox and Early Quaker Culture* (Manchester: Manchester University Press, 2011).
Hinds, Hilary, *God's Englishwoman: Seventeenth-Century Radical Sectarian Writing and Feminist Criticism* (Manchester: Manchester University Press, 1996).
Hockliffe, E. (ed.), *The Diary of the Rev. Ralph Josselin 1616–1683* (London: Royal Historical Society, 1908).
Hopkinson, Charles, *Herefordshire Under Arms: A Military History of the County* (Leicester: Orphans Press, 1985).
Horle, Craig, *The Quakers and the English Legal System, 1660–1688* (Philadelphia: University of Pennsylvania Press, 1988).
Houlbrooke, Ralph A., *Death, Religion and the Family in England, 1480–1750* (Oxford: Clarendon Press, 2006).
Houlbrooke, Ralph A., *The English Family, 1450–1700* (London: Longman, 1984).
Hornbec II, J. Patrick, *What is a Lollard? Dissent and Belief in Late Medieval England* (New York: Oxford University Press, 2011).

Hughes, Ann (ed.), *Seventeenth-Century England: A Changing Culture, Vol. 1, Primary Sources* (London: Ward Lock Educational, 1983).
Ingle, H. Larry, *First Among Friends: George Fox and the Creation of Quakerism* (Oxford: Oxford University Press, 1994).
Jenkins, Geraint H., *Protestant Dissenters in Wales: 1639–1689* (Cardiff: University of Wales Press, 1992).
Jones, Rufus (ed.), *The Short Journal and Itinerary Journals of George Fox* (Cambridge: Cambridge University Press, 1925).
Jones, Rufus, *Spiritual Reformers in the 16th and 17th Centuries* (London: Macmillan, 1914).
Keeble, Neil H. (ed.), *The Autobiography of Richard Baxter* (London: J.M. Dent and Sons, 1974).
Keeble, Neil H. and Nuttall, Geoffrey F., *Calendar of the Correspondence of Richard Baxter, Volume 1, 1638–1660* (Oxford: Clarendon Press, 1991).
King James Bible: 400th Anniversary Edition of the Book That Changed the World (London: Collins, 2011).
King, Pamela M., *Medieval Literature, 1350–1500* (Edinburgh: Edinburgh University Press, 2011).
Lamont, William M., *Richard Baxter and the Millennium* (Guildford: Biddles, 1979).
Lane, Calvin, *The Laudians and the Elizabethan Church: History, Conformity and Religious Identity in Post-Reformation England* (London: Routledge, 2016).
Langford, Paul, *Eighteenth-Century Britain* (Oxford: Oxford University Press, 2000).
Laurence, Anne, *Women in England, 1500–1760: A Social History* (London: Weidenfeld and Nicolson, 1996).
Lawrence, Anne, Owens, W.R. and Sim, Stuart (eds.), *John Bunyan and his England, 1628–1688* (London: Hambledon, 1990).
Lemire, Beverley, *The Business of Everyday Life, Gender, Practice and Social Politics in England, c.1600–1900* (Manchester: Manchester University Press, 2006).
Lindley, Keith and Scott, David (eds.), *The Journal of Thomas Juxon, 1644–1647* (London: Cambridge University Press, 1999).
Lloyd, Arnold, *Quaker Social History* (London: Longmans, 1950).
Lutton, Robert, *Lollardy and Orthodox Religion in Pre-Reformation England* (Woodbridge: Boydell Press, 2006).
MacDonald, Michael, *Mystical Bedlam: Madness, Anxiety, and Healing in Seventeenth-Century England* (Cambridge: Cambridge University Press, 1981).
Macfarlane, Alan, *Marriage and Love in England, 1300–1840* (Oxford: Basil Blackwell, 1986).
Macfarlane, Alan and Harrison, Sarah, *The Justice and the Mare's Ale* (Oxford: Basil Blackwell, 1981).
Mack, Phyllis, *Visionary Women: Ecstatic Prophecy in Seventeenth-Century England* (Berkeley, CA: University of California Press, 1992).
May, George, *A Descriptive History of the Town of Evesham, from the Foundation of Its Saxon Monastery, With Notices Respecting the Ancient Deanery of Its Vale* (London: Whittaker & Co., 1845).
Meekings, Cecil Anthony Francis, Porter, S. and Roy, Ian (eds.), *The Hearth Tax Collectors' Book for Worcester, 1678–1680* (Leeds: Worcestershire Historical Society, 1983).
Moore, Rosemary, *The Light in Their Consciences: Early Quakers in Britain, 1646–1666* (rev. edn., University Park, PA: Pennsylvania State University Press, 2020).

Moore, Rosemary (ed.), *The History of the Life of Thomas Ellwood* (Oxford: AltaMira, 2004).
Morgan, Gwenda and Rushton, Peter, *Banishment in the Early Atlantic World: Convicts, Rebels, and Slaves* (London: Bloomsbury, 2013).
Morgan, Nicholas, *Lancashire Quakers and the Establishment, 1660–1730* (Edinburgh: Edinburgh University Press, 1993).
Morland, Stephen C., *Somersetshire Quarterly Meeting, 1668–1699* (Surrey: Gresham Press, 1978).
Mortimer, Russell, *Early Bristol Quakerism: The Society of Friends in the City, 1654–1700* (Bristol: Bristol Branch of the Historical Association, 1967).
Mortimer, Russell (ed.), *Minute Book of the Men's Meeting of the Society of Friends in Bristol, 1667–1686* (Gateshead: Northumberland Press Ltd, 1971).
Mortimer, Russell (ed.), *Minute Book of the Men's Meeting of the Society of Friends in Bristol, 1686–1704* (Gateshead: Northumberland Press Ltd, 1977).
Morton, Arthur Leslie, *The World of the Ranters: Religious Radicalism in the English Revolution* (London: Lawrence and Wishart, 1970).
Noake, John, *Worcester Sects: A History of the Roman Catholics and Dissenters of Worcester* (London: Longman, 1861).
O'Gorman, Frank, *The Long Eighteenth Century: British Political and Social History, 1688–1832* (London: Arnold, 1997).
Owens, W.R. (ed.), *Seventeenth-Century England: A Changing Culture, Vol. 2, Modern Studies* (London: Ward Lock Educational, 1983).
Page, William (ed.), *The Victoria History of the County of Hereford* (London: Constable, 1908).
Partington, E.V. (ed.), *Extracts from the Registers of the Society of Friends for the Bromsgrove and Chadwick Meetings, Worcestershire, 1635–1797* (Birmingham: Birmingham and Midland Society for Genealogy and Heraldry, 1990).
Penney, Norman (ed.), *The First Publishers of Truth: Being Early Records of The Introduction of Quakerism into The Counties of England and Wales* (London: Headley Brothers, 1907).
Penney, Norman (ed.), Fox, George, *The Journal of George Fox* (New York: Cosimo Classics, 2007).
Pennington, Madeleine, *Quakers, Christ, and the Enlightenment* (Oxford: Oxford University Press, 2021).
Pepys, Samuel, *The Diary of Samuel Pepys: A Selection* (London: Penguin, 2003).
Peters, Kate, *Print Culture and the Early Quakers* (Cambridge: Cambridge University Press, 2009).
Porter, Stephen, Roberts, Stephen K. and Roy, Ian (eds.), *The Diary and Papers of Henry Townshend, 1640–1663* (Bristol: Worcestershire Historical Society, 2014).
Punshon, John, *Portrait in Grey: A Story History of the Quakers* (London: Quaker Home Service, 1984).
Purkiss, Diane, *The English Civil War: A People's History* (London: Harper Perennial, 2007).
Raistrick, Arthur, *Quakers in Science and Industry: Being an Account of the Quaker Contributions to Science and Industry During the 17th and 18th Centuries* (York: Sessions, 1993).
Raymond, Joad (ed.), *Making the News: An Anthology of the Newsbooks of Revolutionary England* (Moreton-in-Marsh: The Windrush Press, 1993).
Reay, Barry (ed.), *Popular Culture in Seventeenth-Century England* (London: Routledge, 1988).
Reay, Barry, *The Quakers and the English Revolution* (London: Temple Smith, 1985).

Rideal, Rebecca, *1666: Plague, War, and Hellfire* (London: John Murray, 2016).
Roberts, Stephen K., *Evesham Borough Records of the Seventeenth Century, 1605–1687* (Kendal: Titus Wilson, 1994).
Seaward, Paul, *The Restoration, 1660–1688* (Houndsmill, Basingstoke: Macmillan, 1991).
Sharpe, James, A., *Crime in Early Modern England* (Longman: London, 1999).
Sharpe, James A, *Instruments of Darkness: Witchcraft in Early Modern England* (Philadelphia: University of Pennsylvania, 1996).
Sharpe, Kevin, *The Personal Rule of Charles I* (New Haven: Yale University Press, 1992).
Shaw, William Arthur, *A History of the English Church During the Civil Wars and Under the Commonwealth, 1640–1660, Vol. 1* (London: Longmans, 1900).
Shoesmith, Ron, *The Civil War in Hereford* (Eardisley: Logaston, 1995).
Siena, Kevin, *Rotten Bodies: Class and Contagion in Eighteenth-Century Britain* (New Haven: Yale University Press, 2019).
Smith, Joseph, *Bibliotheca Anti-Quakeriana & Bibliotheca Quakeristica* (New York: Kraus Reprint, 1968).
Smith, Nigel (ed.), *George Fox: The Journal* (London: Penguin Books, 1998).
Snell, Beatrice Saxon (ed.), *The Minute Book of the Monthly Meeting of the Society of Friends for the Upperside of Buckinghamshire, 1669–1690* (High Wycombe: Hague & Gill, 1937).
Southall, Isabel, *Memorials of The Prichards of Almeley* (Birmingham: Privately Printed, 1893).
Spicksley, Judith M., *The Business and Household Accounts of Joyce Jeffreys, Spinster of Hereford, 1638–1648* (Oxford: Oxford University Press, 2012).
Spufford, Margaret (ed.), *The World of Rural Dissenters, 1520–1775* (Cambridge: Cambridge University Press, 1995).
Spurr, John, *The Restoration Church in England, 1646–1689* (New Haven: Yale University Press, 1981).
Stannard, David, *The Puritan Way of Death: A Study in Religion, Culture, and Social Change* (Oxford: Oxford University Press, 1977).
Stell, Christopher (ed.), *Nonconformist Chapels and Meeting-Houses: Herefordshire, Worcestershire & Warwickshire* (London: HMSO Books, 1986).
Stone, Lawrence, *The Family, Sex and Marriage in England, 1500–1800* (London: Penguin, 1990).
Stoyle, Mark, *Soldiers and Strangers: An Ethnic History of the English Civil War* (New Haven: Yale University Press, 2005).
Symonds, Richard and Long, Charles Edward, *Richard Symonds's Diary of the Marches of the Royal Army* (Cambridge: Cambridge University Press, 1997).
Tarter, Michele Lise and Gill, Catie, *New Critical Studies on Early Quaker Women, 1650–1800* (Oxford: Oxford University Press, 2018).
Taylor, Ernest, *The Valiant Sixty* (York: Sessions, 1988).
Taylor-Lewis, Thomas (ed.), *Letters of the Lady Brilliana Harley* (London: Camden Society, 1854).
Thistlethwaite, W. Pearson (ed.), *Yorkshire Quaker Meeting, 1665–1966* (Harrogate: Printed by the author, 1979).
Thomas, Kathleen H., *The History and Significance of Quaker Symbols in Sect Formation* (Lampeter: Edwin Mellen Press, 2002).
Thomas, Keith, *The Ends of Life: Roads to Fulfilment in Early Modern England* (Oxford: Oxford University Press, 2010).

Thomas, Keith, *Religion and the Decline of Magic: Studies in Popular Beliefs in Sixteenth and Seventeenth-Century England* (Harmondsworth: Penguin, 1973).
Trevett, Christine, *Women and Quakerism in the 17th Century* (York: Sessions, 1992).
Trevett, Christine (ed.), *Women's Speaking Justified and Other Seventeenth-Century Quaker Writings About Women* (London: Quaker Home Service, 1989).
Trevor-Roper, Hugh, *Archbishop Laud* (2nd edn., London: Phoenix Press, 2000).
Trevor-Roper, Hugh, *The Crisis of the Seventeenth Century: Religion, The Reformation, and Social Change* (Indianapolis: Liberty Fund, 1967).
Underdown, David, *Revel, Riot, and Rebellion* (Oxford: Oxford University Press, 1985).
Underwood, Ted L., *Primitivism, Radicalism, and the Lamb's War: The Baptist-Quaker Conflict in Seventeenth-Century England* (Oxford: Oxford University Press, 1997).
Vann, Richard, *The Social Development of English Quakerism, 1655–1755* (Cambridge: Harvard, 1969).
Vipont, Elfrida, *George Fox and the Valiant Sixty* (London: Hamish Hamilton, 1975).
Wagstaff, Thomas, *Piety Promoted in Brief Memorials and Dying Expressions of Some of the People Called Quakers* (9th part, 2nd edn., London: James Phillips & Son, 1798).
Walsham, Alexandra, *Charitable Hatred: Tolerance and Intolerance in England, 1500–1700* (Manchester: Manchester University Press, 2009).
Walter, John, *Covenanting Citizens: The Protestation Oath and Popular Political Culture in the English Revolution* (Oxford: Oxford University Press, 2016).
Walter, John, *Crowds and Popular Politics in Early Modern England* (Manchester: Manchester University Press, 2010).
Walton, Joseph, *Incidents Illustrating the Doctrines and History of the Society of Friends* (Philadelphia: Wm. H Pile's Sons, 1897).
Wanklyn, Malcolm, *Inventories of Worcestershire Landed Gentry, 1537–1786* (Worcester: Worcestershire Historical Society, 1998).
Wanklyn, Malcolm and Jones, Frank, *A Military History of the English Civil War, 1642–1646: Strategy and Tactics* (Harlow: Longman/Pearson Education, 2005).
Watson, Ben, *Cider, Hard, and Sweet: History, Traditions, and Making your Own* (Woodstock, VT: The Countryman Press, 2013).
Watts, Michael R, *The Dissenters: From the Reformation to the French Revolution* (Oxford: Clarendon, 1985).
Webb, John and Webb, T.W. (eds.), *Memorials of the Civil War Between King Charles I and the Parliament of England as it Affected Herefordshire and the Adjacent Counties* (London: Longmans, 1879).
Whiteman, Anne (ed.), *The Compton Census of 1676* (Oxford: Oxford University Press, 1986).
Wilcox, Catherine M., *Theology and Women's Ministry in Seventeenth-Century English Quakerism* (Lampeter: Edwin Mellen Press, 1995).
Wood, Andy, *Riot, Rebellion and Popular Politics in Early Modern England* (London: Palgrave, 2001).
Wood, Jack, *Some Rural Quakers: A History of Quakers and Quakerism at the Corners of the Four Shires of Oxford, Warwick, Worcester and Gloucester* (York: Sessions, 1991).
Wrightson, Keith, *Earthly Necessities: Economic Lives in Early Modern Britain* (London: Penguin, 2002).
Wrightson, Keith, *English Society, 1580–1680* (London: Hutchinson, 1982).
Wrigley, Edward Anthony and Schofield, Roger S., *The Population History of England, 1541–1871* (Cambridge: Cambridge University Press, 1989).

Wroughton, John, *An Unhappy Civil War: The Experiences of Ordinary People in Gloucestershire, Somerset and Wiltshire, 1642–1646* (Bath: Lansdowne Press, 1999).

Wyatt, Martin, *Quakers in Plymouth: A Friends' Meeting in Context 1654 to the 1960's* (York: Quacks Books, 2017).

Book Chapters

Allen, Richard C., 'Living as a Quaker During the Second Period', in Richard C. Allen and Rosemary Moore, *The Quakers, 1656–1723: The Evolution of an Alternative Community* (University Park: Pennsylvania State University Press, 2018).

Allen, Richard C., 'Restoration Quakerism, 1660–1691', in Stephen W. Angell and Pink Dandelion (eds.), *The Oxford Handbook of Quaker Studies* (Oxford: Oxford University Press, 2013).

Allen, Richard C. and Moore, Rosemary, 'The Friends and Business in the Second Period' in Richard C. Allen and Rosemary Moore, *The Quakers, 1656–1723: The Evolution of an Alternative Community* (University Park: Pennsylvania State University Press, 2018).

Amussen, Susan Dwyer, 'The Gendering of Popular Culture in Early Modern England', in Tim Harris (ed.), *Popular Culture in England, c.1500–1850* (London: Macmillan, 1995).

Barry, Jonathan, 'Popular Culture in Seventeenth-Century Bristol', in Barry Reay (ed.), in *Popular Culture in Seventeenth-Century England* (London: Routledge, 1988).

Bell, Erin, 'Quakers and the Law', in Richard C. Allen and Rosemary Moore, *The Quakers, 1656–1723: The Evolution of an Alternative Community* (University Park: Pennsylvania State University Press, 2018).

Birkel, Michael and Angell, Stephen W., 'The Witness of Richard Farnworth: Prophet of Light, Apostle of Church Order', in Stephen W. Angell and Pink Dandelion (eds.), *Early Quakers and Their Theological Thought, 1647–1723* (Cambridge: Cambridge University Press, 2015).

Brown, James, 'Alehouse Licensing and State Formation in Early Modern England', in Jonathan Herring, Ciaran Regan, Darin Weinberg and Phil Withington (eds.), *Intoxication and Society: Problematic Pleasures of Drugs and Alcohol* (Basingstoke: Palgrave Macmillan, 2013).

Brown, Raymond and Sell, Alan P., 'Quakers and Dissenters in Dispute', in Richard C. Allen and Rosemary Moore, *The Quakers, 1656–1723: The Evolution of an Alternative Community* (University Park: Pennsylvania State University Press, 2018).

Canela, Erica and Healey, Robynne Rogers, 'Our Dear Friend Has Departed This Life: Memorial Testimony Writing in the Long Eighteenth Century', in Robynne Rogers Healey (ed.), *Quakerism in the Atlantic World, 1690–1830* (University Park: The Pennsylvania State University Press, 2021).

Capp, Bernard, 'Extreme Millenarianism', in Peter Toon (ed.), *Puritans, the Millennium and the Future of Israel: Puritan Eschatology 1600 to 1660* (London: James Clark & Co., 1970).

Capp, Bernard, 'The Fifth Monarchists and Popular Millenarianism', in J.F. Macgregor and Barry Reay (eds.), *Radical Religion in the English Revolution* (New York: Oxford University Press, 1984).

Capp, Bernard, 'Republican Reformation: Family, Community, and the State of Interregnum Middlesex, 1649–1660', in Helen Berry and Elizabeth Foyster (eds.), *The Family in Early Modern England* (Cambridge: Cambridge University Press, 2007).

Carr, Helen, 'Can our Emotions have a History?' in Helen Carr and Suzannah Lipscomb (eds.), *What is History, Now?: How the Past and Present Speak to Each Other* (London: Weidenfeld & Nicolson, 2021).

Durston, Christopher, 'Puritan Rule and the Failure of Cultural Revolution, 1645–1660', in Christopher Durston and Jacqueline Eales (eds.), *The Culture of English Puritanism, 1560–1700* (Palgrave Macmillan: Basingstoke, 1996).

Dyer, Alan, 'Small Market Towns 1540–1700', in Peter Clark (ed.), *The Cambridge Urban History of Britain, Volume II, 1540–1840* (Cambridge: Cambridge University Press, 2000).

Griffiths, Paul, Landers, John, Pelling, Margaret, Tyson, Robert, 'Population and disease, estrangement and belonging 1540–1700', in Peter Clark (ed.), *The Cambridge Urban History of Britain* (Cambridge: Cambridge University Press, 2000).

Hadfield, Andrew, Dimmock, Matthew, Shinn, Abigail, 'Thinking About Popular Culture in Early Modern England', in Andrew Hadfield, Matthew Dimmock, Abigail Shinn (eds.), *The Ashgate Research Companion to Popular Culture in Early Modern England* (London: Routledge, 2014).

Hagglund, Betty, 'Quakers and the Printing Press', in Stephen W. Angell and Pink Dandelion (eds.), *Early Quakers and Their Theological Thought, 1647–1723* (Cambridge: Cambridge University Press, 2015).

Harris, Tim, 'Problematising Popular Culture', in Tim Harris (ed.), *Popular Culture in England, c.1500–1850* (London: Macmillan, 1995).

Hessayon, Ariel, 'Early Quakerism and its Origins', in John Coffey (ed.), *The Oxford History of Protestant Dissenting Traditions: Volume I: The Post-Reformation Era, c.1559–c.1689* (Oxford: Oxford University Press, 2020).

Hindle, Steve, 'A Sense of Place? Becoming and Belonging in the Rural Parish, 1550–1650', in Alexandra Shepard and Phil Withington (eds.), *Communities in Early Modern England* (Manchester: Manchester University Press, 2000).

Hughes, Ann, 'The Pulpit Guarded: Confrontations Between Orthodox and Radicals in Revolutionary England', in Anne Lawrence, W.R. Owens and Stuart Sim (eds.), *John Bunyan and his England, 1628–1688* (London: Hambledon, 1990).

Ingram, Martin, 'From Reformation to Toleration: Popular Cultures in England, 1540–1690', in Tim Harris (ed.), *Popular Culture in England, c.1500–1850* (London: Macmillan, 1995).

Israel, Jonathan I., 'William III and Toleration', in Ole Peter Grell, Jonathan I. Israel, and Nicholas Tyacke (eds.), *From Persecution to Tolerance* (Oxford: Clarendon Press, 1991).

Moore, Rosemary, 'Gospel Order: The Development of Quaker Organization' in Richard C. Allen and Rosemary Moore, *The Quakers, 1656–1723: The Evolution of an Alternative Community* (University Park: Pennsylvania State University Press, 2018).

Moore, Rosemary, 'Seventeenth-Century Context and Quaker Beginnings', in Stephen W. Angell, and Pink Dandelion, (eds.), *The Oxford Handbook of Quaker Studies* (Oxford: Oxford University Press, 2013).

Moore, Rosemary, 'The Early Development of Quakerism' in Richard C. Allen and Rosemary Moore, *The Quakers, 1656–1723: The Evolution of an Alternative Community* (University Park: Pennsylvania State University Press, 2018).

Reay, Barry, 'Popular Culture in Early Modern England', in Barry Reay (ed.), *Popular Culture in Seventeenth-Century England* (London: Routledge, 1988).

Sheils, William J., 'Catholicism in England from the Reformation to the Relief Acts', in Sheridan Gilley and William J. Sheils (eds.), *A History of Religion in Britain: Practice and Belief from Pre-Roman Times to the Present* (Oxford: Blackwell, 1994).

Sheils, William, 'English Catholics at War and Peace' in Christopher Durston and Judith Maltby (eds.), *Religion in Revolutionary England* (Manchester: Manchester University Press, 2007).

Spurr, John, 'From Puritanism to Dissent', in Christopher Durston and Jacqueline Eales (eds.), *The Culture of English Puritanism, 1560–1700* (London: Palgrave, 1996).
Stevens, Sylvia, 'Travelling Ministry', in Stephen W. Angell, and Pink Dandelion (eds.), *The Oxford Handbook of Quaker Studies* (Oxford: Oxford University Press, 2013).
Stock, Gwynne 'Quaker Burial: Doctrine and Practice', in Margaret Cox (ed.), *Grave Concerns: Death and Burial in England, 1700–1850* (York: Council for British Archaeology, 1998).
Walter, John, 'Faces in the Crowd: Gender and Age in the Early Modern English Crowd', in Helen Berry and Elizabeth Foyster (eds.), *The Family in Early Modern England* (Cambridge: Cambridge University Press, 2007).
Watkins, Morgan, 'Letter from Morgan Watkins to Mary Penington, 18 August 1665', in Abram Rawlinson Barclay (ed.), *Letters &c. of Early Friends* (London: Harvey and Darton, 1841).
Welling, Jacalynn Stuckey, 'Mission', in Stephen W. Angell and Pink Dandelion (eds.), *The Oxford Handbook of Quaker Studies* (Oxford: Oxford University Press, 2013).
William III, 'An Act that the Solemne Affirmation & Declaration of the People called Quakers shall be accepted instead of an Oath in the usual Forme', in John Raithby (ed.), *Statutes of the Realm: Volume 7, 1695–1701* (London: Record Commission, 1820).
Withington, Phil, 'Citizens, Community, and Political Culture in Restoration England', in Alexandra Shepard and Phil Withington (eds.), *Communities in Early Modern England* (Manchester: Manchester University Press, 2000).
Zaller, Robert, 'Wilde, John (1590–1669)', *Oxford Dictionary of National Biography* (Oxford: Oxford University Press, 2004).

Articles

Atherton, Ian, 'Viscount Scudamore's "Laudianism": The Religious Practices of the First Viscount Scudamore', *Historical Journal*, 34, 3 (1991), 567–96.
Ayoub, Raymond, 'The Persecution of "an Innocent People" in Seventeenth-Century England', *Quaker Studies*, 10, 1 (2005), 46–66.
Bailey, Richard G., 'Francis Ellington's Use of Prophecy to Explain the Appearance, Deliverance, and Apocalyptic Role of Quakers in the Last Days', *Quaker Studies*, 3, 2 (1998), 111–32.
Bannister, Arthur Thomas, 'Visitation Returns of the Diocese of Hereford in 1397 (Continued)', *English Historical Review*, 45, 179 (1930), 444–63.
Bauman, Richard, 'Aspects of 17th Century Quaker Rhetoric', *Quarterly Journal of Speech*, 56 (1970), 67–74.
Bastow, Sarah L., '"Worth Nothing, But Very Wilful": Catholic Recusant Women of Yorkshire, 1536–1642', *Recusant History*, 25, 4 (2001), 591–603.
Bell, Erin, 'Eighteenth-Century Quakerism and the Rehabilitation of James Nayler, Seventeenth-Century Radical', *The Journal of Ecclesiastical History*, 59(3) 2008, 426–46.
Bell, Erin, 'The Early Quakers, the Peace Testimony and Masculinity in England, 1660–1720', *Gender & History*, 23, 2 (2011), 283–300.
Ben-Amos, Ilana Krausman, 'Gifts and Favors: Informal Support in Early Modern England', *Journal of Modern History*, 72, 2 (2000), 295–338.
Ben-Amos, Ilana Krausman, 'Reciprocal Bonding: Parents and Their Offspring in Early Modern England', *Journal of Family History*, 25, 3 (2000), 291–312.
Boulton, David, '"Elves, Goblins, Fairies, Quakers and New Lights": Friends in the English Republic', *Journal of the Friends Historical Society*, 63 (2012), 3–19.

Burke, Peter, 'Popular Culture in Seventeenth-Century London', *London Journal*, 3, 2, (1977), 143–62.
Canela, Erica, 'The Commendable Life and Noble Death of Humphrey Smith', *Quaker Studies*, 25, 1 (2020), 3–26.
Clifton, Robin, 'The Popular Fear of Catholics during the English Revolution', *Past & Present*, 52 (1971), 23–55.
Cherry, Charles, 'Enthusiasm and Madness: Anti-Quakerism in the Seventeenth Century', *Quaker History*, 73, 2 (1984), 1–24.
Cressy, David, 'The Protestation Protested, 1641–1642', *Historical Journal*, 45, 2 (2002), 25–79.
Cressy, David, 'Revolutionary England 1640–1642', *Past & Present*, 181 (2003), 35–71.
Cust, Richard, 'Was There an Alternative to the Personal Rule? Charles I, the Privy Council and the Parliament of 1629', *History*, 90, 3 (2005), 330–52.
Day, John I., 'Horse Racing and the Pari-mutuel', *Annals of the American Academy of Political and Social Science*, 269, 1, (1950), 55–61.
Ellis, Henry, 'Letters from a Subaltern Officer of the Earl of Essex's Army, Written in the Summer and Autumn of 1642', *Archaeologia*, 35, 2 (1854), 310–34.
Fincham, Andrew, 'Faith in Numbers—Re-quantifying the English Quaker Population during the Long Eighteenth Century', *Religions* 10, 83 (2019), 1–15.
Foyster, Elizabeth A., 'Male Honour, Social Control and Wife Beating in Late Stuart England', *Transactions of the Royal Historical Society 6th series*, 6 (1996), 215–24.
Gwyn, Douglas, 'James Nayler and the Lamb's War', *Quaker Studies*, 12, 2 (2008), 171–88.
Harlow, Jonathan, 'Preaching for Hire: Public Issues and Private Concerns in a Skirmish of the Lamb's War', *Quaker Studies*, 10, 1 (2005), 31–45.
Horle, Craig W., 'Quakers and Baptists, 1647–1660', *Baptist Quarterly*, 26 (1976), 344–62.
Hughes, Ann, 'Public Disputations, Pamphlets and Polemic', *History Today*, 41, 2 (1991), 27–33.
Jenkins, Rhys, 'Industries of Hereford in Bygone Times', *Transactions of the Newcomen Society*, 17 (1936), 175–89.
Johnson, Rosalind, 'The Case of the Distracted Maid: Healing and Cursing in Early Quaker History', *Quaker Studies*, 21, 1 (2016), 33–47.
Johnston, Margaret Anne, 'The Confrontation Between Quakers and Clergy 1652–1656: Theology and Practice', *Quaker Studies*, 26, 2 (2021), 209–40.
Kent, Stephen A., 'Relative Deprivation and Resource Mobilization: A Study of Early Quakerism', *British Journal of Sociology*, 33, 4 (1982), 529–44.
Kent, Stephen A., '"Handmaids and Daughters of the Lord": Quaker Women, Quaker Families, and Somerset's Anti-Tithe Petition in 1659', *Quaker History*, 97, 1 (2008), 32–61.
Kesselring, Krista L., 'Gender, the Hat, and Quaker Universalism in the Wake of the English Revolution', *Seventeenth Century*, 26, 2 (2011), 299–322.
Kolassa, Iris-Tatjana and Elbert, Thomas, 'Structural and Functional Neuroplasticity in Relation to Traumatic Stress', *Current Directions in Psychological Science*, 16, 6, (2007), 321–5.
Langelüdecke, Henrick, '"I Finde All Men & My Officers All Soe Unwilling": The Collection of Ship Money, 1635–1640', *Journal of British Studies*, 46, 3 (2007), 509–42.
Langelüdecke, Henrick, '"The Pooreste and Symplest Sorte of People?": The Selection of Parish Officers During the Personal Rule of Charles I', *Historical Research*, 80, 208 (2007), 225–60.
Langley, A.S., 'Seventeenth-Century Baptist Disputations', *Baptist Historical Society Transactions*, 6 (1918–19), 216–43.

Little, Patrick, 'Uncovering a Protectoral Stud: Horses and Horse-Breeding at the Court of Oliver Cromwell, 1653–8', *Historical Research*, 82, 216 (2009), 252–67.
Maclear, James F., 'Quakerism and the End of the Interregnum: A Chapter in the Domestication of Radical Puritanism', *Church History*, 19, 9 (1950), 240–70.
Manning, David, 'Accusations of Blasphemy in English Anti-Quaker Polemic, *c.*1660–1701', *Quaker Studies*, 14, 1 (2009), 27–56.
Marston, Jerrilyn Greene, 'Gentry Honor and Royalism in Early Stuart England', *Journal of British Studies*, 13, 1 (November 1973), 21–43.
Matar, Nabil, 'The Barbary Corsairs, King Charles I and the Civil War', *Seventeenth Century*, 16, 2 (2001), 239–58
Miller, John, '"A Suffering People": English Quakers and Their Neighbours *c.*1650–*c.*1700', *Past & Present*, 188 (2005), 71–103.
Nicholls, John (ed.), 'Letters of Lady Brilliana Harley', *Gentleman's Magazine and Historical Review* (July 1856–May 1868), 468–75.
Nuttall, Geoffrey F., 'Another Baptist Vicar? Edmund Skipp of Bodenham', *Baptist Quarterly*, 33 (1990), 331–4.
Nuttall, Geoffrey F., 'Overcoming the World: The Early Quaker Programme', *Studies in Church History*, 10 (1973), 145–64.
Questier, Michael, 'Catholic Loyalism in Early Stuart England', *English Historical Review*, 123, 504 (2008), 1132–65.
Park, Charles E., 'Puritans and Quakers', *New England Quarterly*, 27, 1 (1954), 53–74.
Plumb, Derek, 'The Social and Economic Spread of Rural Lollardy: A Reappraisal', W.J. Sheils and Diana Wood (eds.), *Voluntary Religion, Studies in Church History*, 23 (1986), 11–29.
Reay, Barry, 'Popular Hostility towards Quakers in Mid-Seventeenth-Century England', *Social History*, 5, 3 (1980), 387–407.
Reay, Barry, 'Quaker Opposition to Tithes 1652–1660', *Past and Present*, 86 (1980), 98–120.
Roberts, Stephen K., 'The Quakers in Evesham 1655–1660: A Study in Religion, Politics, and Culture', *Midland History*, 16, 71 (1991), 63–85.
Taylor, Kay, 'Chalk, Cheese, and Cloth: The Settling of Quaker Communities in Seventeenth-Century Wiltshire', *Quaker Studies*, 10, 2 (2006), 160–84.
Thomas, Courtney, 'The Honour & Credite of the Whole House', *Cultural and Social History*, 10, 3 (2013), 329–45.
Thomas, Kathleen, 'An Evaluation of the Doctrine of the Inward Light as a Basis for Mission – As Exemplified by Quaker Approaches to Jews and Muslims in the Seventeenth Century', *Quaker Studies*, 14, 1 (1996), 54–72.
Underdown, David, 'The Chalk and the Cheese: Contrasts among the English Clubmen', *Past & Present*, 85 (1979), 25–48.
van Duinen, Jared, '"An Engine Which the World Sees Nothing Of": Revealing Dissent Under Charles I's "Personal Rule"', *Parergon*, 28, 1 (2011), 177–96.
Wallis, Patrick, 'Apprenticeship and Training in Premodern England', *Journal of Economic History*, 68, 3 (2008), 832–61.
Waugh, W.T., 'Sir John Oldcastle', *English Historical Review*, 20, 79 (1905), 434–56.
Waureghen, Sarah, 'Covenanter Propaganda and Conceptualizations of the Public During the Bishops Wars, 1638–1640', *Historical Journal*, 52, 1 (2009), 63–86.
Webb, John, 'Some Passages in the Life and Character of a Lady Resident in Herefordshire and Worcestershire During the Civil War', *Archaeologia: or Miscellaneous Tracts Relating to Antiquity*, 37 (1857), 189–223.

Whiteman, Anne, 'The Protestation Returns, 1641–1642: Part I, The General Organisation', *Local Population Studies*, 55, (1995). 14–26.
Whiteman, Anne and Russell, Vivian, 'The Protestation Returns, 1641–1642: Part II, Partial Census or Snapshot? Some Evidence from Penwith Hundred, Cornwall', *Local Population Studies*, 56 (1996), 17–29.
Whiteway, John, 'An Account of the Siege of Brampton Bryan Castle', *Archaeologia Cambrensis*, 10, 39 (July 1864), 232–43.

Unpublished Works

Theses
Allen, Richard C., 'The Society of Friends in Wales: The Case of Monmouthshire, c.1654–1836, University of Wales, Aberystwyth, Ph.D. thesis, 1999.
Berry, Simon, 'Responses to Lollardy and the Shaping of the English Religion, c.1400–1450', University of Oxford, Ph.D. thesis, 2019.
Evans, Eric J., 'A History of the Tithe System in England, 1690–1850 with special reference to Staffordshire', University of Warwick, Ph.D. thesis, 1970.
Andrew Fincham, 'The Origins of Quaker Commercial Success, (1689–c.1755)', University of Birmingham, Ph.D. thesis, 2021.
Forde, Helen, 'Derbyshire Quakers, 1650–1761', University of Leicester, Ph.D. thesis, 1977.
Griffith, Patricia, 'Early Quakers in Cornwall, 1656–1750', University of Exeter, Ph.D. thesis, 2004.
Johnson, Rosalind, 'Protestant Dissenters in Hampshire, c.1640–c.1740', University of Winchester, Ph.D. thesis, 2013.
Kightly, Charles, 'The Early Lollards: A Survey of Popular Lollard Activity in England, 1328–1428', University of York, Ph.D. thesis, 1975.
Laycock, Richard G., 'The Quakers in Gloucester, 1655–1737', University of Birmingham, M.Phil. thesis, 2001.
Leachman, Caroline L., 'From an "Unruly Sect" to a Society of "Strict Unity": The Development of Quakerism in England, c.1650–1689', University College London, Ph.D. thesis, 1997.
Mortimer, Russell S., 'Quakerism in Seventeenth-Century Bristol', University of Bristol, M.A. thesis, 1946.
Peters, M. Kate, 'Quaker Pamphleteering and the Development of the Quaker Movement, 1652–1656', University of Cambridge, Ph.D. thesis, 1996.
Pick, Peter R., 'Interjections of Silence: The Poetics and Politics of Radical Protestant Writing 1642–1660', University of Birmingham, Ph.D. thesis, 2000.
Quine, E.K.L., 'The Quakers in Leicestershire', University of Nottingham, Ph.D. thesis, 1968.
Selleck, A.D., 'The History of the Society of Friends in Plymouth and West Devon from 1654 to the Early Nineteenth Century', University of London, Ph.D. thesis, 1959.
Spraggon, Julie, 'Puritan Iconoclasm in England 1640–1660', University of London, Ph.D. thesis, 2000.
Stevens, Sylvia, 'A Believing People in a Changing World: Quakers in Society in Northeast Norfolk, 1690–1800', University of Sunderland, Ph.D. thesis, 2004.
Taylor, Kay S., 'Society, Schism and Sufferings: The First 70 Years of Quakerism in Wiltshire', University of the West of England, Ph.D. thesis, 2006.
Zemaitis, Daniel S., 'Convergent Paths: The Correspondence Between Wycliffe, Hus, and the Early Quakers', University of Birmingham, Ph.D. thesis, 2012.

Bibliography 211

Websites

'5 December 1642 [Earl of Stamford's Letter, about securing the Papists]', *Journal of the House of Lords: Volume 5, 1642–1643* (London: His Majesty's Stationery Office, 1767–1830), p. 475. *British History Online* http://www.british-history.ac.uk/lords-jrnl/vol5/pp475-476 [accessed 11 May 2015].

Bank of England Inflation Calculator, https://www.bankofengland.co.uk/monetary-policy/inflation/inflation-calculator [accessed 23 January 2020].

'Charles I – volume 459: July 1–13, 1640', in *Calendar of State Papers Domestic: Charles I, 1640*, ed. William Douglas Hamilton (London, 1880), pp. 434–74. *British History Online* http://www.british-history.ac.uk/cal-state-papers/domestic/chas1/1640/ pp434-74 [accessed 25 May 2021].

'Charles I – volume 492: September 1642', *Calendar of State Papers Domestic: Charles I, 1641–3*, ed. William Douglas Hamilton (London, 1887), pp. 383–98. *British History Online* http://www.british-history.ac.uk/cal-state-papers/domestic/chas1/1641-3/ pp383-98 [accessed 11 May 2015].

'Charles I – volume 492: October 1642', in *Calendar of State Papers Domestic: Charles I, 1641–3*, ed. William Douglas Hamilton (London, 1887), pp. 398–400. *British History Online* http://www.british-history.ac.uk/cal-state-papers/domestic/chas1/1641-3/ pp398-403 [accessed 21 February 2021].

Green, M. Everett (ed.), *Calendar of State Papers, Domestic Series, [Commonwealth] 1649 –1660, Preserved in the State Paper Department of Her Majesty's Public Record Office. Vol. 3: Jan–Oct 1651* (London: Longman & Co., [21 April] 1651), p. 514 http://go.galegroup.com/mss/i.do?&id=GALE%7CMC4326301667&v=2.1&u=tlemea_spoa&it=r&p=SPOL&sw=w&viewtype=Calendar [accessed 17 December 2013].

'July 1654: An Ordinance prohibiting Horse-Races for Six Monethes', in C.H. Firth and R.S. Rait (eds.), *Acts and Ordinances of the Interregnum, 1642–1660* (London: His Majesty's Stationery Office, 1911), pp. 941–2. *British History Online* http://www.british-history.ac.uk/no-series/acts-ordinances-interregnum/ pp. 941–2 [accessed 10 January 2022].

'March 1654: An Ordinance for Prohibiting Cock-Matches', in C.H. Firth and R.S. Rait (eds.), *Acts and Ordinances of the Interregnum, 1642–1660* (London: His Majesty's Stationery Office, 1911), p. 861. *British History Online*, http://www.british-history.ac.uk/no-series/acts-ordinances-interregnum/ p. 861 [accessed 10 January 2022].

Mary Morrissey, *Confessionalism and conversion in the Reformation*, in James Simpson (ed.), Oxford Handbooks Online, Oxford University Press, 2015, pp. 1, 3, https://www.oxfordhandbooks.com/view/10.1093/oxfordhb/9780199935338.001.0001/oxfordhb-9780199935338-e-73 [accessed 25 May 2021].

Roberts, Stephen. K., 'Smith, Humphrey (bap. 1624–d. 1663)', *Oxford Dictionary of National Biography* (Oxford: Oxford University Press, 2004). www.oxforddnb.com/view/article/25818 [accessed 16 May 2014].

The Unabridged Acts and Monuments Online or TAMO (1570 edn.) (Sheffield: Digital Humanities Institute, 2011), p. 486, http//www.dhi.ac.uk/foxe [Accessed: 24 July 2021].

Index

7000 Handmaids of the Lord, 50

A Sad Caveat to All Quakers, 71, 74–5
Abbot, Henry, 143–4, 149
Act of Uniformity (1662), 44
Adderbury, Oxfordshire, 42, 86
Affirmation Act (1697), 48
Alehouses, 93, 95–6, 99
Algiers, 42
Almeley, Herefordshire, 40, 42–3, 46, 48–9, 56
Alton, Hampshire, 141
Anglo-Dutch Wars, 109, 121
Antichrist, 31–2, 38, 99, 129
Apocalypse, 32, 108, 110, 132
Apocalyptic, 31, 38, 79, 101, 105, 110, 117, 140–1
Armscott, Worcestershire, 40
Atkin, Robert, 138
Atkinson, Christopher, 77
Audland, John, 33–4, 38
Axminster, Devon, 136

Baker, Daniel, 36, 38, 82, 90, 97
Baptists, 23, 26, 28, 118
Barbary Corsairs, 42
Baxter, Richard, xvi, 19, 33, 58–63, 65, 67–9, 71, 73, 75–7, 89–91, 99, 111, 118
Bayley, William, 136
Bellenden, Sir William, 9
Bengeworth, Worcestershire, 40, 43, 132
Beoley, Worcestershire, 13
Bewdley, Worcestershire, 23
Bishops' Wars, 4–5
Blasphemy, 27, 64–5, 73, 91–3, 117
Blome, Richard, 65–6
Bodenham, Herefordshire, 56, 129
Book of Daniel, 135
Book of Exodus, 109
Book of Hebrews, 138–9
Book of Isaiah, 138
Book of Job, 147
Book of John, 138
Book of Matthew, 27
Book of Miracles, 69
Book of Revelations, 108
Boston, Massachusetts, 155
Bourne, Edward, 39, 67–9, 80–1, 84, 86, 89, 92, 101–103, 105, 108, 111–23
Bowater, John, 115
Brampton Bryan, 6, 14
Bridport, Dorset, 139
Bristol, 48, 54–5, 63–4, 73, 95
Bromsgrove, Worcestershire, 40, 115
Bromyard, Herefordshire, 40, 43
Burial Grounds, 35, 43–5, 144
Burrough, Edward, 57–9, 91, 150

Caldicott, Henry, 84–5
Camm, John, 150
Cartwright, Thomas, 132–3, 135
Cater, John, 45, 49–50
Catholic, 2–3, 5, 7, 16, 44, 62, 104, 111–12, 114, 118, 120–1
Catholicism, 2, 9, 111–13, 139
Chadwick, Worcestershire, 34, 40, 59, 89
Chandler, Thomas, 59–60
Charles I, 2, 4–5, 7, 9, 15, 20, 24, 127, 135
Charles I's Personal Rule, 4–5, 127
Charles II, 39, 79, 84, 103, 111, 114
Church of England, 5–7, 79
Civil wars, xv–xvi, 1–2, 9–11, 16, 19–20, 23, 25, 28, 67, 80, 83, 105, 111, 121–2, 127–8, 136, 152, 154
Claines, Worcestershire, 69–71, 73
Clarendon Code, 79

Clubmen, 16–17
Colchester, Essex, 73–4
Cole, Anthony, 34–5
Commissioners of Array, 10–11
Complin, Nicholas, 124, 145–6, 148
Conventicle Act (1664), 83–4, 107
Conventicle Act (1670), 84
Courten, Elizabeth, 66
Cromwell, Oliver, 21, 23, 25, 30, 64, 94, 134
Cromwell, Richard, 102

Danson, Thomas, 90
Declaration of Indulgence, 114
Derby, 27
Diggers, 24
Dolphin, Richard, 86
Dorchester, 1656
Dore, Herefordshire, 3, 8
Drayton, Herefordshire, 11
Drayton-in-the-Clay, Leicestershire, 26
Drew, Sarah, 30
Droitwich, Worcestershire, 40
Dudley, Worcestershire, 40
Dyer, Mary, 155

Eckley, John, 46, 55
Erbery (Erbury), Dorcas, 64, 73
Erbery, William, 129
Essex, 74, 143
Evelyn, John, 63, 74
Evesham, Worcestershire, 40, 43, 58, 66, 78, 96, 132–8
Evesham Gaol, 133–4
Exeter, 73, 135
Exton, James, 49, 54
Eyton, Herefordshire, 24

Fanatic (Fanatick), 65, 91
Farnworth, Richard, 31–4, 36, 38, 57, 59–60, 63, 98, 129–30
Fell, Judge Thomas, 27
Fell, Margaret, 26–7, 30, 34, 36, 53, 75, 110, 122
Fifth Monarchists, 24, 31, 84, 105
First Army Plot, 5
Fisher, William, 35, 45–50
Five Mile Act (1665), 83

Fox, George, 26–30, 32–8, 41, 43–6, 51–2, 54, 56, 64–5, 69, 73–4, 76, 86–8, 90, 96–7, 104, 108, 121–2, 129, 135, 145, 148, 150

Gaol Fever, 89, 146, 154
Gates, Nicholas, 148
General Baptists, 23, 26
Good, Thomas, 118–22
Goodaire, Thomas, 33, 35, 59–61
Gospel Order, 41
Grafton Flyford, Worcestershire, 40
Grand Remonstrance, the, 6
Great Book of Sufferings, 82, 86, 88–9
Great Fire of London, 109, 140
Great Plague (1665), 39–40, 109–10, 121

Hampshire Gaol, 147
Harley, Lady Brilliana, 12–14
Harley, Sir Robert, 5, 7, 12, 14–15
Hat Honour, 24, 27, 80–1, 133, 135
Hereford, 1, 8, 11, 14–20, 24, 32, 34, 39–40, 43–4, 47–9, 56, 84–5, 108, 126
Herefordshire, 1, 4–5, 7–11, 13–18, 20, 23–5, 32–3, 38–45, 47–51, 53–8, 78–80, 82, 84–6, 88, 89, 92, 95, 107, 123–4, 126–32, 134–5, 152
Herefordshire Militia Assessment of 1663, 126
Herefordshire Protestation, 7–9
Hinton, Mary, 136
House of Commons Protestation (1641/2), 5–7, 9
Howgill, Francis, 56
Hubberthorne, Richard, 59, 102, 150
Hyde, Edward Earl of Clarendon, 79

Independents, 23, 25, 33–4, 128

James, Duke of Monmouth, 111
James, Duke of York (later James II), 84
Jeffreys, Joyce, 11

Kendal Fund, 30
Kidderminster, Worcestershire, xvi, 19, 33, 58–9, 90
Kilkinton, Herefordshire, 11

King's Norton, Worcestershire, 40
Kings Caple, Herefordshire, 44
Kittermater, Thomas, 11–12
Knight, George, 69–70, 80–1

Laud, Archbishop William, 2–4, 127
Leominster, Herefordshire, 6, 23, 35, 40, 42–7, 55–6, 84, 86, 89
Levellers, 24
Light or Inner Light, 29, 44, 74, 97, 101–103, 108, 110, 112, 138, 148, 150
Lilburne, John, 24
Little Cowarne, Herefordshire, 124, 126, 130
London, 6, 27, 36, 39, 45, 51, 54, 56, 65, 95, 107, 109–10, 140–1
London Yearly Meeting, 45, 54
Lower, Thomas, 87
Ludgater, Robert, 143

Marlborough, Wiltshire, 39
Marriage, 45–8, 51, 55–6, 126
Meeting House(s), 42–3, 46, 48, 85
Melledge, Anthony, 136
Mercurius Belgicus, 18–19
Mercurius Politicus, 74
Merrick, Elizabeth, 46, 51
Merrick, James, 24, 35, 39, 42, 44, 46–7, 49, 51, 78, 86
Merrick, Joan, 44
Merrick, Mary, 50
Merrick, Thomas, 44–5, 46, 49, 78
Merrick, Walter, 44, 46, 78
Miracle(s), 69, 71, 73–6
Monthly Meetings, 42–3, 46–7, 50, 54

Nayler, James, 26–7, 34, 59, 64–5, 73–4, 76, 91, 101–102, 129, 136
New Model Army, 16–17, 22, 25
Newby, Margaret, 66
Northampton, 42
Nottingham, 10
Nottinghamshire, 73

Oath of Abjuration, 132
Oath of Allegiance, 80–1, 121
One Sheet Against Quakers, 67, 73

Papists, 2, 14, 62, 65, 111–13, 119–20
Parker, Henry, 86–8
Parliament, 2, 4–9, 12, 15–18, 20, 24–5, 50, 64, 67, 79, 83, 114, 122, 128
Parliamentarians, 7, 11–12, 14–19, 21–2, 26–7, 102, 127
Parnell, James, 73–4
Pearson, Susanna *see* Pierson, Susanna
Penington, Mary, 40, 52
Penn, William, 29
Pepys, Samuel, 40, 95, 99, 107, 111
Pershore, Worcestershire, 40, 97
Peter(s), Hugh, 128
Pierson, Susanna, 69, 71–6, 80–1, 90–1
Piety Promoted, 50
Pitt, William, 135
Pitway, Edward, 43, 133
Pool, William, 69–75, 80
Poor relief, 41–2, 51, 116
Popular hostility, 66, 85
Potter, James, 148
Powell, Henry, 45
Powick Bridge, Battle of, 10
Prichard, Edward, 48, 56
Prichard, Elizabeth, 50
Prichard, Mary, 50–1, 56
Prichard, Roger, 43, 48–9, 51, 55–6
Puritan(s), xvi, 7, 9, 19, 50, 58, 64, 98, 102, 109
Puritanism, 2–3
Pym, John, 6–7

Quaker Act of 1662, 83–4
Quaker Peace Testimony, 122
Quarter Sessions, 10, 44, 87–8, 97, 133
Quarterly Meetings (or Quarterly Meetings for Business), 41–3, 45, 47, 49, 54, 56, 85

Ranters, 24, 60, 63, 73, 101
Refusal to Swear, 7, 80–1, 89
Ringwood, Hampshire, 136
Ross-on-Wye, Herefordshire, 24, 35, 40, 42–3, 46–50, 56, 78
Royalist(s), 5, 7, 9, 11–19, 22, 67, 94, 122, 127, 136
Rye House Plot, 84

Scaff, George, 33, 35
Scudamore, John, 3
Scudamore, Sir Barnabas, 1, 16, 19
Second Day Meeting, 153
Seekers, 35, 129
Seward, Abraham, 85
Sherborne, Dorsetshire, 136
Ship Money, 4
Shipston-on-Stour, Worcestershire, 40
Simmonds, Martha, 64
Simpson, William, 78–9
Skipp, Edmund, 129
Smith, Humphrey, xiii, 51, 55, 56, 66, 86, 107–108, 124–51
Smith, Humphrey Jr., 141–4, 148–50
Smith, Mary, 130
Smith, Nathaniel, 47
Smith, Robert, 81–2
Statute of Praemunire, 88
Stoke Bliss, Herefordshire, 124, 126, 128
Story, John, 51
Stourbridge, Worcestershire, 40
Stranger, Thomas, 64
Suicide, 70–1, 75
Swarthmoor Hall, 27, 30

Taylor, George, 30
Taylor, Thomas, 45–6, 48–9
Terrill, Sir Thomas, 141–2
Test Act (1673), 114, 121
Tithes, 23–4, 28, 50, 61, 80, 89, 115–16
Tombes, John, 23
Townshend, Henry, 13
Tredington, Worcestershire, 86
Tub Preachers, 22

Ulverston, Cumbria, 27

Vagrancy Act (1656), 31, 39, 132, 136
Venner, Thomas, 84
Vincent, Thomas, 109

Wakefield, Yorkshire, 27
Watkins, Morgan, 24–5, 28, 35, 39–41, 43–4, 47, 92–4, 96, 98–110, 113–15, 117, 122–3, 128, 140
Weatherly, George, 143
Westmorland, 33, 54, 58, 66, 77
Whitehead, George, 145
Wilde, Major John, 82–3
Wilkinson, John, 51
Willam, Thomas, 30, 75–6
Wiltshire, 31, 39, 51, 54
Winchester Gaol, 134, 138, 141, 144, 148, 150
Winstanley, Gerrard, 24
Women's Meeting, 50–2, 54
Worcester, 3, 8, 10–11, 13–15, 20–1, 29–30, 33, 36, 38, 40, 43, 59, 69, 75, 80–4, 86–9, 95–7, 102, 115–16, 135–6
 Battle of, 10, 20–1
 Gaol, 36, 38, 82, 86–9, 97, 101, 116, 121
Worcestershire, xv–xvi, 1, 4, 9–11, 13–14, 16–17, 23–4, 32–4, 38–41, 43, 48, 50, 53–4, 57–61, 69, 79–80, 82, 84–6, 88–9, 92, 95, 97, 106–107, 115, 123–4, 132–4, 143, 152
Wyatt, Lucy, 50, 143, 149

Young, Edmund, 66

Dear Reader,

We hope you have enjoyed this book, but why not share your views on social media? You can also follow our pages to see more about our other products: facebook.com/penandswordbooks or follow us on X @penswordbooks

You can also view our products at www.pen-and-sword.co.uk (UK and ROW) or www.penandswordbooks.com (North America).

To keep up to date with our latest releases and online catalogues, please sign up to our newsletter at: www.pen-and-sword.co.uk/newsletter

If you would like a printed catalogue with our latest books, then please email: enquiries@pen-and-sword.co.uk or telephone: 01226 734555 (UK and ROW) or email: uspen-and-sword@casematepublishers.com or telephone: (610) 853-9131 (North America).

We respect your privacy and we will only use personal information to send you information about our products.

Thank you!